CONTENTS

MY LIFE
WITH 3 WOMEN

ALAN RICHARDS

Penhurst Books

For information regarding rights or permissions, please contact Penhurst Books at
e-mail -- penhurstbooks@usa.com
Penhurst Books-Miami / Fax 305 675 0940

ISBN 0-9705684-7-9

Library of Congress Card Number: 01-109718

Design and Map by Madrigal Associates

First edition- 2001

Pen*hurst* Books

Printed in the United States of America

MY LIFE WITH 3 WOMEN

THE START

Santa Barbara

Cabo San Lucas

Hawaii

Palmyra Island

$\mathcal{N}$

$\mathcal{W}$ $\mathcal{E}$

$\mathcal{S}$

Ⓧ

RESCUE - LOST AT SEA

Tonga

Fiji
Islands

The Kingdom of Tonga

**FOUR WANDERING
STRANGERS MEET**

| 1,000 MILES |

DEDICATION

To Sandy—who has since become the love of my life.

A WORD FROM THE AUTHOR

For more than five years I lived and cruised in the South Pacific, Asia and Europe. Almost a year of that time—*eleven and a half months*—was with the three women in this book.

Some names and identifying details and locations have been changed to respect and protect the privacy of those involved. If the names used in this book are similar to those of any person living or dead, it is purely co-incidental.

This is not only my story, but is also the story *of three very remarkable women.* Because it's *their* story as much as it is mine, I have written it in the third-person.

We were each in the South Pacific trying to get away from—*or at least find a way to deal with*—some serious problems in our lives when we first met.

We lived together and shared *everything* for that remarkable year. However, this is above all a story *of survival.*

There's no doubt in my mind that none of us would be alive today if we hadn't been there for each other during the horrendous survival-storm. We had some injuries, but by working together we survived.

We didn't know if we were going to make it the night we were attacked by modern-day pirates in Indonesia. We escaped— thanks to everyone's calm courage, a rocket flare and a dark, moonless night.

We survived the storm and escaped the attack, but in some ways the greatest challenge we faced that year was surviving our own pasts.

Four wandering and troubled strangers met and began to live together in a small space.

Alone, we were in trouble.

Together—*well, that's when the magic began to happen*.

Alan Richards
2001

INTRODUCTION

The guests at the resort couldn't miss it. From the hotel breakfast room over-looking the beautiful lagoon in Fiji, they could see it all.

The sleek cruising boat with the American flag was anchored in the blue lagoon in front of the Fijian Yanuca Island Resort---a luxury hotel in Fiji, a country known as the "Eden" of the South Pacific. The boat had slipped into the lagoon and anchored just before sunset the previous day.

They saw a man get off the boat and into a dinghy. He was medium height with a hardened and bronzed body. His head was shaved and covered by a colored bandanna. He had a drooping moustache and a gold earring.

He looked like a pirate. But what happened *next* is what caused the guests to put down their forks and stop eating.

One after another, 3 attractive women in bikinis came up from inside the boat and got into the dinghy with the man. One of them---a tall, blonde young woman---took the oars and expertly rowed them ashore.

The pirate and the three women walked along the beach towards the restaurant. They were laughing and talking with one another as they entered and took a table. One of the women poured the man his coffee and all three kept their eyes fastened on him, listening to every word he said.

Everyone in the restaurant looked at the pirate and asked, "*who is this guy?*"

CHAPTER ONE

FOUR ON THE RUN

Alan Richards had just gone through the *worst week* of his entire life. He had lost the woman he loved.

He and Ann had spent the last 6 months together cruising through the islands of the Pacific. She had been his cruising companion, his lover, his friend—and had saved his life when he was lost overboard at sea. Now she was suddenly gone—back to deal with a family crisis in Seattle.

For six months he had been in one Pacific paradise after another with the women he loved and as captain of his own 40-

foot cruising vessel *ESCAPEE*. *It doesn't get any better than this,* he told himself. Life was great—but then Ann left and it all fell apart.

He had met her in Mexico when she was there on a vacation with a group of girlfriends. After only a few days together, Alan had already started to fall in love and invited Ann to join him on the cruise across the South Pacific.

When he reached Hawaii she took an extended leave from her job as a manager at a software company in Seattle and flew to Honolulu to join him. Ann had cautioned him all along that she had an aged mother to take care of and might have to go back after just 6 months. Alan was never good at facing unpleasant reality and right up to the very end he blocked it all out and convinced himself that he and Ann would continue together around the world.

It was here in The Kingdom of Tonga that the reality hit. Ann called her mother and found things were far worse than she thought and she would have to go back. Her mother was deathly afraid of elderly-care homes and there was no one else to take care of her.

He was 46 and had been in real estate in Santa Barbara until his divorce the previous year. That's when he took some lessons, bought *ESCAPEE* and told everyone who'd listen that he was going to cruise around the world. None of his friends believed he'd get very far—they *knew* he was running away and were certain he'd be back soon. *"Three to four years,"* he said. Three to four *months,* they thought and they were almost right. *Almost.*

He'd managed to get as far as Tonga, but now with Ann gone all the joy had gone out of cruising. During one of his frequent phone calls to Ann he said, *"nothing's the same without you.* I'm not even sure I *want* to keep going on any longer." He was dead serious and had been thinking of turning around and going back to Hawaii to sell *ESCAPEE.* Ann's departure had left such a gaping hole in his life he'd lost all heart for going on.

"Alan Richards, stop that kind of talk right now!" Ann had said fiercely. *"I'm not going to be responsible for ending your dreams. You were cruising before you met me, and you're going to keep on. If you give up and come back, don't bother calling me."* Then her voice softened and she said, "I miss you. I miss our boat—our home. I miss the wonderful life we had together—the islands, the people. Call me once a month Alan, and let me know how you're doing and where you are. Maybe I can come back some time in the future. Who knows?"

Alan hung up knowing Ann was slipping out of his hands. At first he had called her almost daily but now the calls would be only once a month—and what then? The *only* thing that stopped him from turning around and going back was the *certainty he'd lose Ann anyway.* So what was the point of going back? He might as well go on—*alone.*

Alan didn't remember much about the next few weeks or so except that they passed so slowly. He went through all the right motions, but there was no question about it—*his heart just wasn't in it anymore.*

It was August and the South Pacific hurricane season was only a few months away. That *forced* him to snap out of it and make a decision—*move on or stay put.* The hurricane season lasted four to five months and cruising boats couldn't safely go to sea during that time. If he didn't go soon he'd be stuck where he was—and Alan just couldn't face the thought of staying on in Tonga any longer. Every anchorage, every restaurant—*everything*—reminded him of Ann.

He needed a change. He knew he needed to snap out of it and get busy with some demanding project—one that would force him to focus on something else. The passage to Fiji, with some of the most dangerous reefs in the South Pacific, *was just the thing.* He'd have to stay awake and be alert at all times during those three to four days it would take to reach Suva, the capital of Fiji, where he had to check in with the authorities. Some of those passes between the Lau Group of islands were narrow—and dangerous reefs stuck out from both sides making them even narrower. Deadly reefs dotted the entire area and if he drifted off course even a little he could easily lose *ESCAPEE— and his life.*

He studied the navigation charts and talked with some of the other cruisers who were also heading for Fiji. One guy said, *"I'd never do it alone.* Just one slip up and you're on a reef. It's happened to a lot of people—some a lot more experienced than you are."

Alan knew it made sense to take some someone along with him—three to four days *was* too long to stay awake and alert by himself. He started checking the bulletin board at the Paradise International Hotel in the Tongan town of Neiafu— where cruisers hung-out. Neiafu was one of the cruising "cross-roads" of the Pacific and cruising boats were there from all over the world. It was also a major crew-change port and notice cards were put on the bulletin board by crew looking for a boat—or boats looking for crew. He quickly saw that the board was full of cards from boats looking for crew—but there were *no crew looking for boats.* He was out of luck.

The reason was simple—most of the cruisers wanted to take on an extra crew or two for the dangerous passage to Fiji or the long run down to New Zealand. While Alan was trying to make up his mind whether to go on or turn back, all the available crew had been snapped up. He was getting worried when early the next day he saw a new card which had been put up on the board overnight.

A German woman was looking for a crew position "heading west". She was on the big German boat Alan had seen anchored in front of the hotel, so he went right out to the boat to meet her—if he delayed, someone from another boat would grab her as crew for sure. That's where he met Sigrid. She was 25 and an experienced cruiser who'd sailed all the way from the Mediterranean on the German boat as paid crew. The owner—a German businessman—had some financial problems and was taking the boat to California to sell it and fly back to Germany.

Sigrid wasn't ready to call it quits and go back to Germany, she said, and was looking for another boat to join. She was slim and a bit taller than Alan—that German blood, he figured—and had long, blonde hair. Her serious demeanor reminded Alan of a stern, no-nonsense school- teacher.

The only possible drawback Alan could see was her limited English. "I study English," she explained. "I no speak much. *If speak more...speak better*". Alan knew if she had a chance to practice her English it would quickly come back to her. When he finished asking about her—how far she was going, what experience she'd had—it was *her* turn. She asked about him, the boat, its condition, how far he was going west—and when. All were good, intelligent questions.

In the end, she said, " *ja, I come see boot, Ellen. If goot, ve go.*" This was Sigrid—direct, matter of fact and right to the point. There was no beating around the bush and with her accent he was now *"Ellen," the man with a 40-foot "boot"*.

Alan wondered if she really would turn up, but later that same day Sigrid came to *ESCAPEE* to check it out. She went throughout checking *everything*—the safety equipment, engine, the radios and life-raft. She wanted to see her separate sleeping arrangements. She was crew—*that's all*—and she wanted to make that clear from the start. It was a very thorough inspection and she seemed pleased. *"OK, Ellen, ve go,"* she said grabbing and shaking his hand vigorously, pumping it up and down like an old-fashioned water-pump. Alan winced—that woman had a grip.

He had already decided he didn't want to go alone with one woman—it was just *too similar* to the times he and Ann had enjoyed alone. *He needed different.* Two men and one woman—

that would be different, so he was still looking for a guy to join them. He thought he'd found the right guy—a young man from Australia who was heading back that way. He had decided to switch boats at the last minute and Alan quickly reached an agreement with him, but when he was due to move on board *ESCAPEE,* he never showed up. "Oh him," someone in the hotel said, "he took off on that British boat."

"Hello," a quiet voice said from behind while Alan was having lunch at the hotel. "I hear you're looking for crew." He looked up—and quickly stood up. It was a young girl who couldn't have been more than 20. He invited her to have a seat and join him for lunch. Over lunch he found out that she'd flown to Tonga with a charter group from the US and they had chartered two boats from the big Moorings Charter Fleet for a couple of weeks. Her father had paid for the trip as a college graduation present, she said. She was from Atlanta and spoke with a soft southern accent. Her name was Susan.

"Well, did you have a good time on the charter, Susan?" he asked, trying to figure her out. *This didn't make any sense at all*. She had flown out with a charter group and would *fly back* with them—it's a pre-paid, *round-trip* package deal. You come as a group and you go back as a group—so what's all this about wanting to be crew?

"Yes, it was great," she said. "I enjoyed it so much I'm not ready to go back with the group tomorrow."

She saw Alan's confusion and said, "I took a couple of years break during college and finished late—just a few months ago. I don't want to rush right back and get into some job —not yet. I love the South Pacific and want to see a lot more of it before I go back and get myself all tied up in a job. *You can understand that can't you?"*

Oh yes he could. As they ate lunch Alan told Susan about himself and where he and Ann had been. He then asked her to tell him about herself and as she did he saw that she was very pleasant and sweet—a "soft" and gentle girl. She was about Alan's height, with long dark hair and big, brown eyes. She was 23—not 20 as Alan had guessed—and young for her age. She obviously had led a very sheltered life and her soft, slightly pudgy face and those big brown eyes reminded him of a big, overgrown doll.

He asked her if she'd had any experience in big ocean waves and rough weather. She said her father had once taken her on a week's cruise from the Virgin Islands in the Caribbean to Antigua. Alan was impressed—that was right into the teeth of those rough Caribbean seas. If she'd done that, she could handle this. It would be an easy down-wind trip to Fiji, *except for those reefs.*

"Well I've already got my crew," he said and saw a worried, anxious look flash across her face. *"But I guess one more won't hurt."*

"Oh thank you," she said, very relieved. "You won't be sorry."

"OK, but you've got to fax your father and get his approval. He's expecting you back, so fax him the name of my boat and my name"—and he scribbled it out on a napkin and handed it to her. "I don't want an angry, worried father searching the South Pacific for his missing daughter. If he says its OK you can go—*but you've got to get his OK."*

Alan was thinking about his own 22 year-old daughter, Lisa, and how *he'd* re-act if he heard that she'd run off to sea with some vagabond pirate looking like—*well, like he looked now.*

He had left Santa Barbara looking like a guy in real estate is expected to look—*normal.* He'd lost a lot of weight at sea and was now wiry, lean and hardened. He had toughened up, shaved his prematurely balding head and covered it with a brightly colored bandanna. He had grown a drooping moustache and got an earring. He was trying very hard to look like a pirate—at least his Disneyland-inspired idea of what pirates look like. *It was all show of course—"a load of bullshit"* as his best friend, Michael had called it in Hawaii. And Michael was right. Alan was still that straight—even square—family man with a son and daughter of his own about Susan's age.

"OK, Mr. Richards, I'll send the fax to my dad."

"Alan. It's just Alan—not captain Alan, not his royal highness Alan. Just Alan." She giggled—cute kid he thought, but even at 23 a little too sheltered and innocent to be out here in the big world on her own. Anyway, he figured, her father would probably never agree.

"OK Alan, I'll send the fax to my dad." Susan knew he would never agree—*not in a million years*—so she had come up with a plan on the spur of the moment to deal with that. She'd find out what day they were going to leave *and send the fax the day they left*—so that with the time change there'd be no chance for her father to send his *"get the hell home"* reply before they left. In just this short time together Susan had already figured Alan out—a nice enough guy and not the sort to throw her off the boat just because her father "neglected" to reply to a fax in time. And she could already tell that Alan wouldn't sit around waiting for a fax once the departure time had come.

Well, there went Alan's plan for finding both a man and a woman as crew. Now it was just Alan and *two* girls. Can I call even them "girls," he wondered—you had to be careful about those kinds of things these days.

Sigrid and Susan moved onto *ESCAPEE* and settled in. Each had her own single bed—or berth as they're called. *ESCAPEE* had five berths but one was full of stuff—so there were really four. Alan took the private front cabin when they were at anchor and that left three available berths in the main cabin. There were only two cabins on board—Alan's private forward cabin and the main cabin with the 3 berths plus a separate toilet-shower room—called a "head". While underway at sea Alan's forward cabin bounced around too much to be used and everyone would just crash and sleep in the main cabin, in one of the three berths. Anyway at least one or two of them had to be on watch at all times. Off to the side of the main cabin was a small galley—or kitchen.

Sigrid and Susan got along very well and Sigrid was soon practicing her English with Susan every chance she got. Sigrid took over the job of making lists of things to buy for the trip to Fiji and reorganized the galley—the kitchen. Alan had it all jumbled up from those weeks as a bachelor and the disorder greatly offended Sigrid's German sense of order. He couldn't help but notice that Sigrid had a large bust for someone so slim. And she was strong—*very strong*. He watched in amazement as she lifted the heavy outboard motor off the inflatable dinghy and put it in its locker on *ESCAPEE*. *He couldn't do that.* With his back problem he had to use a winch to lift it onboard. Sigrid said she preferred rowing "for the exercise" instead of using the outboard motor. She swam non-stop an hour a day, cutting through the blue water of the bay like a speeding torpedo. Alan thought to himself—*that woman's a fish!*

Susan showed a lot of interest in the chart and navigation. Alan taught her how to use the GPS—the Global Positioning System, which is a network of satellites which fixed their position at sea. He taught her how to put in "way-points"— that is key positions where they'd have to alter their course to stay off the reefs. She was a very fast learner and Alan never had to repeat himself. Without anything being said, Susan also took over washing the dishes and keeping the cabin clean and in order—considered the 'dirty' jobs on a vessel.

He also soon found out she was a *neat-freak*—always picking things up and putting them away. *"A place for everything—and everything in its place,"* she said at least two or three times a day, scolding both Alan and Sigrid for leaving things lying around. Sigrid wasn't all that orderly after all, but then neither was Alan, so Susan started to pick up after both of them. Her willingness to do any job impressed them both and Alan recognized that even though she was a soft, sweet "southern lady," she certainly wasn't spoiled.

Susan still hadn't sent that fax to her dad. She would though—she prided herself in keeping her word the way a lady should. She had it written out and was just waiting for the *right time* to send it—the day they left. She could then truthfully tell Alan, *"no reply back yet"*.

The next day Alan was doing a last-minute check of the weather bulletin in the hotel when a sailor friend approached him with a woman at his side. Alan thought it was his girlfriend.

"This is Alan," his friend said to the woman. "He's headed for Fiji—when is it Alan, tomorrow?"

"Yes, tomorrow about four in the afternoon. Just checking the weather," he said, still concentrating on the chart.

"*...and he's looking for crew,*" the friend said to the woman. "So he's probably your man."

Dammit, Alan thought, the guy obviously hadn't heard that he *already had crew—two of them.* Alan turned and started to say just that when the woman said, *"oh, that's great. You're about my last chance.* Seems like I got here too late and everybody else is already gone. I thought I might even have to fly home."

"Look, I already have crew—*two in fact,*" he said. "I'm sorry, but you're a little late. If I'd known earlier…"

"*Isn't there room for just one more?* I don't take up much space. Just this back-pack," the woman said. Alan was ready to close it off and say no, but he knew his was one of the last boats to leave.

"You said something about having to fly back home," he asked, "didn't you come on a boat?"

"No, I've been back-packing with my boy friend from island to island, hopping flights, taking small inter-island boats. But we had a disagreement of sorts and he took off, leaving me stuck here. As a woman I can't backpack on my own down here—these Polynesian societies just aren't ready for that. If I don't find a place on a boat—and yours is about the last to leave—I'll have to fly back home from here."

"Where's home?" Alan asked.

"I was born in a small town in Ohio, but I work at a mutual fund management company in Chicago and decided to take some time off. I've still got four more months to go. I sure don't want to go back four months *early*—so couldn't you fit in *just one more? I promise not to eat much, never talk and sit in a quiet corner and be a good girl.*"

Alan laughed in spite of himself and the tension was broken. She had a sense of humor. He now looked at her closely for the first time. She was in her mid-thirties, medium height, slim with short, reddish hair and had some freckles—probably Irish, Alan figured. She was clearly smart and self-reliant—that much was clear at first glance.

"Have you ever been cruising before?" Alan asked. She knew this was the key question, but had already decided to answer it truthfully.

"No, never. Just out on a fishing boat a few times in Lake Michigan."

Alan was impressed with her honesty—she was telling the truth even though it might hurt her chances. "Well, look, I can't decide this on the spot. I need to talk to the other two. They're the ones who'd have to squeeze you in. Meet me back here tomorrow morning. *Oh, what did you say your name was?*"

"*It's Carole—as in Carolyn.*"

"OK Carole, I can't promise anything, but I'll see you here tomorrow, let's say about nine. Is that OK with you?"

"Done deal and however it turns out, thanks"

Now what? Alan thought on his way back to *ESCAPEE.* How do I ask the girls—women—about Carole? I really don't *have* to ask—it's my boat. But on the other hand, I really should—it's only fair since they're going to have to make room for her.

That night after Sigrid had cooked dinner and he and Susan had finished the dishes, they were sitting in the cockpit talking. Alan said, "you girls...I mean women. Look, I need to get something settled. Which do you want me to call you--*girls or women?* You know, as in *did you girls enjoy your day?*"

Sigrid and Susan looked at each other. "Ve wimmen und girls. You choose, ja?" Sigrid said, looking at Susan who added, "girl is OK with me, Alan."

"OK, girls it is, and just to be equal you can call me a boy—anyway, everyone tells me I never really grew up. Now I've got to ask you girls about something. Today another wom...girl...met me and asked to go to Fiji with us. I know it might be a little crowded so I thought I'd ask you first. She's never sailed before so if we all agree, it's just to Fiji—*no further.* If we don't take her with us she's going to have to fly home to Chicago several months early."

"That'd be a shame," Susan said, thinking of herself.

"Ja, ve make room," Sigrid said. "But vat if she sick?"

"*Sick?*" Alan asked, thoroughly confused. "What do you mean sick, Sigrid?"

Sigrid struggled to explain in her limited English and decided to not even try. Instead, she gave a highly realistic *imitation* of someone throwing up all over the boat—*complete with all the nauseating sound effects.* Susan was startled and jumped, expecting to see vomit all over the boat. Alan thought that was about the most graphic vomiting he'd ever seen—or heard—and he'd been pretty seasick a few times himself.

"Oh, *seasick.*"

"*Ja!*" Sigrid smiled, very pleased that she'd managed to overcome the language barrier.

"Well, it's just to Fiji," Alan said. "No further until we find out if she gets seasick. That's about three, maybe four days."

"Ja, ve do it," Sigrid said.

"OK, I'll tell her in the morning," and they decided where her berth would be.

Alan's head was spinning. He'd started out planning to go alone but then he found the *only* crew available—a woman. *Now, he'd wound up with three women*—all in the space of two days! It had all happened so suddenly and unexpectedly—*what had he gotten himself into?*

The next morning at nine he was at the hotel as promised. Carole had been waiting there since eight and Alan could tell she was nervous and worried about the answer. She'd checked around during the previous afternoon and found that *ESCAPEE* really *was* her last chance to leave on a cruising vessel. Alan had sent Susan off to the post office to see if a fax had come in from her dad. Instead, Susan was *just now sending the fax to her father.* It would be tomorrow before the irate fax demanding she return home *immediately* could possibly arrive. They'd be at sea by then.

"*Morning Carole,*" Alan said, "*let's go to Fiji.*"

"Thank you—*thanks very much.*"

"Well, thank the girls, too. It's their decision as much as mine. They didn't want to leave you stranded here either."

"That's really nice of them. I can't wait to meet them."

"OK, let's go. Oh, just one thing, Carole. Let's make this just to Fiji—it'll be a little crowded on board. Is that OK with you?"

"It sure is… and thanks again."

"And one other thing. Sigrid and Susan have agreed to be called girls—you know as in 'you girls' ready to go?' I know you're women, but we're pretty informal on *ESCAPEE*."

Carole got it at once, "hey, if they're girls, I'm a girl. In Chicago I'm a woman. Out here I'm just another girl," she said smiling.

"And you can call me a boy—I am at heart anyway and I guess this adolescent pirate get-up sort of proves it. *OK, we raise anchor at four. Next stop, Fiji*"

By the time Alan and Carole got to the boat Susan had returned from sending the fax and Alan introduced Carole to Susan and Sigrid. "I really want to thank you guys for taking me aboard. That was really nice of you," Carole said.

"No problem Carole, we just put ourselves in your shoes," Susan replied.

"*Ja, you are velkum*" Sigrid said, grabbing and vigorously pumping Carole's hand up and down, just as she'd done with Alan. *German through and through*, Carole thought, but very nice.

"Oh, Susan, what about the post office? Any fax in from your dad?" Alan asked.

"No, nothing in," which of course was absolutely true.

"*Damn*," Alan said, "*we can't wait around. We'll have to leave today anyway—fax or no fax*." Susan gave him her sweetest smile.

"OK, time to stow everything for sea," he said.

Sigrid jumped right in—she'd done it a hundred times before. Susan copied her and Carole did her best to help. Getting a cruising boat ready for the open sea is serious business. Everything that can be moved has to be secured or put away. Lockers have to be closed and latched shut and anything that's not in use at the moment put in its place. *"A place for everything and everything in its place,"* Susan chirped happily. She loved organizing things and "being tidy," as she called it. *That girl's a definite neat-freak,* Alan said to himself again and while Susan happily tidied up below Alan, Sigrid and Carole went up on deck to get *ESCAPEE* into its sea-going mode.

Everything on deck had to be stowed and secured, the cockpit sun awning put away—the inflatable dinghy hauled up on deck and secured—and on and on. By around 5 PM *ESCAPEE* was ready for sea. Alan looked at the sun and said, *"it's too late to head out to sea now.* This is the first time on board for you all and I don't want you to have to learn your way around a new boat at sea in the dark—so we'll go to that anchorage out near the pass and stop for the night. Early tomorrow we'll take off and you guys can get familiar with *ESCAPEE* in broad daylight—*much better."*

They nodded their heads and appreciated Alan's decision. Everything *was* completely new to them—even Sigrid had to learn her way around, almost the same as Susan and Carole. Alan overheard them.

"Considerate guy, isn't he?" Carole asked Susan.

"I have good feelings about him," Susan said.

"Ja" Sigrid added, "I sink so"

Alan motored out into the channel, showed Sigrid the engine controls and turned *ESCAPEE* over to her—after all she was a pro. She expertly steered through the maze of narrow, winding channels towards the anchorage. *"OK, Sigrid, we're going to drop the anchor over there,"* Alan called out when they had reached the anchorage. He lowered the anchor and she backed up very slowly until the boat suddenly jerked to a stop, telling them the anchor was safely set for the night. "Thanks Sigrid," he said while she shut the engine down. They'd worked well as a team on that first anchor drill—*good sign for the future.*

"*That's enough work,*" Alan said. "I *now declare 'social hour' on ESCAPEE. Let's get the wine and drinks up—and how about some sandwiches or cheese? Anyone hungry?*" They all were and Carole and Susan busied themselves with sandwiches while Alan showed Sigrid the sail handling equipment.

"*Last call for drinks,*" Alan said when the sandwiches were brought up. There's no booze when we're at sea." They sat around in *ESCAPEE'S* large, comfortable cockpit and *four complete strangers* started going through the often-awkward and sometimes lengthy process of getting to know each other. Carole started it off by asking Alan about his trip from his homeport in Santa Barbara to Tonga. Ann was part of everything and he just wasn't ready to talk about her yet—it was still much too painful. But he did tell them a little about the day he was lost overboard at sea—and how Ann had come back to save him after he'd already given up all hope.

They listened in wide-eyed horror and looked at him as though they were looking at a miracle—*and in a way they were.* Alan had a point in telling the story. He wanted them to be very aware of the danger of going overboard.

"*So, why did Ann leave?*" Susan blurted out.

A look of sadness instantly flashed over Alan's face. He had never learned to mask his feelings—whatever he felt was right out there on his face like a neon sign. And it was *pain* they saw. Carole and Sigrid shot Susan a look that could kill for asking that question *but it was too late*—the question was already out in the open. Alan told them where he and Ann had met, how long they'd been together, where they'd gone and how they had fallen in love. He left out a lot, of course, but they got the picture—a man who'd shared 6 months alone with a woman he'd come to love. She had saved his life and they had shared *everything* together, but circumstances beyond their control had torn them apart. By the time Alan finished, it was very quiet on *ESCAPEE.* Susan was almost in tears over a love story with such a sad ending, and was wishing she'd never asked that damned question and put Alan through all this. *"Stupid question"* she later admitted to Carole and Sigrid. *They certainly agreed.*

"Enough of this reminiscing," Alan said. *"That's all in the past.* Tomorrow we start the future, so you'd better get some rest. We're having a big breakfast and move out right after daybreak." Alan went up to the forward cabin, closed the door and fell into his berth thinking of Ann—what *had* been and what *might* have been. It was the *might have been* that broke his heart all over again. As he fell asleep he could still hear talk coming from the main cabin.

He awoke at dawn and saw the sprawling bodies of the three girls—*OK to call them that* he reminded himself—spread out on their berths every which way. They had talked late into the night and were still sound asleep. He tried to quietly make coffee, but rattled the pot. Carole looked up with sleepy eyes and said quietly, "here, let me do breakfast. You take it easy and have your coffee." She climbed out of her berth, took off for the bathroom, called the *head* and soon came back to start making breakfast. Susan rolled over sleepily, pulling the sheet off and leaving her naked body sprawled out in the open—she'd slept in the nude because it was so warm. Alan quickly pulled the sheet back over her and as his eyes met Carole's, she smiled and rolled her eyes. Alan grabbed his coffee and went up on deck *fast.*

One thing was becoming very clear to him—living in such a small space *with three women* was going to take some getting used to—*that's for sure!* He knew he better get used to scenes like this morning—*there were certainly going to be a lot more.* In many ways living on a small cruising vessel *is like living in a very small house*—except at sea you can't leave the "house" and get away. You live on top of each other so you'd better get along—and you've got almost no privacy. Alan had just had a graphic reminder that *he was now living in a very small "house" with three women he didn't even know.* Oh well, he went to sea to have adventures—and it looked like he was going to have *more* than he bargained for.

"*OK, everyone up. Breakfast's ready*," he heard Carole shout out. Sigrid got up slowly but Susan just rolled over and went back to sleep. Carole slapped her lightly on the rear end—and that woke her up. She leaned over and told Susan what had happened—about Alan and the sheet coming off—and Susan went bright red. She wrapped the sheet tightly around her and took off for the head. Alan wondered just how long any attempt at privacy would last. *Not long, that's for sure.*

After breakfast he said, "let's all take a look at where we're going. You'll enjoy it more if you guys know what's ahead of us." As they gathered around the chart table Alan showed them the route to Fiji he had marked up. "We're going to '*thread the needle*' right here," he said, pointing to where the route went through a narrow pass between two Fijian islands. "Reefs stick out from both islands, so it's a lot more narrow than it seems. We've got to thread this needle in daylight. If we see we're getting there at night, we'll have to slow down..." and he then traced *ESCAPEE'S* route on into Suva harbor in Fiji. "We should be in Suva in 3-4 days, depending on a lot of things. *But we've really got to watch it here*," he said, tapping that narrow and dangerous channel.

"Everyone wears a safety harness attached to the boat when it's rough," he said. "No one goes overboard. *Been there—done it. No fun*. Alan then showed Carole how to haul up the anchor with the electric windlass—which pulled the anchor and chain back on board—while Sigrid steered them out into the channel. Alan and Carole raised the sails and Sigrid expertly steered them out the pass and into the open seas.

The trade-winds were coming from behind them and it would be an easy "down-hill" run all the way to Fiji—*like a skier gliding down a mountain*—a little bumpy at times, but effortless. *ESCAPEE* gently moved ahead being "pushed" along by the wind and rolling waves coming in from behind. With

Sigrid steering, Alan started to show Carole and Susan the things they needed to know.

"First, as I said, no one goes overboard. So keep these safety harnesses hooked onto the boat at all times," and he showed them how to connect their harnesses. "When you need to go down below, hold on all the time. Believe it or not, more people are hurt being thrown around *down below* than are injured up on deck—or go overboard. Carole, if you or Susan get to feeling a little queasy let me know right away—I'll get you some honey in warm water and that should get rid of the queasiness and stop it from turning into sea-sickness." He wasn't concerned about Sigrid. She'd done all this far more than he had and her experience gave him more time to help the other two. Carole seemed to be doing just fine, too, so far. It'd take her a day or so to get her sea legs of course but she was an outdoors woman— clearly self reliant, capable and smart. He was sure she'd adjust very well.

Susan—*poor Susan*. First, she wasn't used to getting up that early and it'd been a long time since she did that rough sail in the Caribbean. She was quiet and withdrawn which for talkative Susan was a sure sign she was feeling queasy—the first stages of being seasick. "Here, drink this," Alan said, handing her a glass of honey in warm water and some graham crackers. That settled her stomach and made her feel better. Soon she was sitting up and chattering away non-stop. *That girl's a neat-freak and a talker* Alan said to himself.

Around 3 in the afternoon the winds increased, bringing even larger waves from behind them. *The "downhill skier" was picking up speed.* ESCAPEE surfed down the front of the waves—like a 40-foot surfboard—as they swept harmlessly under her. "What a great ride," Carole called out. Alan said, "this is as good a time as any to teach you to steer."

There are three ways to steer *ESCAPEE*—electric autopilot, mechanical wind-vane and hand-steering. The *autopilot* was only good in calm seas, since it was far too weak to work in big waves. The *wind-vane* is a mechanical device bolted to the back of the boat. It has a big "paddle" sticking up in the air, and as the wind moves it back and forth, it pulls a rope, which is led through pulleys to the wheel—and turns the wheel. It's good for most steering at sea, but can be unreliable in really bad weather. That's where *hand steering* comes in. When the weather is really bad the boat must be hand steered. Alan wanted to teach Carole and Susan how to steer—for safety, of course, *but also for the sheer fun of it.* It's far more enjoyable to actively steer and sail a cruising boat in good weather than just sit around as a passenger..

"Everybody does everything on board—no separate jobs. Everybody steers, everybody cooks, everybody does the dishes, everybody keeps watch, including me," Alan said. "*No 'galley-slaves' on board.*" Carole was really glad to hear that— as the last to arrive, she thought she might be stuck just cooking or doing the dishes. She was already fascinated by this strange new world at sea and wanted to learn to sail the boat, know how it worked—*everything!*

About the most difficult thing to learn on a sailing vessel is how to steer in large "following" seas—big waves that sweep in from behind constantly trying to shove them off course. As soon as Alan told them how difficult it was, Carole wanted to learn to do that *first*. She took it as a personal challenge and as Alan was about to learn—*Carole loved challenges*. After a quick lunch in the cockpit, Carole said, "I want to start with the hardest job. If I can do that, everything else is easy—*right?*"

"Right," Alan said.

He started showing Carole how to hand-steer. If she steered too far one way, the wind would get behind the mainsail and they'd be "back-winded" and could tear the sail or even have a "knockdown"—knocking the boat over on its side. *That was a definite "no-no".* But if Carole steered too far the *other* way, they'd "broach"—that is, they'd swing sideways, turning back up into the wind and face back towards those big waves. One of them could sweep across the boat and do some damage. So Carole had to get it right—*every wave, every time.* She wanted a challenge—*she got one!*

She was good—*really good*—and steered the 40-foot "surfboard" straight down the waves. At first she was white-lipped with concentration, but as Alan began to say, *"that's it. You've got it. Good going,"* she started relaxing and smiling. *"You're a natural, Carole.* You've got a feel... "

"Hey, this is fun," Carole said, turning to look back at Sigrid.

"Look out!" Alan shouted and grabbed the wheel. In just that moment of inattention, *ESCAPEE* started into the beginning of a broach. Carole quickly corrected it and said "sorry, wasn't paying attention for a moment"

"You're doing great, Carole," and Alan started to move away, to show her his confidence in her.

"Don't leave me!" she pleaded, but Alan looked at Sigrid who nodded her head. They both agreed Carole was ready to be on her own. *"Wow, this is fun. This is great!"* Carole exclaimed. Not only was Carole not going to get seasick, she was turning into an excellent helmsman or helmsperson—or whatever the right term was. She was fast, intelligent and not at all intimidated by the big waves, the speeding boat and newness of it all. Alan figured there wasn't much that would intimidate that woman.

"Three cheers for Carole" Alan called out—and all three joined in. Carole was beaming—just like an enthusiastic little girl with a new toy. She obviously thrived on adventure—and was getting a hand-full. Now it was Susan's turn. Poor Susan—she had no "feel" for the boat at all. Time and again, Alan had to grab the wheel and correct it, so he said, *"Susan, you didn't learn to ride a bicycle by jumping on a Harley-Davidson. And this is a Harley ride.* Let's wait for calmer waters—and I promise you, you'll be steering in no time."

"You promise you'll teach me?"

"I sure will. I'm going to make a first-class helmsgirl out of you!"

By the end of their first day together some things were already becoming clear to Alan—*and he liked what he saw.* Sigrid was as solid as a rock. She clearly knew a lot more about sailing than he did but was just too nice to show him up. Her English was improving and she had loosened up a lot after being around all the informality and friendliness of Susan and Carole. That "severe" look she'd had at first was going away. She was not only a skilled sailor but also a stable, mature person. Alan already knew he could depend on her, come what may.

Carole was a very fast learner—a lifetime of self-reliance had obviously taught her how to adapt fast—and she clearly loved having new challenges being thrown at her. And when something was explained to her once she got it. She wasn't satisfied knowing just *what* to do—she also wanted to know *why*—and that was one of the things that marked her as a "natural". She still had a lot to learn but Alan had never seen *anyone* learn to steer in rough seas as quickly and as well as she had. *He sure hadn't!* And on top of all that she didn't have that "chip on the shoulder," he thought at first she might have.

Carole was a little more intense and "hard" than Susan or Sigrid—that was just her personality—but there were no hang-ups he could see. Even so, he knew he wouldn't call her a "girl" back in Chicago—she'd probably shove him out the window.

Susan—once again, what could he say about Susan? She was sweet and willing to do any job. Her fetish about "*a place for everything and everything in its place*" kept the cabin neat and "tidy" as she called it—even if she got a little frustrated with them all for leaving things lying around. She was beginning to show a real aptitude for navigation and chart-work—skills that would be *critical* in the dangerous, reef-strewn islands they were heading towards. Also very much in her favor was that easy-going personality and the willingness to do any job that needed doing.

Alan still had to give her some honey in warm water with crackers a few times—but she was slowly getting her sea legs. She once said she needed to lie down and started to go down below to her berth. That would only make her seasickness worse so Alan gestured to her and she laid her head in his lap and went sound asleep up in the fresh air of the cockpit. Before long Alan needed to get up and help Sigrid adjust the sail, but couldn't move without awakening Susan. He just shrugged his shoulders—and Carole jumped in and helped. In an hour or two Susan's queasiness was a thing of the past and she was chattering away non-stop.

Around 10 the first night Alan went down to study the chart. *"We've got a little problem,"* he said when he came back up to the cockpit. "At this speed, we'll hit the narrow channel between those two islands about 4 in the morning—in the dark. No way. So we'll have to take down one of the sails to slow us down and make sure we get to the channel entrance about dawn—not a minute sooner." *The skier was hurtling down the mountain too fast.*

Alan explained to everyone what had to be done—*and done very carefully* in the pitch darkness of night with the boat rolling and bouncing and heavy seas coming in from behind.

"Sigrid and I have got to go on deck to the front of the boat and haul that sail down to slow us. It's a two-person job. We're going to be exposed and out in the open up there and we can't count on the wind vane—not with us on the front deck. Carole you've got to hand steer and keep ESCAPEE lined up straight. If we broach or get knocked down while we're up there we'll probably be thrown overboard. We've got these harnesses on but it would still be dangerous. *So steer her straight down the groove."*

Carole gripped the wheel tightly while Sigrid and Alan hooked their safety harnesses on and left the safety and peacefulness of the cockpit to go forward. It was like a *hostile* "*war-zone*" on the bucking and bouncing front deck of the boat as wind driven spray lashed them without mercy. It was so different from the quiet, dry safety and comfort of the cockpit. A broach now would certainly sweep them both overboard, harness or no—but they trusted Carole. Sigrid and Alan dropped to their knees and worked together in the darkness and managed to get the sail down and secured. They then literally *crawled* back on their knees along the wet, bouncing, spray-lashed deck to the quiet, comforting safety of the cockpit.

"*Thanks, Carole. You made it easier for us,*" Alan said.

"*Double scotch! No, double-double scotch!*" Carole called out to an imaginary bartender.

They slowed down and Alan stayed up the rest of the night, making sure the current didn't push them too close to the island and its reefs. A lot of boats had been lost in the beautiful South Pacific due to strong, unpredictable currents pushing them onto reefs. Alan warned Carole and Susan, "you can point the boat in one direction *but go another*—and the reefs are there waiting to grind you to pieces. So we *really* have to keep our eyes open."

He drew a "*no-go*" line five miles from the narrow entry to the *eye of the needle* and said, "no way do we cross this line until daylight." Throughout the long night he and Susan checked their position with the GPS every thirty minutes to make sure that strong current hadn't pushed them across that line towards the dangerous reefs. An anxious night finally ended and dawn broke, finding them right on that line. They were now ready to head down one of the most dangerous navigable channels in the Pacific. It would take them about an hour to get through and free of all the reefs which extended out from the two islands and into the safe, open waters on the other side.

"OK," Alan said, *"here we go."*

Sigrid expertly lined *ESCAPEE* up right in the middle of the narrow channel. Alan handed Carole the binoculars and said, *"keep an eye on those reefs on both sides Carole. You've got to see them off to the sides at all times. If you lose sight of them, call me at once. With these currents, they could turn out to be right in front of us."* Susan's job was to help Carole spot the reefs and keep the precise time they started through the pass with the stopwatch.

Once they entered the channel there'd be no turning back. *The "skier" couldn't stop the downhill run and go back up the mountain.* No one could turn around and go back against those winds and waves. They were committed now. Everyone was doing their job and Alan was down below studying the chart when Susan called out, *"Alan, get up here fast!"* Alan shot up and looked at Susan who was pointing *behind* them. He had been paying so much attention to the dangers ahead   *he'd forgotten to look back* to see what was coming at them from behind—*and at sea you always look back.*

A large and dangerous *"black squall,"* with heavy rain and flashing lightning was sweeping down on them from behind—coming right at them. A black squall is a short, fast moving and *very violent storm*—with extremely heavy rain, lightning and high winds. They don't last long—usually only minutes—*but you'll never forget those few minutes.*

A squall caught the huge "tall-ship" *PRIDE OF BALTIMORE* by surprise and knocked it over on its side before the crew could reduce sail. The captain and several of its crew died as it roared out of the black night and caught them by surprise. According to one report, it was a "black wall" coming at them in the black night—*black against black*—and the crew couldn't see it coming. The huge tall-ship was instantly knocked down, the seas poured into open deck hatches and it went straight down—before the captain and crew below could get out. They went down with the ship. *There wasn't even time to send a distress signal* and the survivors drifted in a life-raft for days until they were rescued. Squalls can be awesome and deadly.

The crew of *ESCAPEE* had no more than two or three minutes at most before their own black squall hit and when it did they'd lose all visibility—*right there in the middle of that dangerous channel.* When that incredible deluge of rain and lightning hit they wouldn't be able to see a thing until it passed. Alan's heart sank. They were about to go speeding down one of the most dangerous channels in the Pacific—with no visibility. *The skier was going to be hurtling downhill—blind.*

"Carole," Alan shouted over the rising wind, "get a compass bearing on the reef on both sides—where it sticks out the farthest. Shout it out.   Susan, grab a pen and write it down when Carole calls it out. No room for mistakes." Alan rushed down and got rain jackets for them all. He knew the blasting rain would hit with the force of hailstones—*hailstones shot from shotguns.*

Sigrid had already taken a final bearing over the boat's big compass—right down the center of the channel. They put on their rain jackets and Carole called out the bearings to the reefs sticking out into both sides of the channel.   They were now entirely at the mercy of the currents—*God help them if those currents pushed them very far sideways.* They were as ready as could be when it seemed like someone "*turned out the lights*".

The squall hit with rain driving sideways like pellets from a shotgun—so hard they hurt. The sky went dark and all visibility was lost in the ferocious rain. They couldn't see anything beyond the front of *ESCAPEE* and at times *couldn't even see the front of the boat.* Susan and Carole huddled against each other on the side trying to protect themselves from the stinging force of the rain. Sigrid and Alan stood next to each other at the wheel, taking the full force of the blasting rain and concentrated on steering.

Black squalls are a thing apart. They have to be experienced to be believed. The ferocity of the rain can take your breath away—*literally*. The rain can be so heavy it sometimes seems to stop you from breathing. There seems to be *no more air* left and you feel as though you're breathing water. Large, powerful birds have been known to drown in mid-flight in these tropical squalls. *ESCAPEE* was now hurtling *blind* down the channel at full speed—barely under control—driven by the much stronger winds of the squall. Alan and Sigrid stood side by side—ignoring the stinging rain, watching only that big compass. They could see nothing else. Every time the boat swung off course, he and Sigrid together muscled the wheel over to bring her back on course. *It was all they could do now*.

Susan and Carole huddled together on the side—a dark blob. Alan could see their frightened faces, frozen in the flashes of lightning, which were all around them. *They were afraid. So was Sigrid. So was Alan*.

Alan called out, "*Susan, how long's this been going on?*"

She checked the stopwatch and shouted, "*eight minutes*". It had seemed like an hour.

"*Damn, this is a long one,* " Alan shouted to Sigrid who could hardly hear him though standing right next to him. Lightning made everyone look like a ghost when it hit—freezing the tense, anxious expressions on their faces.

Alan and Sigrid looked at each other, wondering the same thing—*what were those currents doing to ESCAPEE?*

"*Unfasten your safety harnesses!* " Alan shouted to Carole and Susan, trying to be heard over the noise of the furious rain. They didn't understand—he had told them to keep them fastened. Sigrid already had hers off—*she understood*. *ESCAPEE* could crash into one of those reefs at any moment now and he didn't want anyone to be trapped in the wreckage and killed. If they hit, their best chance for survival was to be thrown free of the wreckage and Alan watched to make sure they disconnected their harnesses from the boat. They had been speeding ahead *blind* for eleven minutes now—and those deadly reefs had to be very close by now.

"*How long now, Susan?*" Alan called.

"*Fourteen minutes,*" she called back over the noise the rain, thunder and flashing lightning.

Then—*just like that*—the squall was gone. That's how tropical squalls are—they hit suddenly and hard and they pass suddenly. The black wall had now passed over them and was moving on ahead, leaving them behind in the bright morning tropical sunlight, which beat down on their huddled bodies. Everyone looked around quickly to see where they were. They were *far* off course—much too far to the right—and Sigrid quickly brought *ESCAPEE* back into the center of the channel and away from those reefs which they would have hit in a few more minutes.

"*Three cheers for Sigrid,*" Alan called out and they loudly cheered Sigrid, who stood behind the wheel with a huge grin on her face. "*OK, now you guys—three cheers for us all!*" They were so relieved they cheered, hugged and congratulated each other while taking off the rain clothes. They were soon back to their bikinis and drying out in the brilliant morning sunlight. Their world was completely different from just *two minutes ago.* That's the tropics.

They'd worked perfectly together as a team under extreme pressure—*and it was extreme.* Alan later admitted that this was the worst situation he'd ever been in except of course when he was lost overboard. Sigrid agreed that was one of her worst experiences at sea.

After clearing the channel they entered open, safe waters and the winds eased off and it was suddenly a typical sunny tropical day with gentle trade-winds—and no reefs. Carole said, "*Alan, you've been going since yesterday. Take some time off and get some solid sleep. We'll take care of things up here. We've got it all under control.*"

Good idea—he'd have to be at his best when they entered Suva harbor—so he went below, stripped to his shorts and crashed in the nearest berth. As he drifted off into a deep sleep he heard the girls talking and laughing.

The squall had "broken the ice" between them. They had discovered they could count on each other when the chips were down and the pressures and danger had welded them into a "team". They were also discovering something else—*a personal "chemistry" was at work between them.* They genuinely liked each other and were on their way to becoming very good friends. The possible personality clashes and common problems and frictions of several people—especially strangers—living together in a small space just weren't happening.

By the time *ESCAPEE* sailed into the harbor at Suva everyone was feeling really good about themselves and each other. She had become what's called "a happy boat"—where people enjoy *each other's company* as well as the adventures they're having. They had left Tonga as complete strangers and didn't know what to expect or how they'd get along. During the cruise *they discovered they got along very well* and could count on one another in a crisis. They had learned a lot about the sea, *ESCAPEE,* themselves *and each other* during those first few days together.

It had been a very good first cruise.

The arrival of *ESCAPEE* in Suva with one man and three good-looking women in bikinis created quite a sensation. *It's not often you see one man with an all-female crew.* It does happen from time to time of course, but it often ends in a spectacular flop. It's the dream of a lot of men but if they're the macho, controlling type, expect sex as their "right" or are on some kind of power trip it usually ends in a high-profile blow-up. One guy sailed into Suva with four women on board, but as soon as they had anchored the women quietly packed up and called for the guy to come and look over the side into the dirty, oily water of Suva bay. *"Look at this,"* they called out to the guy. When he did, they pushed him into the filthy water in front of all the other boat crews—and quickly found crew positions on other boats. The guy was such a laughing stock he left the next day—*by himself.*

No one ever found anything offensive about Alan. There was no power trip going on here—no macho bullshit. It just wasn't Alan's way and besides he was still learning a lot himself and *knew* he didn't know it all. Also, the more he was around these women, the more he liked them. They were what his grandfather who had raised him back in Iowa called "good people".

The skippers of other boats were fully expecting another *"all-girl crew"* break-up. They love that because several women are suddenly available and looking for crew positions. As Sigrid rowed them ashore to the yacht club for dinner, all eyes were on them for any signs of tension. Several of the skippers would have offered a crew position to the women at a second's notice if they sensed any problem. The *"vultures"*—skippers at the bar needing crew—watched them closely. To their amazement they found the group of four obviously happy in each other's presence. They didn't seem to want to get away from each other—although they had just been cooped up together in a small space for several days. That *really* surprised the vultures.

They ate, had their drinks and talked until the dining room closed, re-living that frightening passage through the channel. *Carole was on a high*—she had started off afraid of seasickness and knowing *nothing* about boats or the sea, but wound up being able to steer and handle *ESCAPEE* in large waves. She was very happy with what she'd discovered about herself and that Alan had called her *"a natural"*.

Susan was still wide-eyed at that experience and proud of how she'd handled herself, working right alongside Alan and the others. Sigrid had been through a lot of close calls in her time at sea but admitted that was one of the scariest.

They were all so absorbed in talking with each other they hardly noticed any of the others around them. The vultures were ready to pounce but after that seeing how well they got along together they gave it up as a lost cause. When they returned to *ESCAPEE* Carole said, "Alan, I know you agreed to bring me only as far as Fiji, *but do you think there's any chance I could stay on with you guys? At least* a *little while longer?*" Sigrid and Susan looked towards Alan, waiting for his answer.

Alan knew that question was coming. Carole had been the big surprise of the cruise, so he said, "well, let's see now," pretending deep, agonizing thought. "Let's be democratic about this and take a vote. *Everyone in favor of Carole staying with us, give her a big hug.*" Everybody did—*Alan too.*

"*Carole, don't even ask. You're one of us now.*" Alan wanted to keep this winning team together—at least a little while longer.

Fiji is called "*the South Pacific Eden*" because of its beautiful islands and beaches. However, the British put the capital in Suva—the wettest, most disagreeable, rainiest spot in Fiji—much the same as the Dutch put the capital of Indonesia in the hottest, most disease-ridden place they could find—and then died by the thousands. *Figure that.* Alan was going to get some supplies and parts and get out of Suva to the sunny, warm western part of Fiji—which really *is* a south Pacific Eden.

They would've left within two days, except for a minor inconvenience—an appendectomy. Alan had awakened with a tenderness in his abdomen, but ignored it while he and the girls went shopping at a street market. By mid-day, he couldn't touch it without pain. Afterwards the pain grew severe and he could hardly stand. The girls grabbed him to keep him from falling and someone called an ambulance. He was rushed to the local hospital and diagnosed as having an inflamed appendix, which had to be removed.   All he could think of was *thank God it didn't happen at sea.*

The procedure was simple and was expertly done later the same day. He was soon recovering back in his room when a huge Fijian nurse came in and said, *"my name's Margaret, you know, like Princess Margaret. My momma named me after her."* Her big smile and friendly face quickly put Alan at ease.

"What's troublin' you honey? You don' look like no sick man to me," she said and laughed. She looked at his chart and said, "You look fit and ready to go home soon. You just keeping restin' and we'll have you out of here in no time. Now I want to tell you something," and she got close to him, almost whispering, *"you better get well and get out of this hospital fast or these Indian doctors will kill you, that's for sure."*

"What?"

"These Indian doctors are all butchers," she said, "and they'll kill you if you don' get yourself out of here soon's you can. People like you come in here a little sick and they take'em out the back door in rubber bags. It's those Indian doctors." With that up-lifting, encouraging word Big Margaret continued her rounds, leaving a very shaken Alan behind.

Soon afterwards an Indian doctor arrived and looked him over. "Well, you're doing just fine. But you need another two days recuperation before you go. We want to be sure everything's healing well. The doctor then looked around and said, *"but be careful of these Fijian nurses. They don't know what they're doing. I can prescribe the right medication for you, but there's no telling what they'll give you. You could get some very bad stuff stuck in your arm or down your throat—happens all the time."*

What the hell is this? Alan thought. The nurses said the doctors were butchers and the doctors said the nurses would stick anything into his arm or down his mouth. The girls came for a visit and Alan told them what the nurse and doctor had said.

Another foreigner—an Australian who was a patient—walked down the hall and they motioned for him to come in. "Do you live here?" Alan asked. He did. "What's going on around here?" and told the man what the nurse and doctor had said.

"Yes, it's a big problem here," the man said. "Here's the story in a nutshell. The British set up big sugar plantations in Fiji in the late 19th century or so, but they couldn't get the Fijians to work. I mean, why do all that hot, backbreaking work? The Fijians have everything they need. Everything grows here, they build their own thatched roof houses from natural materials and food literally drops off the trees into their laps. They help one another if they get in trouble and need something—that's their tribal social security system and custom. So why did they need to do all that back-breaking work in the hot sugar fields just so the British could make some money?

"Anyway the British smelled profits and brought in thousands of Indians all the way from India and put them to work in the fields. Now, you've never seen *two people more different* than the big, easy-going, laid-back Fijians and the intense little, hard-working Indians. *You could scour the earth and find no two people more different from each other.* And the British brought the Indians to the Fijian Islands and dropped them here. The Indians grew in population far faster than the Fijians—just look at how crowded India is. Now almost half the people are Indians—here on *South Pacific Fijian islands*.

"The Indians out-worked them and now own almost all the businesses. They can't own the land, but they control the economy. But they're not satisfied with that. They want the money *and* the power. They want to run everything—and that's where the Fijians draw the line. At least that's what the Fijians tell me. So this conflict is not going to get any better."

"*That's why the Fijian nurse doesn't like the Indian doctor...*" Carole said

"*...and why the Indian doctor bad mouths the Fijian nurses,*" he added. "*These people really don't like each other.*"

"They kept separate and seemed to get along fine until the Indians started trying to grab it all. That's when the Fijians dug in and things got bad. They don't want to be underprivileged minorities on their own islands. Anyway, that's just my own personal opinion and how I see it."

"*Well, we're here to see the beauty of Fiji,* not get mixed up in politics," Carole said, and everyone nodded their heads in agreement. "We just want to enjoy these islands along with Alan—*or without him* if either the Indian doctor or Fijian nurse kills him," she said laughing.

"*Hey, wait a minute.* This is no fun. I want outa here," Alan protested.

After the girls had gone, Big Margaret stopped by to see how he was feeling. "Who're those three women who came to see you?"

"*Oh, I live with them*"

"You live with *three* women?" she asked unbelievingly.

"*Yes*"

"*Which one's yours?*" she asked

"*All three. They're all three mine,*" Alan said, joking with her.

"*No....no...that can't be!*"

"*Sure it is,*" he said. "We live together and they're all three mine..."

"*No...go on. You're making fun with me,*" Big Margaret said with a very skeptical look on her face.

"*Just ask them when they come to see me next time.*"

The next day they were back and Big Margaret barged right in and asked them directly. *She had to know—now.*

"This man says you alls his women. Now that ain't true, is it?"

They got the picture and played the role. *"Sure, he's our man. He may not look like much, but he's sure man enough for us all,"* Carole said. *Isn't that right girls?"* she asked, looking at Sigrid and Susan. *"Right,"* Susan said, *"we take turns and he keeps us all happy."* Sigrid nodded her head in vigorous agreement.

"Well, I never...." Big Margaret said and rushed down the hall. They started laughing, but Big Margaret was back in a flash bringing a group of big Fijian nurses with her.

"This here man's got all them ladies there," she said. *"Can you believe that?"* The nurses shyly covered their faces and laughed so hard their big bellies were shaking. Alan soon became the hit of the hospital and nurses came and went at all hours just to get a glimpse of the man who had all those women. *It was absolutely scandalous—*and they loved every minute of it.

Two days later, Alan said goodbye to Big Margaret and the group of nurses who came to see him off. *"Got to go take care of those women,"* he said—and they shook with laughter all over again.

"Now, you wait a little while and don't go getting too active so's that heals real good," Big Margaret said.

"You don't know these women, Margaret. They won't let me wait," he said and they laughed again.

Sigrid and Carole arrived in a taxi to take him back to the boat where they had a big "welcome home" dinner on board *ESCAPEE.* In Alan's absence they had shopped and loaded up with fresh food from the street markets and got *ESCAPEE* ready to go. The next day they left rainy Suva for the sunny and beautiful *"real Fiji"* at the western end of the main island of Viti

Levu. Because of the dangerous reefs they could sail only during the daytime and towards sunset of the first day they pulled into the beautiful, blue lagoon in front of the Fijian Yanuca Island Resort—a luxurious resort complex.

The next morning they went ashore for breakfast, wearing only their bikinis, which by now was "standard uniform" on *ESCAPEE*. As usual Alan had his pirate outfit on— or as Susan jokingly put it—*"everything but the parrot and the eye-patch."* Sigrid rowed them ashore and her bikini top barely contained her abundant breasts as she moved forward and backwards while rowing. They were an accident waiting to happen. The hotel guests having breakfast had a view of it all— three striking women in bikinis on that boat with one man. As they entered the dining room which over-looked the magnificent bay where *ESCAPEE* was anchored, every eye was on them. They ordered breakfast and Susan poured Alan's coffee. Carole asked him where he wanted to cruise for the next year or so and their eyes were fastened on him in rapt attention as he talked of New Caledonia, Bali and Singapore.

Everyone in the room looked at the pirate surrounded by three women in bikinis and asked, *"who is this guy?"*

As they finished their breakfasts and were lingering over coffee, Alan slipped away to call Ann from the hotel phone. It was the day before in Seattle due to the time change and Ann was there with her mother.

"Ann, it's Alan. I'm calling from Fiji. How are you?"

"Alan! It's great to hear from you. I'm fine...how're you?"

"We had a good trip from Tonga—a little scary at times. I'm in Fiji now. How's it looking with your mom? Any chance of you coming back down?"

"I'd love to—you know that—but it's just not going to work. I can't see any possibility at this time. Mom's not doing well at all and she's still afraid of a nursing home. She'd be dead within a year. I'm so sorry Alan, but I have to be truthful. *I just don't see it happening.*"

"I'm really sorry to hear that Ann. I was hoping....."

"I know Alan, but I've had to face the facts. It's just not going to be possible. You'll find someone else to sail with you. You're a nice man. You need someone with you...."

"But I want you Ann. You."

"I know Alan. I miss you too, but some things just don't seem meant to be."

"I'll call you in a month or so Ann"

"You do that Alan—and keep sailing."

Well, that was it, Alan realized. He'd kept his hopes alive but now he had to face the fact—his life with Ann was over. He returned to the dining room to find the girls talking and laughing with each other. He needed to get out of there and *do something.* "Why don't we do a little snorkeling on these coral reefs? I hear they're incredibly beautiful. Then we'll head out around mid-day when the sun's high—better visibility."

They snorkeled for a couple of hours taking in the breathtaking beauty of the live coral and the multi-colored fish swimming all around them. It was another world down there just a few feet beneath the surface. They floated on the surface, watching the incredible show just beneath them. One spectacularly colored fish after another swam by, painted a combination of outrageous, brilliant colors no artist would ever be bold enough to try. Sigrid took pictures with her underwater camera. No description prepared any of them for the beauty of Fiji's coral reefs and the incredibly multi-colored fish. By now the lunchtime crowd was in the dining room and watched the pirate and the three women in bikinis have lunch in the cockpit of *ESCAPEE* after their swim. These hotel guests had flown all the way to Fiji to have an adventure, and here was this pirate—

captain of his own world-cruising boat and living with three good-looking women in bikinis. *Now that was a real adventure.*

Alan wanted to leave when the sun was high so they could see to thread their way out of the twisting, unmarked channel and around those dangerous clumps of coral. That's called *"eyeball navigation"*—and the best time to do it is when the sun is high and behind you. Carole raised the anchor and Sigrid motored slowly in a circle while Susan climbed to the spreader about halfway up the mast to give her better visibility for the tricky channel.

ESCAPEE'S spreader consists of two aluminum *arms* that stick out of the mast on either side, about halfway up. They *spread* the wire cables running through their ends, which help to hold the mast up. Susan was up the mast in a flash and perched herself on one of the spreaders. From up high she had excellent visibility of the dark clumps of coral and called directions down to Sigrid, who steered through the twisting, unmarked entrance. Alan stood on the bow with Carole, watching the coral reefs slip by on each side.

He'd tried to climb to the spreaders once with Ann steering but his bones and his back just couldn't take it. Susan was like a monkey—up in a flash. They soon cleared the channel and headed out towards the open sea and the rolling waves of the Pacific.

"Susan, come on down" Alan called.

"You should see the view from up here. Just a little longer."

"No...down now!" Alan called out and Susan scampered down as *ESCAPEE* started rolling in the ocean swells—she would've had trouble hanging on. Alan apologized for having to shout at her but Susan understood. She knew he was right, she said, and gave Alan that sweet smile of hers which would melt any heart.

They were headed westward along the south coast of Viti Levu island and were now getting close to *the real topical paradise*—the one that fully justified Fiji's tourist slogan, "*The Way The World Should Be*". At the western end of the main island of Viti Levu, there is a gigantic, protected lagoon which is sheltered from the ocean by a massive reef complex. The reef creates the sheltered, tranquil and unspeakably beautiful waters of western Fiji.

Inside the massive lagoon are many islands, some with villages and a large number of small ones that are uninhabited. There are also a number of famous resorts, such as the Turtle Island Resort, where the move *The Blue Lagoon* was filmed. The massive lagoon is shallow and has uncharted coral reefs and shifting sand banks, so boats move around only during the day when they can see. *ESCAPEE* was headed for an island, which is the home of the Malolo-lai-lai Yacht Club—a hang-out for cruising boats from all over the world. Around four, they realized they couldn't make it safely all the way that day and decided to anchor in a small, sheltered cove for the night. Within five minutes everyone was in the water and swam around the little bay and onto the white, sandy beach.

" *I know—how about dinner on the beach tonight,*" Susan said.

"*Ja...gut..wunderbar!* " Sigrid shouted and Alan looked at her in surprise—that once-somber German girl was getting downright enthusiastic and really loosening up. She was a lot more relaxed now and Alan figured it was the happy, informal ways of Carole and Susan, all the informality on board *ESCAPEE*—and just getting to know everyone better. Whatever it was, that stiff German girl was changing in front of their eyes.

Susan and Carole gathered some driftwood for a fire while Alan and Sigrid swam back to *ESCAPEE* to get some of the fresh fish they'd caught that day on the way there and the other things they would need for the barbeque. That night they had a fresh fish barbeque on the sandy beach while *ESCAPEE* rocked gently at anchor. When the fire went out the moonless sky above was filled with more stars than any of them had ever dreamed possible. *It was wall-to-wall stars.* It seemed as if one layer of stars was behind every other layer—off into infinity— but still close enough to reach out and touch or scoop up. They talked and sometimes just sat there, absorbed in the magic of the moment.

Carol said, "*this is just so great.* I never noticed the stars living in Chicago—you just lose touch with Mother Nature. Then, all this! *I've got an idea.* Sigrid, you're heading back to Germany and are in no hurry. Susan, why don't you tell your father you're taking a year off and I'll put my plans on hold. *Why don't we just keep on going with Alan—and keep him out of trouble? Look how we saved his bacon with that appendectomy—he would've collapsed helplessly in the street. And can you picture him up on those spreaders? No way! We all know old Alan here couldn't make it on his own without us, right?*"

"*Right,*" Susan chimed in.

" *Ja, Ellen no make it mitout us,*" Sigrid added.

Come on guys," Alan said, "*give me a break.*" But he really was hoping they could all stay together a little longer.

"*And who in their right mind wants all this to end?*" Carole finished off. They sat looking at the wall-to-wall stars above, everyone lost in their own thoughts.

The seed of an idea had been planted.

The next morning Susan calculated the zigzagging course they had to take through that maze of islands and coral patches to get to the Malolo-lai lai Yacht Club. She'd become really good at navigation and piloting through reefs by now. "Alan, check this out," she said. "I think we should plan to be at worst of the coral patches around 11. The sun will be behind us and high, so we should have great visibility for the next couple of hours. By then I figure we should be at the yacht club."

Alan took a look and said, "*looks good to me. Let's do it.*" Susan was precise and exact and really got the hang of tricky coastal piloting among reefs and hazards. They raised the anchor and were soon surfing down the rolling waves of the open ocean. A few hours later they went through the channel entrance into the massive lagoon and it was as if someone suddenly slammed the door shut to the big ocean waves. They stopped rolling, the waters were calm—and there was nothing but flat water so clear you could see the bottom.

For the last hour Susan sat high on the spreaders, guiding them through the maze of dark coral patches and around the small sandbanks sticking up out of the shallow water of the huge blue lagoon. By three in the afternoon they approached the bay in front of the Malolo-lai-lai Yacht Club and everyone's eyes popped out—there must've been thirty cruising boats from all over the world anchored there.

Yacht Club? Any member of a stuffy yacht club in the US would've had a heart attack to see what called itself a "yacht club" here. Membership "fees" were a dollar a year and anyone who arrived by boat qualified as a member. It was a center for sailing boats from all over the world—they anchored in the sheltered bay, the crews ate in the dining room and relaxed at the huge, waterside bar. Most of the buildings were large, round, thatched "huts" with just a floor and thatched grass roofs overhead and no walls—all open to the gentle winds. As a "member" of the club, they gave you a card and carved the names of all visiting boats in the big beam above the bar. So many had been carved into the beam it looked like it might collapse with just one more name. There were even a few laundry machines on the island—*every sailor's wet dream.* In short it was a relaxing and well-run haven for wandering cruising boats from all over the world.

As *ESCAPEE* entered the bay and started to anchor, all eyes—in the bar, in the restaurant and on the anchored boats—watched the new boat arriving with three women in bikinis and one guy trying very hard to look like a pirate. Every guy was asking himself, *"do they, or don't they?"*—thinking of only one thing. The vultures looking for women crew were already sharpening their knives. Long before *ESCAPEE'S* anchor was firmly set more than one sailor had decided to move in on the guy who was trying to look like a pirate and take his women. The way they saw it this guy had a couple of women to spare and if he wasn't man enough to keep the one he *might* be entitled to—well, that's the pirate's own tough luck.

The vultures saw *ESCAPEE* as a sort of *supply truck* bringing a priceless tank of water to a thirsty desert—and the men were getting their drinking cups ready. "Thank you, kind sir, for bringing these lovely ladies to us," they were clearly thinking as they planned their moves, *"we'll take it from here."*

Every eye watched them get in their dinghy as Sigrid rowed them ashore, her large breasts once again almost popping out of her bikini top as she moved forward and backwards. Alan was sure that bets were being made at the bar as to whether they'd stay inside or not. And every eye stayed on them as they walked up to the bar and ordered a few cold beers. The *hunting season* had opened. The *water truck* had arrived on the thirsty desert and woe to the phony make-believe pirate who had innocently brought them there.

Alan stepped out to see if there was a fax awaiting him—he'd given the fax number to his best friend, Michael, to pass to his kids. In just the short time he was gone, the men moved in and soon encircled the girls. Like everyone in Suva, they figured this *"one man --all women crew"* business wasn't working out. It usually didn't—everyone knew that—and these women would surely be ripe for the picking by now. One thing was clear—that guy trying to pass for a pirate was *certainly* no great specimen of manhood. By the time Alan got back he found a tight circle of men around the girls and pushed his way through. By this time Carole had about had enough.

"*Hey, hey,*" she said, "*back off you guys. Haven't you seen a woman before?*" Her firm but humorous approach did the job—and soon Alan was alone at the bar with the three girls. Every guy in the place envied him. But it was just a *temporary truce*—every man there was planning his *next* move. Carole knew that and had an idea how to deal with it.

"*Sigrid, Susan, let's show these guys we're really with Alan so they leave us alone from now on.*"

Alan heard Carole but didn't know what the hell she was talking about. These three were intelligent, smart—*and fast thinkers*. Not even Alan's best friend would claim he was a fast thinker. Solid and reliable—*yes*. Persistent—*hell yes!* But fast—*no*. Alan was about to discover a basic fact of life of living with these three women—*he'd never be able to keep up with them*. Carole had already told Alan that he seemed to have a "*comprehension problem*" when it came to understanding women—*especially them. Alan was about to find out how true that was*.

Soon—*to his utter astonishment*—they had their arms around him and were stroking his hair, handing him his beer, massaging his shoulders and were draped all over him. He was shocked and *still* didn't know what the hell was going on. Sigrid leaned over to try to hug him and accidentally shoved her abundant breasts right into his face. Everyone in the bar stared in envy—and Alan was totally flustered and struggled with that "*comprehension problem*" of his. But the girls got their message across loud and clear—*they were with Alan. Hands off.*

When they went back to the boat the girls started laughing and couldn't stop. "*Did you see the look in their faces when we fell all over Alan?*" Susan said. Sigrid was laughing as hard as Alan had ever seen her. "Hey, what an act we've got, huh," Susan said.

"*And you, my friend*," Carole added, "*have one hell of a reputation.*"

That was really true. For the first time in his life *everyone wanted to be Alan Richards—pirate and lover.* And Carole had been right as usual—after that scene in the bar, whenever they went to shore for lunch, dinner or just to hang around the beach no one bothered them. They were clearly Alan's—and every man there asked himself the obvious question—"*what the hell's this guy got that I haven't?*"

People living on cruising boats are a very social bunch and this group was no different. They often had beachside barbeques and potluck dinners. By far the largest group of people at Malolo- lai- lai were couples—solid couples or even families with children —not those pushy, women-hungry single guys hanging around the bar. They got together to socialize at barbeques and potluck dinners every few days. Alan and the girls went to each one and drew stares as Sigrid rowed them ashore. They were the rare exception—a man with an all female crew on an obviously "happy boat". The girls added to that "*happy boat*" reputation by what they called "*the performance*" which they soon perfected. The girls arrived at the barbeque or potluck dinner carrying all the plates, food and a folding chair for Alan. He carried nothing—just walked up from the dinghy at the water's edge as though he was king of the world. Carole unfolded the chair and he sat down. Sigrid opened and served him a cold beer while Susan brought him a sandwich. Sigrid re-filled his beer and Carole slowly massaged his shoulders.

Every man there—*however happily married*—stared at Alan in open, undisguised envy. The wives and girlfriends looked angrily at their staring, daydreaming husbands or boy friends and one woman was heard snapping, "*quit hallucinating Henry. Don't even think about it!* " No one ever seemed to get upset with Alan or the girls—just at their husbands and boy friends for their unabashed staring and "hallucinating"—*like poor Henry.*

Every man—every single man without exception—
wanted to be Alan Richards, *make-believe pirate* and up until
now, *make-believe lover*.

After a few days the crowds of sailors, the crush of boats
and all the busy activity began to get old. *"Let's go find some
remote, uninhabited island and just hang out,"* Alan said and the
girls were more than ready. They got the chart and guidebook
out and found a group of islands a few hours away. The
guidebook said one large island had a traditional Fijian village
"where you can see life the way it's been lived for centuries".
That got their attention. And to make it even better, there were
several nearby small islands with no one on them where they
could swim, fish and just take it easy.

Alan sent Susan ashore to fax her father that she was
fine and sailing westward with *ESCAPEE.* As usual she
arranged the timing so he could never reach her to order her back
home. Alan had once suggested she call him and she re-acted
with such a horrified expression Alan let it drop, sensing a real
tension between Susan and her father.

When she came back, Susan worked out the winding,
zigzag course necessary to keep them off the coral patches and
shifting sand banks that were scattered throughout the huge
lagoon. They left around nine the next morning and reached the
island about three in the afternoon, after several hours of
dodging sandbars and big patches of coral. Coral is a living
growing thing—and no charts could ever show where they all
were. It had been intense *eyeball navigation* all the way. Out of
respect for the traditional village, when they went ashore the
girls had loose dresses over their bikinis and Alan wore a sun hat
instead of his usual wildly-colored bandanna. The guidebooks
were very firm about it—when you visited the "old Fijian"
villages, you wore proper clothes and respected their traditions.
One of those traditions was the presentation of the Kava roots to
the chief upon arrival.

Kava has played a major role in Fiji's culture for centuries. When Captain James Cook was in Polynesia in 1769, he saw the Kava ceremony for the first time. Kava is one of 2,000 members of the pepper family. In the old days, after pulling the plant from the ground, virgins were selected to chew it until it turned into a pulp. They then spit the messy results into a bowl of coconut milk, which was then strained through a cloth. The results of all this were then served to the chief and his honored guests who ceremonially sipped it in small quantities.

When *sipped* properly Kava sometimes leaves a slight tingling on the lips. Sometimes the lips go numb—similar to how a person might feel after a visit to the dentist. Others will even feel a little tipsy or sedated—all depending on the person. It's been called *"Mother Nature's Valium"* and "the root of tranquility".

It's supposed to be sipped in small quantities in a ceremonial setting. Taken in larger quantities the effect can be *seriously* mind-altering, sedating, hallucinogenic or "intoxicating"—all depending on the person. There's no alcohol in it, but when taken in excess, the effects on some people make them act plain drunk.

Kava roots are a traditional gift to the chief of the island to be presented by the visitors upon arrival and Alan had a bundle ready. The tradition called for Alan and the girls to wait on the beach until a boy came and escorted the group's leader to the elaborate tribal "greeting hall," where the chief would be awaiting him. These greeting halls are often magnificent high–domed structures made of thatch and bamboo, with floors of highly polished wood. Some are so beautiful they should be in museums.

Word of their arrival quickly spread and a boy was sent to get Alan while the native chief put on his ceremonial finery to meet them. When the chief was fully dressed and ready to receive them Alan was brought in to meet the chief who was, by then, resplendent in his tribal finery and sitting cross-legged on the highly polished wood floor of the ceremonial hall.

Alan had been instructed to sit cross-legged in front of the chief, keeping a respectful distance away. The chief said *"Bula"*—which is both a greeting and a hello—welcoming Alan "and his people" to the island and asked why they had come. Alan said they came to learn about their traditional Fijian way of life and then placed the tied bundle of Kava roots in front of the chief—half way between himself and the chief—as he had been told to do.

If the chief accepted the bundle of Kava roots they were welcomed on the island as his guest. If the chief didn't like his looks and decided not to accept the bundle of Kava they would have to leave. Much to Alan's relief, the chief reached over and pulled the bundle of Kava to him and said, *"you and your people are welcome on my island. You may come and go as you please."* Alan bowed his head to thank him, and the chief was gone. He returned to the girls waiting at the beach and said, *"we're in,"* and explained what had happened.

They strolled through the traditional grass-thatched huts of the village while the naturally warm and friendly people smiled at them and said *"Bula"*. Some said *"Bula, Bula"*— meaning they were *very* welcome.

They saw a dive shop at the edge of the village and went in. It was run by a New Zealander—a Kiwi—who explained that the village allowed him to bring guests to dive on the incredibly beautiful reefs of this and nearby islands and this earned the village some money. The Kiwi said, "You folks are here at a good time. I've got a new dive boat arriving tomorrow and the village is doing the entire traditional welcoming ceremony for a new boat—just like they've done for centuries. *Don't miss it.*"

The next morning they went back on shore and the island was hopping with activity. Everyone was dressed in traditional garb. The men wore the traditional Sulu skirts and some had charcoal slash marks on their faces, which made them look very fierce. A thatch "arch" had been built along the beach and some pigs were roasting in the pit. The entire village had stopped everything for this great celebration to welcome the new dive boat. Alan and the girls dressed modestly and stood on the beach next to six very large, young Fijian girls in huge, white bras and grass skirts with white panties underneath. They were giggling and laughing with excitement and Alan asked a Fijian what was happening.

He said that, as in the old days, the new boat would arrive and anchor in the bay. The "women-hungry" crew just in from a long absence at sea would jump overboard and swim to shore and chase the "virgins"—those six big, fat young women—down the beach. If they caught the virgins *before* they got safely through the arch, they got the girls. If the girls made it through the arch first, they were safe.

"They don't want to be safe," he whispered to Alan. Everyone stood along the beach as the new dive boat entered the bay, anchored and the randy, women-starved crew jumped overboard and started swimming ashore. By this time the six fat "virgins" were jumping up and down and squealing with excitement. The second the women-hungry sailors reached the beach, the virgins shrieked and started running—as fast as their big bodies would carry them—and the lusty sailors took out after them.

Alan was shocked at how fast those huge, fat girls could run. They flew along the beach towards the safety of the arch as all the villagers cheered them on. But as the virgins ran they looked back over their shoulders and *seemed to slow down a little* so the men racing after them could catch up. The man was right—they *wanted* to be caught. Those six fat virgins timed it just right. The moment they reached the safety and protection of the arch, the women-hungry sailors caught up with them and piled on top and all the bodies—the fat virgins and the randy sailors—all rolled into the makeshift arch and knocked it down.

The villagers, the virgins and the sailors dissolved into howls of laughter.

"They didn't even *try* to get away," Susan said in surprise.

"Susan, honey, they *wanted* to be caught" Carole said. *"They were tired of being virgins. Weren't you?"* Susan blushed.

Next was the formal "boat welcoming" ceremony in the same large ceremonial building where Alan had been welcomed the day before. This was a somber ceremony and everyone was in full tribal regalia. The Fijians honor and preserve their tribal culture perhaps more than any other people of the South Pacific. The fierce-looking Fijian sitting next to Alan wore the Sulu skirt and had charcoal slash marks on his face. He was a bank manager on the main island who'd come back to his home island for this ceremony.

The chief sat on the polished wood floor in the middle and the elders sat in a semi-circle in front of him. Everyone else sat on the floor farther away and Alan and the girls were allowed to sit off to the side. The drums stated beating and some men brought in several large hollowed-out gourds full of Kava. One of the men dipped a half-coconut shell in it and took it to the chief who had the first sip. Next he gave a sip to each of the tribal elders. One half-shell of Kava was enough for four or five men to have a sip.

Drums kept beating during the Kava drinking ceremony, but as soon as the last sip was taken the drums began beating even faster and tribal dancers started a foot-stomping dance ritual that held Alan and the girls in awe. The chief nodded and someone came over with a half a coconut shell of Kava for the guests. Alan drank the first sip. It was the color of muddy water and had no taste to it. Then Sigrid, Carole and Susan were offered sips. The Kiwi dive shop manager next to them leaned over and whispered, "this is quite an honor. Usually, outsiders aren't allowed to participate. You guys are really lucky."

A speech in Fijian followed and then it was over. Everyone got up and left and Alan was talking with the Kiwi when he noticed Sigrid, Carole and Susan over by the gourds, helping themselves to more of the leftover Kava. As far as they were concerned the ceremony was finished, everyone was gone and all this Kava was "leftovers'—*so why let it all go to waste? That would be a shame, so they helped themselves to more— much more.* They passed the half-coconut shell around, drank it all down, refilled it and then guzzled it again. Each girl had at least two full half-shells—*or more*—several times more than the huge Fijians had sipped.

"*Hey, be careful with that stuff,*" the Kiwi said.

"*I no feel nuzing,*" Sigrid said

"*Me neither,*" Susan said. "This stuff's got no taste. None. *What's the big deal, here?*" she asked, swallowing the last of her second coconut shell full of Kava. "*I've tasted soft drinks with more punch to it than this.*"

Carole was on her *third* coconut shell. "It's has no taste at all," she said. "*So this is all there is to it, huh?*" she asked, sounding disappointed. Sigrid had matched her drink for drink.

"Well, you know in the old days, the Kava root wasn't pounded as it is now," the Kiwi said. "The root was chewed by virgins. They chewed little pieces into pulp and spit it into bowls. When they had enough fully-chewed Kava, they added some coconut milk and the chiefs drank it."

"*Wooeeee!*" Carole shouted, "*any virgins here? Count me out.*" She looked at Susan who turned bright red, "*no, not me,*" she said shyly.

"*Weellllll,*" Carole said slurring her words, "*how's bout Sigrid? Sigrid old girl, you a virgin?*" Carole was feeling no pain—*the Kava had started its work.*

"*She's getting high and doesn't know it,*" the Kiwi said. "Watch. In a minute she'll probably start trying to feel her lips and can't. They'll be completely numb—they're usually the first to go. *You'd better get these women back to the boat. The Fijians don't like any public display of drunkenness—and these women are getting there fast.* I think you'd better get a move on. Need some help with them?"

"*Sure do, thanks,*" Alan said and he and the Kiwi took the coconut shells from the protesting girls who wanted more and guided them away from the village, straight towards the beach and the dinghy.

By now Carole couldn't feel her lips at all and was desperately running her fingers over her face, searching for them. They were totally numb and she couldn't feel them at all. Sigrid started walking in slow, giant exaggerated steps—trying to make each step longer than the last—and laughing hilariously at her sand-covered feet. Susan had started dancing and twirling around like a ballet dancer doing a pirouette—moving to music no one else heard.

"*This stuff's treacherous,*" the Kiwi said. "*It has no taste and you can't tell when you've had too much—then the delayed re-action hits you—and I mean hits.* It affects people differently and you never know how they're going to re-act. I've seen people drunk, sedated or convinced the sea was blood or full of dragons. One woman thought her hair had become snakes—she was running around screaming and trying to pull her hair out. We had to wrestle her to the ground and pin her arms down. You just never know how they'll re-act. *One thing I can tell you— they're going to have a 'hang-over from hell'.*"

Somehow they got the high stepping, laughing Sigrid, the ballet-dancing Susan and the lip-searching Carole into the dinghy. "You need some help getting them back on board?" the Kiwi asked. "I don't think so," Alan said. "Got to go. Thanks."

He rowed back to *ESCAPEE* with the three women who were by now somewhere off in their own Kava-induced fantasy worlds. When he reached the boat he had the job of getting them all safely back on board. *Dammit*, he thought, *I should've asked the guy to help me.* How am I going to get them back on board? When he tried to get tall, strong Sigrid up she turned belligerent and said, "*no, I want go back*". Susan had fallen asleep—she was probably sedated—and lay on the floor of the dinghy.

Carole had started moaning, "*my lips are gone, my lips are gone*" and was convinced they had fallen off into the water. She started trying to get out of the dinghy into the water to search for them.

"*No, Carole*," Alan said. "*Not now.* Wait a minute and I'll go with you."

"*You shuuur?*" she asked.

"Yes, now sit right where you are. *Don't move!*"

Alan somehow managed to push and pull an unresisting Susan on board, but there was no way he could get Sigrid or Carole back on board if they didn't want to go. Then the problem solved itself—Sigrid needed to go to the bathroom and *willingly* climbed on board. *What a break that was!* Alan could never have made the strong German girl do anything she didn't want to do. He finally talked Carole into going on board and changing into her blue bikini—the one she liked best. He promised that *if* she did, he would definitely—*absolutely*—go swimming with her and together they'd find those missing lips.

By the time he got all three safely on board and in the cabin, Carole had started sobbing and crying over her missing lips. She staggered to the mirror and stuck her tear-stained face right in it to *see* if her lips were still there. In her condition she couldn't focus her eyes, so *now she not only couldn't feel them – she couldn't see them either. The mirror only confirmed her worst fears—those lips were gone!* She burst into deep sobbing over the tragedy of her lost lips and forgot all about going into the water to find them—just as Alan had hoped. At least she didn't think her hair had become snakes like the other woman, Alan thought gratefully.

Sigrid had gone to the potty and then stripped off her lava-lava skirt, her bikini top and was starting to pull her bottom off when Alan got her to sit down. *"I'm hot"* she muttered and then lapsed into a stream of German Alan couldn't understand. She kept trying to take her bikini bottom off and Alan kept telling her it wasn't hot. They got into a ridiculous argument— one in English and one in German—over whether it was hot. *This is dumb!* Alan thought, arguing in two languages over whether it's hot. He turned for a moment to look at Susan and Sigrid already had her bottom off and was sprawled asleep on her back, totally naked and muttering in German.

Carole was still at the mirror *trying to feel her lips or at least see them.* She could do neither and was sobbing and crying. Between her heaving sobs, she said, *"why can't I feel them? Where did they go?"* Then through all her mental and physical haze she suddenly figured out *why* she couldn't feel them. *They were gone!* That great tragedy was just too much to bear and her body shook with deep, wracking sobbing.

Susan was lying asleep on her berth one moment and the next she was sitting on the floor examining her hands up close, as if they were some wonderful marvels she'd never seen before. She moved them up and down with fingers in motion—like *little birds* or *butterflies* fluttering around and her eyes followed them in complete fascination. In her Kava-induced fantasy, her moving hands and fluttering fingers must have become those beautiful birds and butterflies, Alan figured. She was totally absorbed in her moving, turning and twisting hands. Then she fell over on her side, sound asleep and clearly sedated.

Alan pulled her up and put her gently back in her berth—*two down and one to go. Carole was still at the mirror looking for those missing lips* and was sobbing her heart out as she stared into the mirror, trying to focus her eyes and find them. Her body shook—wracked with heavy sobbing. She was devastated by their loss. *How would she ever live without them?* Sigrid was sprawled on her back naked, snoring and sometimes mumbling in German. Alan tried to cover her but she pushed him away. *"Hot"* she called out. He wasn't about to start *that* argument again.

Alan looked at the cabin with the three "drunken" women. They weren't *technically* drunk with alcohol of course, *but what a meaningless distinction that was!* Well, just let them sleep it off. *Tomorrow—oh, Lord tomorrow.* Those poor girls, Alan thought. The Kiwi said they'd have a *hangover from hell.*

He gently led a highly distraught Carole from the mirror where she'd given up all hope of finding her lips and got her to sit down on her berth. By now she was an absolute mess—one breast was out of her bikini top and her eyes were swollen almost shut from crying so hard. She collapsed into her berth and lay there, shaking and sobbing. Then she was gone—sound asleep.

At last they were all safe in their berths—in various stages of wreck and ruin. Alan poured himself a big brandy and went up to the cockpit and looked down at the wreckage below—these three intelligent women in states of total disaster. If they could only see themselves now. No, he thought, best not to. He slept in the cockpit that night to make sure no one came up on deck in that condition and fell overboard. That had led to the death of more than one intoxicated sailor—*and he wasn't about to take any chances.*

He slept uncomfortably, awoke at first light and looked down into the main cabin to see the disastrous carnage below. *It looked like a scene from a WW II battleground with casualties lying all around.* No one was moving. Carole had taken her bikini off and was sprawled out naked and Sigrid was right where he left her, lying on her back—also naked and snoring loudly.

Sometime during the night, Susan had ripped her dress and bikini off and was lying there stark naked, just like Sigrid and Carole—Alan figured the Kava must have made them feel hot. He was worried about Susan. She seemed to be having trouble breathing so he reached down to feel her forehead and when he did, she mumbled something, reached out and pulled him down to her—clutching him to her like a teddy bear. He tried to break her grip and ease back, but she held on. *"No', no"* she said as he tried to pull away. He finally wiggled free, pulled the sheet over her and started to make coffee—*they'd sure be needing lots of it.*

No one moved a muscle for a couple of more hours and that suited Alan just fine—he needed some peace and quiet after that unforgettable night. He had gone to sea to have new adventures and experiences—and here he was *with three naked women.* He remembered one of the old *Candid Camera* television programs, *What Do You Say To A Naked Lady?* Well, what do you say to *three* naked ladies? *Candid Camera* sure had nothing on him!

Sigrid slowly got up and headed for the bathroom where she violently and loudly threw up—making that same horrendous, nauseating, and truly impressive vomiting noise she'd only *pretended* to make before when asking if Carole might get seasick. *This time it was for real.* She staggered back to her berth and crashed, sound asleep.

Susan was mumbling something again and Alan was still worried about her. He moved close and heard her saying, *"got to pee, got to pee"*. Alan pulled the sheet off to let her get up, but she just lay there mumbling, *"got to pee"*. Damn, if he didn't take her, she'd do it right there!

He raised her up into a sitting position and got behind her, held her under her arms and sort of "walked" her to the door of the head. She stopped at the door and didn't move. *Oh no*, he thought, *have I got to pee for her, too?* He sat her down on the stool and held her steady as she swayed back and forth and peed. Alan lifted her back up and walked her back to her berth where she collapsed and softly mumbled something. Alan couldn't hear her and leaned down to hear what she was saying. *"Don't have to pee anymore."*

"*Well*, g*ood for you kid,* " he said as he pulled the sheet back over her.

Caroie jerked and moaned in her sleep as if she was having one nightmare after another.

It was at least *one* in the afternoon before they were more or less awake—each lost in her own misery, pounding head, private hell—whatever. They each had one thing in common—*they wished they were dead.* And if they couldn't have *that* wish, they wished yesterday had *never* happened. Alan just stood by ready to help do whatever he could—just be there for them and help them pass through the *hangover from hell.*

This bunch was going to need a *lot* of help getting squared away and back to normal. As far as the villagers could tell, there was no sign of life on *ESCAPEE* that day—*it was a deserted, dead boat.* No one got off. No one was in sight—Alan was down below, making coffee and food and trying to help each one pull themselves back together.

By one-thirty, he had a big pot of hot coffee and eggs and toast ready. He was going to *make* them drink coffee and get something in their stomachs to ease the effects of the Kava. *But they wanted only one thing—to die.* They were now clearly in that *hangover from hell* stage.

Alan brought aspirin and anything else that might ease their throbbing heads and then set out to force them to eat something. He spoon-fed Carole and Susan. Sigrid was sitting up and holding her head, rocking back and forth, refusing to eat anything. Alan tried to spoon-feed the first bites to her but she growled her refusal, pushing the food and Alan away. *He wasn't about to mess with that strong German girl in the mood she was in now*. After Carole and Susan ate a little they went back to a restless sleep. *By three* that afternoon Alan made sure everyone had some food—even Sigrid—and was making more coffee.

About three-thirty Carole had a spectacular throw-up— one that rivaled Sigrid's in nauseating noise—and just made it to the head. Alan wished he could get Susan to throw up. She really needed to. *By four–thirty* the first faint signs of intelligent life were beginning to return to *ESCAPEE*. Everyone was more or less awake and holding their heads and moaning. Susan and Carole were beginning to ask what happened yesterday after their memories took the rest of the day off. Carole asked, *"did you get the license number of the truck that hit us?"*

By six they were in a condition to listen and Alan told them everything that happened—*everything*. He spared no detail. He told of his struggle to get them safely on board and into bed. He told Susan about having to help her pee—and thought she'd crawl into a hole from embarrassment.

"And you, Sigrid" you lay there all night, naked on your back."

" *So, ja, what's* ze *big deal. Bodies natural, ja?"* She was right about that—that European frankness about bodies.

"What about me?" Carole asked slowly. *"Did I do anything stupid?"*

Well, she asked for it.   Instead of just *telling* her Alan did a graphic pantomime of Carole with her face touching the mirror, looking for her missing lips—the lips she could no longer feel or see—-and her body wracking with sobs because they were gone—*gone!*

"Oh my God," Carole said holding her head. *"I'll never live this down."*

By seven they were ready for some solid food—the first of that *day from hell* as it was later called. Alan fixed a simple dinner and they sat down and silently ate their food. Alan made them eat it all, even though his cooking wasn't all that good. Not a word was said and he then made them drink lots of water, to help flush the Kava out of their system.

About eight that night as the night-air cooled and the stars came out, they staggered up from the cabin, one by one, and sat silently beside Alan in the cockpit. More than 24 hours had passed since they had their Kava orgy and still no one felt like talking. Sigrid sat next to Alan on one side and Susan on the other. He put his arms around them both and they leaned their throbbing heads on his shoulders, looked up at the stars and desperately wished that yesterday had never happened.

Around nine Sigrid and Susan went down below to go to bed—this time to have a good, sound sleep. Carole moved over next to Alan and he put his arms around her. She slumped against him, laid her head on his shoulder and said, *"I'm sorry we put you through all this. What a stupid, stupid thing to do."*

"Carole, that's just part of life. We're not perfect and you know something nice—*we don't have to be. In Chicago maybe—but not out here.* Anyway, why use the word 'sorry' when we're just being ourselves? *And, tell me, what's wrong with being ourselves?* People get themselves into trouble when they aren't themselves—*that's where the trouble lies—not in being themselves.* So out here, just be yourself and never apologize for it.

"You're a nice man," she said and kissed him lightly on the mouth. "Good night" "Good night. Sleep well."

It was a *very* subdued boat the next morning as everyone awakened and tried to get busy as usual—*pretending that nothing had happened.* They each felt badly about what they'd done and what they'd put Alan through, so they just avoided the subject—if they didn't talk about it maybe it would go away.

But there was no mistaking it—a lot of the joy was gone from *ESCAPEE.* It had always been a relaxed and "happy boat," but now things just weren't the same anymore.

After a tense, silent breakfast, Alan had enough of it and said, *"now look, you guys, get over this. You did nothing wrong."*

"But we let you down," Susan whimpered.

"No you didn't. If we'd been at sea, yes. You bet! I would've used you for shark bait. I would have keel-hauled your asses. I would have tied you to the masts. I would have flogged you with cat-o-nine tails. I would have made Captain Bligh look like a saint. *But not here in a safe anchorage."* Alan was trying to make a joke of it but it just didn't work.

"We shouldn't have behaved that way," Carole added gravely.

"Look, you guys," Alan said, *"two things we don't allow on board—drugs and guilt. We're all out here to live life and living means being ourselves—maybe even being a little less than perfect sometimes. It's OK to be yourself you know--and why feel guilty for it? Come on, you guys are being much too hard on yourselves."*

They were still much too somber for Alan's tastes. "So the next one of you who says she's sorry—I'm going to throw you overboard." They laughed—*just a little.*

"Besides"—and he paused for effect—*"next time it's my turn. You want to know what pisses me off—I mean really pisses me off? Now, I'm going to lay this one on you—straight from the shoulders—no mincing words. I'm pissed off that you had all the fun. So next time, it's my turn!* You'll have to drag me on board, and guess what—Susan gets the personal pleasure of taking me to the potty. Then you'll have to work all night just to get me sober again. *Am I ever looking forward to that!"*

This time they really laughed.

Life was slowly getting back to normal on *ESCAPEE.*

CHAPTER TWO

THE "ARRANGEMENT"

What they really needed now was a few days of peace and quiet—swimming, resting, relaxing and recuperating from "*the Kava thing*," or *the day from hell* as that unforgettable experience was now delicately referred to.

Carole motored *ESCAPEE* out of the bay and they headed out to look for one of the small, uninhabited islands the dive manager had marked on Alan's chart. They planned to anchor there and spend a few days pulling it all back together. They needed time to get over what had just happened and a little, uninhabited island with a calm bay would be perfect. They soon found it. The island was too small to support a village but was big enough to wander around on. It was as beautiful as any of those postcards at the tourism office and they had the entire little island to themselves. Carole steered *ESCAPEE* into the small, sheltered bay and they anchored in about 15 feet of water which was so clear they could see the anchor lying on the bottom. Best of all, they were alone. After "the Kava thing," they all desperately needed this.

As Sigrid got ready to dive into the sparking, clear water, she ripped her bikini top off and said *"I don' need zis,"* And it was just as well—those large breasts just weren't meant to be confined in that tiny bikini top. It was an "unnatural relationship"—one that just couldn't last.

Carole said, *"why not? You've seen it all anyway,"* and took off her top and plunged in.

"Me too," Susan said as she removed hers and dove in.

"Hey, I'm topless too," Alan shouted and dove deep into the clear, blue water after them. They swam, laughed, played in the water and then went up on the powdery, white sand beach.

"Let's explore," Susan said, so they all took off walking down the beach and followed it as it curved all the way around the island. They circled the entire island—their *own* deserted island—in about fifteen minutes and were back where they started. Alan swam out to the boat to bring back the cooler with drinks, some beach towels and sun tan lotion. He rowed back with it in the dinghy—and they all flopped on the sand and dozed off, each still recovering from that unforgettable "day from hell".

They woke up hungry so Carole and Alan volunteered to row back to the boat to make lunch and bring it to the beach. That was fine with Sigrid and Susan, who just kept snoozing. As soon as Carole and Alan got back to the boat Alan started to get the bread for sandwiches.

"Just a minute, Alan," Carole said and moved up closely to him, shoving her bare breasts up against him. They had touched before by accident in the confines of the boat, of course, *but this was no accident.* Carole had something on her mind and didn't leave Alan in any doubt as to what it was.

"I've got a problem. I'm getting horny and I don't dig girls," she said. *"So that leaves only you, my fearless captain. We're alone now so how about just you and me having a little fun together? You wouldn't let a girl go around horny, now would you?"* Once again, Alan was "behind the curve" as Carole put it—and just didn't get it at first.

"Carole" he stammered, " *I don't know...."*

"Well, I do," she said. "I always know what I want and right now—it's you. Come on Alan, don't try to tell me you haven't fantasized about us girls with us all living together and running around almost naked. *Any man would."*

He sure had but was convinced he'd covered it up. *"No, no, I haven't,"* he lied—and went red in the face which of course only proved to Carole that he certainly *had.*

"Oh yeh, caught you, didn't I? I knew it. Well, guess what—you don't have to fantasize any more." She pulled her bikini bottom off and in one fast movement, jerked his bathing suit down before he knew what was going on and pulled him over to her berth. It had been a long time since Ann had left and living around these three women in all states of nakedness *had been getting to him—that's for sure.* He was more than ready—what man wouldn't be?

They were soon making love. They got used to each other in a short time and went on from there—and were both soon moaning in mutual pleasure. The normal "first-time" awkwardness was overcome by the sheer pleasure and—for Alan—surprise of it all. Carole was a thoughtful and experienced lover and in no hurry. Afterwards they lay together for a few minutes and she whispered into his ear, *"not bad for a start—beats a vibrator anytime.* But I've got some bad news for you. I'm 35 and we all know a woman's sex drive is at its highest around the mid-thirties—so it looks like you're going to have your hands full. *Think you're man enough to handle it?* "

Alan was caught by surprise *again* and before he could gather his wits and respond, Carole jumped up and said, "*sandwich time*". They made the sandwiches and headed to shore in the dinghy and when they got there, Sigrid looked at Carole and said, "*you gone long time.*" Carole just smiled and tipped her head slightly towards Alan. Sigrid got it immediately.

Something often happens when a few people are alone together, cut off from the rest of the world and having the time of their lives—*they create their own little world.* They let their hair down, drop their inhibitions and do things they probably would never do—*or dream of doing*—back in the world they'd left behind—the world where they have to maintain appearances, live up to other people's expectations or be afraid of someone passing judgment on them.

All this was beginning to happen on *ESCAPEE* as they lay at anchor for days at that uninhabited island. They created their own little "world". Inhibitions were dropped and nature took its course. Soon, there were no more bikinis—*tops or bottoms.* Sigrid and Carole swam nude and didn't bother with clothes on board anymore either, except occasionally putting something on to protect themselves from the sun.

"*You, too, Alan*" Carole said. " *I know what you've got under there and believe me, it's no big deal. Off with it.*" Sigrid grabbed his bathing suit and jerked it down, took one look and agreed with Carole, "*no beeg deal*".

Susan was shocked at first and was the last holdout. Before long, wearing no clothes was "no big deal" and everyone went about life on *ESCAPEE* not even thinking about it and not paying much attention to it—except Susan. Sometime during the second day, she called out, "*OK, are you guys ready for this?*"

She came up from the cabin into the cockpit wearing a big smile *and nothing else.*

"*Bravo!* " Sigrid said. *"Three cheers for our Susan"* Alan called out—and they *hip-hip-hooray'ed* a beaming Susan into the cockpit. She was grinning from ear to ear. They knew that to her it was a big deal and she was very proud of herself. Susan had lost any remaining "baby fat," as she called it, and now had a trim, well-rounded figure.

"S*ee, it's easy once you do it,*" Carole said. Susan was still a little self-conscious at first but within hours that passed and she was soon chattering away without a stitch on—and not giving it a second thought. Day after day, they lived, ate and slept in the nude—decompressing from the unforgettable *Kava thing.* One day they had a ceremony—complete with the symbolic burning of one of Alan's old bathing suits—declaring *ESCAPEE* to be *"a clothes-free zone".* The official "proclamation" Alan wrote and read out before the bathing suit burning ceremony said, *"we the undersigned four, declare that henceforth and forever more ESCAPEE shall be a clothes-free zone—except when it's too damned cold or someone else is around."*

Life was just about as perfect as it could get in the little world they had created on *ESCAPEE.* But as the days passed Sigrid began to realize she *was* missing something from their near-perfect world. She knew very well what it was and had a good idea how to fix it. Being Sigrid, she didn't waste any time setting out to fix the problem in her own direct, straight-to-the-point way.

As they all sat in the cockpit reading under the sun awning one lazy afternoon after lunch, Sigrid said,

"Ve share sailing, ja?"

"*Yes*"...they said, wondering what she was driving at.

"OK, ve share boot."

"*What boot?*" Susan asked, looking at Carole.

"I think she means 'boat'," Carole replied

"Ja, boat" Sigrid corrected herself.

"Und," she went on, "ve share chobs"

"*Jobs.*" Carole didn't wait for Susan to ask this time.

"Ja, is what I say, *chobs*"

What *is* she driving at, Alan wondered.

"*So...ve share mans, too*"

Carole got it at once. Susan didn't have a clue.

Alan didn't either of course. As usual, he couldn't keep up with what was going on with these women—it was that damned c*omprehension problem* of his. Carole had even told Alan he was, "*comprehensionally challenged*" as far as women were concerned. And as if to confirm that very point it took Alan *a full day* to figure out what the hell she was talking about. Now, they *were at it again,* leaving him "behind the curve" and confused.

Carole saw both Susan and Alan with the confused looks on their faces and said, "*what she's saying, Susan, is that we share the boat, we share the jobs—so we should—you know— share Alan, too.*"

Susan went red in the face.

"Relax, honey," Carole said, "no one's forcing you to do anything. But on the other hand you don't mind if Sigrid and I work out some arrangement to share our honored captain do you?"

"*No...*" Susan stammered, "*I just—just never heard of such a thing.*"

"*Well, there's a first time for everything and we have to sort of improvise some time, especially out here by ourselves.*

OK, we all agree Alan's not the greatest catch in the world. He thinks he's fit and wiry—*"lean and mean"* as he puts it. I think he's just plain scrawny—you know, like a scrawny rooster. But if you ever learn just one thing about men, Susan, it's this— *always give a man his illusions. Men really do need their illusions, poor things.* And anyway, he's all we got."

"But—I just couldn't," Susan said.

"Honey, don't you hear well? I already said you don't have to do anything you don't want to do. Absolutely. Now relax and Sigrid and I will divide this poor excuse for a man up and save you a share in case you ever want one."

Susan still looked flustered, so Carole said, *"look, here's how Sigrid and I see it.* We've got everything we want on *ESCAPEE*. Right? Do we want to leave and go home? Not yet. This is where we want to be, doing what we're doing. Do we want to switch to another boat and take our chances with someone else? Not us—we've seen those guys at the bar. *So when you really think about it, it's perfect here and we've got everything we need—except for one thing –and you know what that is.* So what are we going to do about it? Give all this up to go find that one thing *somewhere else*—with someone we don't know? All this little arrangement does is give us about the *only* thing we're missing in this otherwise perfect little world of ours. *And we know Alan—he's no prize but he's a decent enough guy. So this is all completely logical when you think about it."*

"Alan" Carole barked, *"you're drooling.* Sigrid, hand him a towel."

Alan wasn't drooling even though Carole was right—*he really did look like he was.* When he was shocked his mouth usually hung open and he had that "vacant" look—the kind that causes people to say, *"the lights are on but nobody's home".* That look could very easily be mistaken for drooling. And there was no mistaking it—he was truly shocked by all this talk going on right in front of him *as though he wasn't there.* He had heard everything being said about him and if he understood it right, these two women were talking about dividing him up like some piece of property. Being a little slow on the uptake it took him a while to get it. But as it finally dawned on him what they were talking about, he said, "*hey, no one's asked me what I think about all this.*"

"*Do you hear someone talking?*" Carole asked Sigrid and smiled. "*Nein, I hear nuzing.*"

"*I said,*" Alan went on, "*no one's asked me what I think about this little arrangement.*"

"*OK, vat you tink,* Ellen? Sigrid said."

"If I have to, *I have to,*" he said with a big grin on his face. "What'd you think? I love it. Yes! *When do we start?*"

"*Calm down Ellen,*" Carole said, deliberately using Sigrid's name for him. "We're in charge of all this from now on in case you didn't notice. You're in charge of anything to do with the boat—it's yours—*but we're in charge of the 'social life' and we'll let you know when. Right Sigrid?*"

"*Ja, ve tell you, Ellen!*" Sigrid said forcefully.

Carole said, "*so there you have it, Alan. The bottom-line about life on ESCAPEE from now on is pretty simple—you're on call.*"

Alan couldn't believe this conversation. But what the hell—he was living with these women and he really did like them and after all, he was a man. *Of course he was for it!* He could hardly believe it and was certain—absolutely certain—that at any minute Carole would say "*just a joke, Alan. Just pulling your leg.*" But no, it really looked like they were serious. *I can't believe it,* Alan thought, *these women are serious.*

Susan just sat there taking all this in, shaking her head slowly and mumbling, "I just couldn't."

"Read my lips, Susan" Carole said. "I finally found them you know after that *Kava thing*—so read them. You don't have to do anything, honey. Just relax."

"But how do we do this?" Alan asked, confused—his increasingly normal state with these women. He could picture methodical Sigrid making up a schedule and sticking it up at the navigation table, right next to the radio schedule—one schedule for the weather broadcasts and another for Alan. Then Carole made it all clear. *"Alan, from this moment you're on stand-by— on call—that's all you need to know.* We'll let you know everything else."

"Ja, ve tell you!" Sigrid said again, forcefully and thrusting her figure sharply at him. *"You on call!"*

Damn, that's the *second* time Sigrid had said that, Alan thought. That German girl's on a power trip and then he remembered what they said about pushy Germans—*"they're either at your throat or at your feet."* But Sigrid's interest clearly wasn't in his feet *or* his throat but somewhere *about halfway in between.*

"Don't worry about it, Alan," Carole said, trying to make it simple for him—*she knew Alan needed simple.* "It'll just happen—you know, like it did with us. This is really no big deal. Sigrid will give me a hint when she wants to be alone with you and I'll do the same. Then the other two will head for the beach. That's all there is to it. Hey, it ought to be great for you—think how many men would trade places with you."

"What if *I* want some action, what then?" Alan asked.

"Well, it's like we said, you're *'on call'* from now on and *ve tell you,"* Carole said. "Of course we're on call to you, too. That is, if you're man enough—*but I sure have my doubts about that,"* she said and smiled.

"OK," Alan said, "but we leave Susan out of it. She's young enough to be my daughter. I even think of her as my daughter—well, more of less."

"Susan's still in a little shock. Let her get over it and you might be surprised what that girl decides to do. After all, she's almost Sigrid's age—though I agree that she has a lot less experience. Sigrid's been around—Susan hasn't. Anyway, I'm not at all sure she looks on you as her daddy—her suger-daddy maybe, but definitely not her daddy," she said, glancing at Susan.

Susan sat in stunned silence as they talked about her as though she wasn't even there—and in a way she wasn't. She was still in shock and struggling to mentally process what had been said about *five minutes before*—so what was being said now just didn't register with her. I can't believe this is happening, Alan told himself again. He still had a sneaking suspicion that this was one of Carole's jokes and at any minute she'd say "*surprise. Just kidding.*"

With the "arrangement" out of the way, everyone settled down and enjoyed the lazy days on their own uninhabited little island. Two days later as they got ready to go to shore for some beach-combing and sun, Sigrid said, "*Ellen...you stay mit me? Bitte.*" Carole rowed to shore with Susan who still couldn't quite deal with it all. Sigrid was a tall girl and barely fit into her berth, but Alan's berth in the forward cabin was longer and wider. As soon as they got into his berth, Sigrid pulled his face down between those impressive breasts. He briefly remembered that close-up view he got in the bar at Malolo-lai-lai when Sigrid embraced him and accidentally shoved those breasts into his face. *But it was nothing like this.*

As they began making love, the energetic and athletic girl took charge, deciding *what, when and how*—and "*Ellen*" just went along for the ride. Before long, he was exhausted and gasping for air. At long last, Sigrid jumped out of bed and said

"Gut, ja?"—in her matter of fact way, as though she was scoring some Olympic competition on a scale of one to ten.

"Yes, Sigrid, yes!" Alan said, gasping for air as he got out of the berth *"very, very good"*. *That was no exaggeration* and Sigrid beamed.

"Gimme five!" she suddenly said and Alan instinctively raised his open hand as she slapped it with hers in a "high-five".

"Where did you learn that?" Alan asked.

"Carole tell me all American mans, after zey make luf like to say, *'gimme five'* and hit hands mit girl. What zat mean, Ellen—*'gimme five'? Why you American mans all time like to say 'gimme five' and hit hands after you make luf? I no understand."*

Alan swore he'd kill Carole the first chance he got!

They dove over the side, swam to the beach and as soon as they got there Carole asked, "Hi guys, what've you been up to?" Alan rolled his eyes and Susan turned her head to look at something else.

"Gimme five," Alan snarled at Carole out of the side of his mouth and she burst into laughter.

They hung out on their own beautiful, uninhabited island for a week and then headed out to two more islands the dive shop manager had marked on their charts. They were even more beautiful—small sandy islands, too small to support a population, but big enough to live on for a week or two. Each was a little bit of paradise and it belonged only to them. Once in a while a dive boat would come by and they'd put something on, but other than that, they had the deserted, small islands to themselves. Those islands were also *clothes-free zones*—just like *ESCAPEE*.

Sometimes they had barbeques on the beach. At other times, they just sat and read, swam, took the dinghy out fishing and had their dinners in the cockpit in the moonlight. One day they decided to take the camping gear Alan carried on board and camp out on the island for a few days, sleeping under the stars to get a better "feel" for it. They only went back to *ESCAPEE* to get water and food. Whenever they needed fresh fish, Sigrid took the snorkel gear and spear gun and brought dinner back to "*CAMP ESCAPEE*," as it was called.

Another time, they played "*castaways*," pretending to be ship-wrecked castaways on an uninhabited island "thousands of miles from any other land"—3 desperate women and 1 man having to survive on whatever washed up ashore and what they could scavenge. The cheated a little—actually, at Alan's insistence *they cheated a lot*—and took some basic food and supplies ashore. The idea was they would remain castaways until one of them could no longer handle it and gave up. They would then then go back to the comforts of *ESCAPEE*.

At first everything went very well—they even made up a "love nest" on the other side of the island where Alan went with Sigrid or Carole from time to time. They made it for five days when the girls began to see signs that Alan was going go to be the first one to crack. The signs were pretty clear—he often wandered over to the beach and longingly looked out at *ESCAPEE—that fridge, the cold beer, that soft berth*. On the fifth day he suddenly said, "*enough! I give up. I want my boat!*"

"*Well, we sure separated the men from the boys, didn't we?*" Carole said as they returned to ESCAPEE. "*Poor baby*. If we're ever ship-wrecked castaways with this guy we're going to have our hands full burping him and taking care of him."

"Carole," Alan said, "*give me a break*."

Alan didn't know it then but a break was about the *last thing* these women would ever give him. They loved to "rattle his cage" as Carole called it. It was *just so easy*. As they saw it, it was Alan's own fault—it wouldn't be nearly so much fun if he wasn't so easily bugged. How could *anyone—even a saint—* possibly let such an easy target go by?

After playing castaways, life returned to what passed for "normal" with these four. Each night they sat in the cockpit or on the beach watching the incredible show of stars above them— clear and un-obscured by the pollution of civilization. Life was lazy, unplanned—and just happened. It was a romantic setting and every so often Alan and one of the two girls would row back to the boat to be alone. By now it had become a normal part of their lives. One day the conversation turned to the lives they had left behind in "the real world"—and would go back to some day. The girls usually talked with each other late into the night before falling asleep but as far as Alan could tell, this was the first time the subject had ever come up. When it did, it opened up a Pandora's Box of unexpected emotions and feelings.

Late one afternoon they were sitting on the beach watching the sunset over the larger, populated island to the west, when Susan suddenly said, "*I lied to you, Alan. I lied to you all.*"

"*What do you mean, Susan?*" Carole asked. This had come completely out of the blue. They had sensed that something had been bothering Susan lately, but had no idea what it was.

"I told Alan I wanted to stay here in the Pacific and not rush back to a job I had waiting. There's just no way I could go back then—or now—so I lied. It wasn't a job I didn't want to go back to—*it was a marriage.* That's what everyone back there's expecting from me after I go back." Susan explained that she was from an "old money" family in Atlanta and her father was insisting—*demanding*—she marry someone her "equal"— financially that is— *and do it now.*

"*Money marries money,*" he had angrily said more than once when she tried to stand up to his pressures. The scary thing, she said, was that he really believed it. That was his way *and his way was the only way.* He was a strong, blustering, domineering man—the head of several companies—who got everything his way or else. When anyone dared stand up to him or crossed him, he'd just say, *"two of us will go into that room but only one of us will come out"*— leaving no doubt as to who that would be. Susan's mother went along with anything he said. When she tried to raise her voice on Susan's behalf once or twice she was put right back "in her place," so she just gave up and quit trying. She once told Susan in despair *"you just have to make the best of what life hands you."* Susan knew that's what was expected of her, too.

"A Southern lady of our standing doesn't work," her father told her—*"she gets married and has kids. She doesn't have a career—she has a family. Got it?"* he barked at her more than once. He bullied her and talked to her like one of his salesmen who hadn't met his quota and always made her feel like a total failure, she said.

While he didn't exactly try to pick the right guy for her, he certainly had picked the *circle* she had to choose from. She was the only girl in a family with three high-achieving sons— "chips off the old block," she called them—and they added their own voices and pressures to their father's. All four of them were ganging up on her, bullying and pressuring her to pick the right man—*right in their view, of course—and pick him soon.* In their circle any daughter who wasn't "settled" in life—meaning married with a financial "equal"—by the time she was 25 was a deep embarrassment to the family. And families like hers don't like to be embarrassed, she said. Their image and face is everything to them—just behind money.

She said she had a boyfriend at the expensive, private college she attended and he would have met her father's expectations—*but not hers.* He was a nice enough guy but there was just no spark of love there. They had made love a few times and each time left her wondering, *"this is it?"* He was certainly from an "equal" family if you went by bank balances, *but she didn't want to marry a bank account.* She said she had seen enough dead marriages and unhappy couples in Atlanta high society to last a lifetime—and she wanted none of it.

After graduation her father gave her this charter trip to Tonga as a graduation gift and made it crystal clear that after the charter she was expected to return home and "get settled in life,"—find that man of equal money and get married—*and do it soon!* She was going back to face all that bullying and pressure from her father and brothers and knew she'd never stand up to them.

"If I'd gone back instead of meeting you guys, I just know I would've caved in to them and married the wrong guy and lived unhappily ever after—just like a lot of girls I know. I'm sorry I lied to you, Alan, but I didn't know you that well then and I was so worried—I don't know what I would've done if you hadn't let me come on ESCAPEE. Those two weeks on the charter boat were absolute hell—all I could think of was what was waiting for me back home. By the time I met you I was really desperate."

"It's OK now, Susan, you're with us here now and we're behind you." Alan said.

Carole, Sigrid and Alan had listened with deep concern to what Susan was saying and were astonished that she had been able to keep all this bottled up inside her all this time. *No wonder she seemed worried!*

She explained that she had *no one to talk to*—certainly no one in college or among her friends. Nothing said in those circles stayed confidential for long. For the first time—sitting here on a beach in paradise with real friends—she was able to open her heart and the long pent-up emotions poured out.

"Why are they doing this to me? They say they love me, but they're killing me inside."

Carole put her arms around her and said, *"Susan, just stand up to them. Do what* you *want to do. It's your life—not theirs.* Don't let them make you do anything *you* don't want to do. If you do, you'll regret it for the rest of your life."

"Ja," Sigrid said, *"is best, Susan. Is best."* She had a very concerned look on her face.

"It's just great being with you guys, here," Susan said. *"I'm getting my perspective back.* I'd lost it—surrounded by everyone ganging up on me, bullying and pushing me around. Every day I'm here with you guys, I'm seeing things a little more clearly. Whenever I do go back—and I hope it's not for some time yet—I'm going to be a lot stronger than any of them think. They're not going to push me around any more."

"Susan," Alan said, *"we love you and we're with you all the way. No one's going to pressure our navigator. Right?"*

"Right!" Carole and Sigrid joined in. Sigrid gave Susan a long, supportive hug and Susan said she felt better than she had since she was a kid—back in those days when life was simple and no one was trying to run her life. She said she had felt *so alone—for so long,* but now she had three good friends who stood with her and could feel herself thinking more clearly—and getting stronger—every day.

It was clear to them all that there was now no way she was going to do as her mother did and *"just make the best of what life hands you".* That girl wasn't going to sit around passively waiting for life to hand her *anything.* She was going to *take what she wanted*—that much was now clear to them all.

There was only one thing Alan couldn't figure out—with a pushy guy like that for a father, why didn't he just reply to those faxes Susan had sent and *order* Susan to return home? *But the guy never even bothered to reply to her faxes. Strange.*

The next day they were on a beachcombing walk around the deserted island and took a break in the shade of a cluster of palm trees when Sigrid said, *"I not go back to be married, like Susan. I married. But no good for me."*

She said she was raised on a farm in Bavaria, south of Munich—the youngest of six children. It was a large, close farm family with traditional values. She attended the local schools and when she was 12, she was drawn to the sailboats on Lake Starnberg—the *Starnbergersee*—near her family's farm. She joined a sailing club on the lake and soon became an expert sailor and was eventually the champion in the Laser class of sailboats. She was tall, strong and athletic and also joined the swimming team. With her on it, they swept the swim meets. She loved sailing and swimming, but eventually went off to college in the north of Germany—in Hamburg. There were local universities, of course, but her swimming prowess had become well known and a university in Hamburg wanted her.

The people and culture there were very different—much colder and more formal than the more easy-going people of Bavaria—and she was often very lonely in the big city. She found it hard to make friends, she said, but became a star of the university women's swim team. That's where she met Rolf, the son of one of the leading insurance families of Hamburg. He made her feel at home in a city where she had always felt like an outsider. He paid attention to her, presented her at elegant dinner parties hosted by his parents and, in the end, proposed marriage. She was only 21 at the time—innocent in the ways of the world and at heart was still a farm girl from Bavaria .

The following year they were married in a wedding, which was one of the main events of the Hamburg social season. But even before the ink on the marriage certificate was dry, Rolf "parked" her in luxurious splendor and isolation in one of the family's mansions and forgot about her. He had her now so the "chase"—the romance, the courting and attention—was over. She soon discovered she was just another one of his trophies—a "trophy wife" who was trotted out to look good on Rolf's arm at certain functions and then put back "in the barn," as she called it.

She went to classes and languished "in the barn" until Rolf was ready to display her at his side once again. Too late, she realized she was just another "trophy" to him—someone to hunt and get—and then hang up on the wall, like one of those trophies from his hunting in Africa—and wait for the next summons to appear.

Later, she found out that Rolf had someone else. She had expected that, of course, since he'd shown no sexual interest in her at all. But she hadn't expected it to be *another man*. Rolf was secretly gay and Sigrid's *sole function* and role in his life was to be a "stage prop" or window dressing to help him keep it a secret. Sigrid's gay friends at the university were outraged at the fraud and almost as upset about it as she was. She was frightened, angry and intimidated—only 22 years old, a long way from home, emotionally shattered and married to a man who didn't want her and used her as a "front" for his deception.

Soon after discovering her real role in Rolf's life, she had a big confrontation with him, and as usual, he brought in his parents to rescue him from the situation he had created. Mommy and Daddy had to save Rolf's skin—again. *No divorce* the mother thundered—that would drag the family name into the mud. Take a lover the mother said—*take many lovers,* but be discreet about it. Don't shame the family name. *You can have lovers—but no divorce!*

For two more years Sigrid kept up the appearance—the stunning wife appearing faithfully on Rolf's arm wherever he wanted. She did take on a lover—*several lovers over a period of time*—she said but knew she was caught in a trap. She could find lovers anywhere but said she would *never* be in a position to fall in love with anyone and have a family of her own.

"It was for me a terrible trap. In all ways, I lose."

The previous summer she flew to Mallorca in the Mediterranean for a few weeks. Rolf thought it was to be with a lover and didn't care, but Sigrid had enough of those quick, empty affairs, she said, and instead flew to *another love*—sailing. She got a summertime job as a sailing instructor at a German-run sailing school. After the season was over, she hung around the big marinas in Palma and saw a large, eighty-foot German boat being prepared to leave for a long voyage. She met the owner and found he was assembling a professional, paid crew to help him sail around the world. They'd be gone two years and he would leave the boat and fly back to his business in Germany from time to time, he said. He asked about her experience and checked her credentials with the sailing school and the next day offered her a job as crew. She went back to the hotel where she was staying and thought about it most of the night.

This *could* be her chance to get out of a loveless, phony marriage without a big blow-up and divorce at this time, she said. *If she left for a couple of years, it would be clear to everyone that the marriage was over.* That was far better than going back now and confronting the family and forcing a divorce. That would lead to an explosive, ugly fight. Rolf had found the names of two of her lovers and threatened to use them against her if she filed for divorce. He had the money to "convince" them to say anything he wanted and it would be very messy. With his money and connections there was never a doubt that Rolf would come out the winner over a farm girl from Bavaria.

Sigrid said she knew that *time itself* often takes care of problems that seem insurmountable. By the time the sun rose the next morning she had decided to go away as crew on the German boat for two years. She called Rolf and *told* him what she was going to do. It's either this or a divorce—*now*—she told him. Faced with that ultimatum, Rolf made the face-saving choice of letting her go, but he made her promise to tell no one where she was going—*absolutely no one*—except her family.

She flew back to Munich to say goodbye to her parents and explain to them what she was doing and—for the first time—*why*. She had never wanted to worry them about her problems and had kept it all to herself. Her family lived in a world of old traditions—far from the madness she had been trapped in with Rolf. When they heard what Sigrid had been through they were all behind her decision to go away—*especially her father*. She was his "baby girl" and they had always been very close. She said a tearful farewell to her family and flew back to the cruising boat in Mallorca.

She said she knew that with his usual cunning, Rolf would eventually figure out a way to explain her absence—and even make it work to his own advantage. Much later, she said, she found out through the grapevine that when people began to notice she wasn't appearing with Rolf at any of the usual functions, he had a ready explanation—she was off in Africa, working as a volunteer with a relief organization helping feed the starving in one of Africa's periodic crises.

It was the classic "*big lie*". Rolf let it be known that he was not only generously giving up his beloved wife's companionship and affection to help the needy, but he would fly out as often as possible to spend time with her, nurture their loving marriage and of course "quietly" do his own share for the needy. According to Sigrid's grapevine that outrageous story impressed everyone with Rolf's previously unknown humanitarian streak. The word was out that not only was he willing to make the sacrifice of letting Sigrid go help the needy, but he went to be with his beloved wife as often as he could and do his own share.

What a fine man!

"*Son of a bitch!*" Carole exploded. "*Someone should castrate the bastard.*"

"*Vat castrate?*" Sigrid asked.

"*Just cut his balls off,*" Carole replied.

Sigrid thought that was funny and said, "*Zat his problem, Carole. No mine. If he liar, is his fault. It has nuzing to do mit me.* He is for me—how you Americans say it—*history. Ja, for me he is history.*"

"*What a fraud that bastard* is," Carole said.

Not only was the marriage a fraud, Sigrid said, but so was everything to do with Rolf. But she had decided that was Rolf's problem—not hers—so she promised to say nothing about where she was and took off on the German boat. By the time they got to Tonga the owner had run into business problems and had been forced to put the boat on the market and return to Germany. *She wasn't about to rush back to all that,* she said— and put the note up on the bulletin board looking for another boat. *That's when she met Alan.*

The three of them listened in amazement as Sigrid told of that long road from being "parked" in a mansion in Hamburg to being out here in Fiji, sharing *ESCAPEE* with them.

"*You did the right thing, Sigrid,*" Susan said. "You've got to get out of that marriage."

"*Ja, I know*" she said. "So, I no hurry to go back," she said. "Ven I go back, I get divorce and start again."

"It sounds like a cheap Hollywood movie," Carole said, still *very* angry. "The whole damned thing was all a sham and a fraud from day one—a show, with false props, false characters and a trophy wife as a stage-prop in a false marriage. *And can you imagine that son of a bitch coming out the hero in all this?* Going off to Africa to help his devoted wife feed the hungry! The bastard painted you guys as a couple like—well like *Albert Schweitzer marries Mother Theresa*—one happy couple out to save the world. That's outrageous and really pisses me off."

Alan had never seen Carole so angry.

"*Ja*, Carole," Sigrid said. " *I angry also—I too much angry. But zat his problem—no mine. I try be no more angry. I try look what in front me, not behind me.*"

"*Well, you're right. So what are your plans, Sigrid?*"

"*Vell, I like zis boat and zis people—'you guys'—as you Americans always say it. So, I like stay mit 'you guys' long time—if OK mit Ellen.*"

"*It sure is, Sigrid,*" Alan said, deeply moved. "*It sure is—for just as long as you want.*"

It was now clear to Alan that far from being the tough, hard German he first thought she was, *Sigrid was a softie—a deeply wounded softie.* She was an innocent, trusting young woman from a simple farm family who had been deceived, used and very badly hurt. That severe, stern exterior she had when they first met was *just a cover* for the deep hurt and deception she had suffered. Now—living with Carole, Susan and Alan and with all the fun and easy-going informality on *ESCAPEE*—that stern exterior had disappeared. Among these real friends Sigrid had let her protective guard down.

Sigrid was becoming Sigrid again—right I front of their eyes—a happy, trusting and sharing girl.

Carole was *still* pissed off. "When you divorce this bastard they'll probably make you sign a confidentiality agreement—and then spread the story that you died tragically of some disease you got helping people in some hell-hole in Africa. Then everyone will feel sorry for 'poor Rolf'. *What a bastard!*"

"*Zat his problem Carole, no mine. He gone from me. He history. I look for new life.*"

They were each imagining the living hell Sigrid had been through for almost three years. She went on to explain that *the hardest thing was to turn loose of her anger at being used.* She said there were times when it was just too much and she wound up in a deep depression, locking herself in the mansion for weeks at a time, seeing no one and missing her classes. Her spirit was broken, she said, and she finally gave up and dropped out of the university altogether. She said she knew she was in a downward spiral and needed some professional help, but Rolf's family was against it. They were afraid it would somehow get out and make *them* look bad. By now, she said, her will was crushed and she was fully dependent on them, beaten down, confused and depressed—and just went along with whatever they said.

Many times, she said, she felt as though she was losing her own personality and her own "self" and was slowly disappearing—*ceasing to exist*—like the figure of a person she often pictured disappearing into one of Hamburg's dense fogs, never to come out again. She said she saw the image of that figure disappearing into the fog over and over—in dreams, in daydreaming, in her imagination—*until she finally realized that person was real. It was her.* During one particularly black period, she found herself holding a large kitchen knife and looking at her wrists.

That was the blackest moment of all, she said—*but it was also the start of her salvation.* It shocked her so badly she finally woke up and decided to get back in control of her life *and do it now.* Two days later she took off for Mallorca and got that job in the sailing school.

Even now, she said, she sometimes finds that anger trying to come back. She was especially sad—*and angry*—about having to be so far from her family as though she was in some kind of exile. Every sea-mile she sailed from Germany to Tonga made her feel she was going deeper into that exile, she said. By the time she got to Tonga she said she was emotionally beaten-up from it all.

"Before I meet you guys, I no remember last time I have a happy day. I no remember when I laugh."

She said she knew there was still a divorce and a battle waiting for her back in Germany, but that was somewhere off in the future. As much as she wanted to go back and be with her family, she just wasn't up to going back now and facing all that. *For now, she said, life here on ESCAPEE and being part of this group was just what she needed.*

After a few days on the island the girls wanted to explore another of the uninhabited islands the dive manager had marked on the chart. After all, every island was better than the last—they just kept getting better. It was only a few miles away, so they raised the anchor and caught the gentle afternoon breeze. They arrived well before sunset and had drinks on board, as the sun went down in an incredible, tropical "light-show". They had dinner in the cockpit that night—tomorrow they'd hit the beach and start exploring this new island. Carole was unusually quiet—all this talk of what Susan and Sigrid faced when they went back had brought her own situation to the front of her mind. It had been easy to ignore it until now, but no longer. After dinner, they relaxed in the cockpit with cognac and Frangelico. It was very clear that something was on Carole's mind and she *wanted* to talk about it but Alan could tell that sharing her feelings didn't come easily with Carole. *She was tough and self-reliant and it just wasn't her way*

Alan had discovered the hard way that there's a *second level of truth—the truth beneath the truth.* When people really let go of all the protective, defensive barriers they've built up against the things they fear or that hurt them—*with people they can really trust*—and open up, they often dig a little deeper and reach a better understanding of themselves. They're not only explaining things to trusted friends, *but to themselves as well.*

It had happened to him as he had talked with Ann about how he screwed up his own marriage. The end of 23 years of marriage is a deep personal failure and left a *million fingers of blame—his own fingers*—pointing at him. No amount of rationalizing could ever paper that over, but after talking it out with Ann he had come to realize he had to quit condemning himself, learn the hard lessons that were certainly there to be learned—and then get on with his life.

Something similar had happened with Susan and Sigrid as they talked about what they faced. They came to a better understanding of it—and of themselves—and got the clarity and strength to move on. That kind of opening up takes real friendship—*trusting friendship*—the kind that had grown between the four of them.

Alan saw Carole struggling with whether to share her feelings. She didn't say anything that night. Alan knew she would—when *she* was ready. As it turned out the next evening she was ready.

They were having a fish dinner on the beach, cooked with the dried driftwood they had gathered from around the little island when Carole said, "*I've listened to Susan and Sigrid share things. I really admire how you guys can do it.* I can't. I never could do what you've done—open up and share my feelings. I've always wanted to and knew I *should*, but just never could. For one thing, I learned early on to take care of myself. I found there was one person I could trust and count on—*only one*—and that was *me*. So this is all kind of hard for me. *Kind of hard? Hell, I've never done anything like this before.*

"Anyway I don't have any 'man problems' like you guys—I've never been married like Sigrid and no one expects me to be, like Susan. When I was 6 my parents and two brothers were killed in a car crash. I had some injuries but came out of it OK. My parents had no close, living relatives who could take me—just an aunt who was much too ill to take care of a child. So one thing led to another and I eventually wound up in a foster-home with a childless couple. They were really nice, but when I was 8, they died when their car—*can you believe my bad luck*—was hit by a train at a rural rail crossing. But this time I was home playing with some neighbor kids or I would have been dead too—the car was mangled—you couldn't even tell it was a car anymore. So off I went again, back as a ward of the state and was put into another foster home.

"When I was 13 I was sexually molested in the home. *Molested, shit! I was raped.* My "foster-father"—*what a term*— warned me to say nothing to anyone or he'd kill me. I was terrified and it went on for two years. When I was 15, I finally told a girlfriend at school and the police questioned me. I was given a medical examination and the police went out to arrest the bastard. He was alone at the time and barricaded himself inside the house. When the police barged in he blew his brains out with a shotgun and that's when the shit hit the fan.

"*His wife blamed me—said I had made it all up and drove her innocent husband to suicide.* She just went wild, telling the press and anyone who'd listen how I had falsely accused her husband and drove him to his death. Well, you know how people are—some people believed her in spite of the statement put out by the police. My name was never published of course, but everyone knew it was me. You don't keep that a secret in a small town—and that woman was telling anyone who'd listen.

"*I was known all over town as either the girl who was raped for two years—and probably enjoyed it and wanted it—or the girl who falsely accused an innocent man and drove him to his death.* Take your pick. One or the other—*that was me.* Those were the two stories about me and everyone chose the one they wanted to believe. Some believed one—some believed the other. I was then placed with a family from a church and they were OK, but I just couldn't go on living in that small town anymore.

"You can't believe what some of the kids at school said right to my face—they asked how I enjoyed being raped and what was it *really* like—*or* why I drove a fine, innocent man to his death. *I just had to get the hell out of there.* I ran away from the foster home twice but was caught and returned each time. After the second time some bright brain at social services *finally woke up to the fact that I had a big problem in that town.* To make a long story short, at age 16 I wound up in Canton, Ohio staying with a family and going to high school there.

"No one knew me there and I finally had a chance to hide in peace from those accusations. I still lived in fear that someone in Canton would find out who I was so I never let myself develop any close friends. Whenever anyone tried to get close to me, I just pushed them away. Anyway, I figured, *who needs them?*

"As soon as I was out of high school I took off on my own. As I said, life had taught me I had one person to count on—*me*, and one person I could trust—*me*. If you're weak and count on others you're screwed. That's just life. *You can rail and scream about it all you want, but that's just the way it is.*

"So I worked my way through college and majored in economics. I turned out to be good with numbers and statistics—they're not nearly as messy as people—and got a job with a mutual fund management firm in Chicago. I had boyfriends in high school, college and while working in Chicago, but my relationships never seemed to go anywhere. We'd date, go out a few times, maybe make love, but as soon as it got serious it always fizzled out—*I mean every time.*

"My friends were getting married right and left and here I was—32 years old and couldn't keep one special guy. I like men and often wished I had the right guy, but every time I tried it just died out. *Look, I know I'm* supposed *to hate men because of what happened to me, but I don't—that was just one sick bastard.* At least I don't *think* I have a problem with men. *Lord, I hope not!*

"Anyway, that really wasn't much of a problem to me and in a lot of ways it turned out to be a big plus. I was working very long hours and had climbed up through the company. Eventually I became a financial analyst, recommending companies we should add to our mutual fund portfolios and specializing in tracking certain companies for the various funds we have. Millions of dollars were being moved around and invested based on my financial research. It took over my life and the pressure was enormous—you don't invest that kind of money on a whim. But I had a knack for understanding financial reports and what moved the equity markets in general and was on my way up. I was only 34—that was just last year, come to think of it. *Time flies*.

"My business life was great, but my personal life—*hell, I had none*. I couldn't seem to get close to anyone for very long. I started a lot of relationships over the years—but like I said, the moment they got serious, something *always* happened to break us up. Last year my company offered to promote me to a management position—now that's a whole, new ball game. If I took this on I'd probably be dealing with a lot more problems.

"Managing people is a hell of a lot different from managing numbers. Anyway, I can't let them put me there if I'm not ready to make it my life—my *whole* life and nothing but my life so I asked for some time off to think about it. I really wasn't sure I wanted to go that way. I needed a little breathing space to think things through before taking that big a step, so that's when I came down to the South Pacific with my latest boyfriend who was between jobs, to bum around the islands and island-hop.

"One day we were 'sharing' our life stories with one another over dinner—you know, really opening up and letting it all hang out and just saying what was on our hearts. I let it slip out about what had happened to me as a kid. *Big mistake! I was really, really stupid I guess, but I thought I could trust the guy.* The very next time we got into an argument over some little thing—I even forget what it was—he threw it all right back in my face. *'Now I know what's wrong with you—you're all screwed up about men. No wonder you can never keep a man. And you never will. You're damaged goods. That's what you are—damaged goods.'*

"I called him a choice name or two and he took off—*story of my life with men*. I know being raped as a kid doesn't exactly make you feel all 'warm and fuzzy' about men—but as I said, I *really* think I've put all that behind me. *I sure as hell have tried to.* I like men. I'm just not very good with them—never have been. Anyway, I wasn't ready to go back to Chicago and make that decision yet—and why should *I* have to go back 4 months early just because that bastard cut out on me? So in Neiafu I thought I'd see if I could find a boat going somewhere—anywhere—*and well, here I am.*

"*So, Alan, what you see is what you get,*" Carole said, looking straight at him.

"*I like what I see,*" Alan said without a moment's hesitation. "*I like it a lot. And if you're 'damaged goods' then bring me more! There's not a damned thing wrong with you and you know something, Carole—in your heart you know it!*"

"*What a bunch of misfits we are!*" Susan said despondently.

"*No way!*" Carole said. "*What Alan just said is absolutely true.* In our hearts we know what we're doing is right for us at this time. No one else may believe that—but we do and that's all that counts. *What the hell else matters?* Sure we've had our share of problems—who hasn't—but at least we're facing them. A lot of people are like Susan's mother—sorry Susan—just staying quiet and unhappy all their lives. An awful lot of people who look successful and who we might envy are really living—what do they call it—'lives of quiet desperation'.

"The one thing the three of us have in common——other than living with Alan here on *ESCAPEE*—is that we're going to fix our problems and live our own lives from now on *as we choose.* We're not going to stay trapped in unworkable situations or be pressured by anyone. Not you, Susan. Not you, Sigrid—and I sure as hell am not. We're here in paradise just taking a break.

"Remember that old saying, '*stop the world, I want to get off*'? Well, that's kind of what we're doing out here with Alan. We've stopped the world for a little while—long enough to get our thinking clear and decide what *we* want to do. When *we're* good and ready, we're going to go back home, confront our problems and damn well do what *we* want to do. We're just backing off a little to get a perspective, figuring out what *we* want to do—and then we're going back and do it.

"*As for me,*" Carole said, "*I may just go back and have a baby of my own. I've really been thinking about that a lot lately, especially here on ESCAPEE. I'm 35 and it may be time. I'd like to have my own child and raise it the way I want—the right way. I wasn't raised in a home full of love, but I sure think I could create one.* I've damned well seen how *not* to raise a kid so I really think I could be a good mother. If I found the right guy—all the better—after all two good parents are better than one. But I want to tell you guys something—*one good, loving parent is better than two bad ones any time.*

"So maybe I can find the right man, but if not I know I could be a very good single parent on my own. I'm really thinking that's what I'd like to do. As I said, if there's a good man involved that's the best, but if not, no big deal. As far as men are concerned, when you need a man you can always find one—*like Alan here,*" she said smiling at him. "Well, anyway, that's what I'm working out in my mind here on *ESCAPEE*—and what better place than out here in all this beauty?

"You just can't rush or force these kinds of life-decisions. *Sometimes these decisions aren't even made—they just happen*— and mine is slowly happening here with you guys. If I take that management position I wouldn't really have time to raise my child the way I want, so I'm thinking about staying at my present level—at this or another firm and raising my child instead. *That's becoming really important to me.* Anyway, I'm re-thinking everything out here—and that's what I'm coming around to."

Carole took a deep breath from that outpouring of feelings and said, "*so there, Captain Alan Richards, it looks like you're stuck with us for a while yet—at least Sigrid and me.*"

"*Me too,*" Susan blurted out, "*me too. Don't leave me out.*" She had caught Carole's spirit. "I'll go back *when* I'm damned well ready, marry *who* I damned well please, *when* I damn well want to—and my father and brothers can go stick their heads 'where the sun don't shine,' as they say down South."

"*Well, there you have it, Alan,*" Carole said. "*Looks like you've got yourself hooked up with three trouble-makers who're going to go back someday and 'rock the boat'—pardon the pun. Think you can put up with us?*"

"*You know what?*" Alan said thoughtfully and much more to himself than to them—"*something just dawned on me. I just discovered why I like you guys so much. You're for real! Each one of you. ESCAPEE'S my home and it's yours too*—for just as long as you want."

"*Ahh, our Alan's getting all mushy over us,*" Carole said, trying to lighten things up a bit. But all kidding aside, they each knew he meant what he'd said—*his home was their home for as long as they wanted.*

That night as Alan dropped off to sleep he couldn't help but be amazed at these three women. *Each had been knocked down hard—especially Carole and Sigrid—but had pulled themselves right back up. Sigrid was turning loose of all that anger that had been killing her. Neither of them were sour or bitter or out to blame anyone—and that really impressed him.* They were just determined to put it behind and get on with their lives. And if they could do that, it was high time for him to get over his guilt about screwing up 23 years of marriage and move on.

He had seen how deeply moved Susan was by what Carole and Sigrid had gone through. That girl had probably *already* absorbed enough truth about life from those two to keep her out of trouble for the rest of her life! *What a benefit Carole and Sigrid had already been to her, just by their examples.* After hearing all this, there was no way she would ever settle for less than what *she* felt was right for her. *Never.*

Quite an amazing three! Alan said to himself as he fell asleep.

The next afternoon around five—after a full day of swimming, beachcombing and just lying around—they had some cold beers in the cockpit. Sigrid, Susan and Carole had been talking, and Carole was their "spokesperson"—as usual.

"OK, Alan, we've opened up our lives to you and each other—and we're glad we did. We know each other much better now—where we're coming from, what we're dealing with and how we can help each other. And guess what? *Now it's your turn.*"

In her own unique way, Carole asked, *"what about you, mystery man?* Is there a nasty, sleeping dragon or 'Jack the Ripper' type hiding behind that nice person you let us see? Left any bodies buried back in California? When you look back over your shoulder, *who's gaining on you?* Running away from any paternity suits?" *We want to know all about the man we're living with—and Sigrid and I need to know who we're sleeping with. A girl really should know those things."*

Alan knew he'd never talk these three strong-willed women out of it.

"It's a long story," he said, hoping for a reprieve.

"So, who's going anywhere?" Carole said.

CHAPTER THREE

THE START

Well, *you guys asked for it*. Let's get some fresh drinks. *Where do I start?*

After my divorce I bought *ESCAPEE*, took some sailing lessons and loudly announced to anyone who'd listen that I was going to cruise around the world. What a big mouth! My best friend Michael told me, "don't make *any* decisions just after a divorce. They'll all be wrong." Other friends told me the same. *But what did they know?* I've always had a problem listening— to my wife, my friends, to anyone. *Still do*—and the girls nodded their agreement.

On the day I left Santa Barbara, Michael threw a big farewell party at the local marina. Everybody came. One of those free, weekly newspapers covered it with an article "*Local Man Leaves to Sail Around World*". Next to the article was my photo with a goofy, silly grin and a caption—"*Man of the Sea*". Even my ex-wife Shirley was there to say goodbye. As I pulled out of the marina I turned to wave to everyone and missed the sharp turn in the channel and *ESCAPEE* was stuck fast on a sand bank. While everyone drifted away, the "*man of the sea*" had to be rescued by a passing boat. And I hadn't even left the marina yet. *What a start!*

After two miserable, seasick days I got to San Diego, took a break and then headed for Mexico. Just one day out of San Diego I had this overwhelming desire to turn around and "*go home*".   But how could I face all those people who'd said goodbye? Then I had an idea—I'd just go back to San Diego, put the boat in a nice marina and live—*OK, hide*—on it quietly for a few months. No one there knew me and after six months or so of hiding out, I'd sell the boat and go back home with some story about losing my boat on a reef in the South Pacific. I could even see the story in the paper—"*Local Adventurer Loses Boat in South Pacific.*" But I was never a good liar. Oh I could lie as well as anyone but it always showed on my face like a sign—so I had to keep going.

Let me back up a little. I married my college girlfriend, Shirley, when I was just out of college. Shirley's two years older than me and had already graduated. Soon we had Carl and Lisa wasn't far behind. Two kids put a lot of financial stresses on me, but I worked at two jobs, both in real estate. I sold real estate and was soon invited to join a new firm being set up by some friends. I was sales manager by the time I was 30 and a full partner at 35. By the time I was 40, I had my own firm and was not only selling properties, but building homes.

Carl and Lisa left for college and Shirley was trying to keep busy selling homes for another agent. I launched a housing project in San Luis Obispo—about 120 miles north of Santa Barbara and soon had to be there most of the week and could get home only on week-ends. Shirley complained about our lack of a life together, but she'd done that before. *I hadn't listened to her then and didn't now.*

Until one day when I was served with a legal notice and then I then heard her *loud and clear—-and much too late.* She had filed for divorce. Through all the long talks into the night which followed—all my promises to change, the counseling—Shirley was still firm. She wanted a life of her own and I can't blame her. The day the divorce was final, Michael and I went to a bar to have a drink. "Alan, my boy, drink up," he said, "you've just been 'sub-divided'."

"More like drawn and quartered," I shot back.

"Well, you're a free man now. Look at it that way."

I told him freedom stinks. I'd always wanted the security of a home, a wife and kids—the whole domestic thing. I was never one of those guys who sought "freedom"—whatever the hell that was. After the housing project was completed, I didn't have much to keep me busy, so I started working out and jogging on the beach. One day I jogged all the way to the Santa Barbara marina and watched all the busy activity—fishing boats coming and going—and saw the masts of all those sailboats, which never seemed to go anywhere.

I went into a shop and picked up a couple of fishing and sailing magazines and spent hours watching the fascinating activity in the marina. That night I read the magazines with their stories of men and women sailing down here in the South Pacific. The photos grabbed my attention—were there really places *this* beautiful—with people *this* happy? I saw an article entitled "*You Can Do It Too*". Well, I sure as hell doubted that, but read it anyway. It was by a guy who'd been a farmer in Iowa and sold out to a large farming company. He and his wife moved to San Diego, took sailing lessons, bought a cruising boat and took off.

The ex-farmer went on to explain that it cost only about $2,000 a month to cruise full time—far less than they lived on back home. They had no car or house expenses or insurance and couldn't spend money while out on the ocean or anchored behind islands. *"The wind is free,"* he said.   That shocked me—-I thought all those people were the idle rich.   The ex-farmer said he'd paid $120,000 for his boat—and that *really* surprised me. That was *less* than a small, one-bedroom home in Santa Barbara. *If I turned my rental units over to an agent I could do that. Forget it. Quit dreaming!* That's when I picked up the magazine that pushed me over the brink—*Latitude 38.* It's articles, photos and letters from *normal* people getting away from it all and cruising around the world was the clincher. That magazine quickly administered the *"coup de grace"* to my old life.

How do you learn all that stuff? I wondered. I walked the docks, talked to sailors and was introduced to a sailing instructor. I finally got up the courage to take some private lessons and was soon able to sail out to the nearby islands by myself on a small rental boat. When I could handle a smaller boat, I'd rent a larger one and take lessons on that. After that, I graduated to a larger size. With my instructor's help, I finally worked myself up to being able to handle a 40-footer on my own—not bad for a guy who'd never sailed.

As I improved my sailing skills I bought this boat and renamed it *ESCAPEE*. It's the biggest I could handle by myself. I had an autopilot, wind-vane steering and other equipment put on to help me handle it without having to find crew. My plan was to go to San Diego, load up with fuel and food and head south down the coast of Baja California to Cabo San Lucas, at the tip of the peninsula. I was deathly afraid of getting out of sight of land and wanted to hug the shore, so I could see land at all times and run for cover if bad weather came up.

About 60 miles south of San Diego, I had my "crisis". *I desperately wanted to turn back and go home.* But the apartment I lived in alone sure wasn't home. The cold reality was *I no longer had a home to go back to,* so I just kept on heading south. By the 4th day, the seasickness had gone and I was slowly getting my sea legs. After a week of slowly sailing close to the coast, I made it to Cabo San Lucas at the tip of Baja California. Cabo is a kind of "jump-off" point for boats heading across oceans and I figured when they go, I'll go with them. If—or more likely *when*— I get into trouble, they'll save my skin. When I started sailing, I'd stopped eating so much and had lost a lot of weight. I had even shaved my head—*what the hell, I was losing my hair anyway.* I'd decided to get this earring—maybe even a couple of tattoos.

One special day that changed my life, I was sitting on my boat at anchor near the beach at Cabo when three women swam around it. I invited them to come on board for a cold drink and they told me they had flown down from Seattle for a few days of sun and swimming. Yes, they loved sailing, they said, so I invited them to go sailing on *ESCAPEE*. I was especially attracted to Ann. She was a brunette, about my height with a great figure and a smile a mile wide. I quickly learned that she was a happy person—positive, up-beat and saw the best in everything and everyone. It was *just great* to be around her. Ann was 38, divorced with no kids and worked for a computer software company. She was an excellent sailor and loved hiking, camping and anything to do with adventure.

Ann and her friends sailed with me for a few days and I told them I was on my way around the world. By the third day I had fallen for Ann and she seemed to like me, too. We took long walks on the beaches and she told me about her failed marriage and I told her about mine. We packed endless hours of talking and being alone with each other into those few days—the rest of the world just ceased to exist—and we made love here in the cockpit of *ESCAPEE*.

Afterwards, we held each other and I asked her to take some time off and join me in Hawaii and sail with me across the Pacific. She had told me how much she loved the tropics and how sick and tired she was of the rain in Seattle, so I really laid it on. Of course, it was all a little fast for her, and she said, *"I'll go back and think about it some more. Who knows? Maybe I can. Let's just wait and see.* Anyway, when you get to Hawaii give me a call. I'll be thinking about it and we can talk about it then."

I knew she really meant *"if"* I ever reached Hawaii. Up until now, it was all just talk—I had leveled with Ann and told her I'd never been away from land. Anyway, at the airport Ann told me once again that she'd seriously consider coming to Hawaii to meet me and I promised to call her when—*if* – I ever made it that far.

I was on a "high." I had met a wonderful woman and she promised to think about sailing with me across the Pacific—and maybe even around the world. Now I was *really* motivated to get to Hawaii. I bought a chart covering the route from Mexico to Hawaii and saw that Hilo on the big island of Hawaii was almost 3,000 miles from the jump-off point of Cabo. I transferred that 3,000 miles onto a road map of the United States and it stretched all the way *from San Diego to the northern tip of Maine!* That distance over the ocean was just water and I couldn't relate to it, but that distance across the US was *very real.* Just imagine driving a car *at 5 miles an hour*—the fastest I could sail—from San Diego to the northern tip of Maine! And all that way there's no gas stations, no repair garages, no medical help and worst of all, no place to run and hide from storms.

"Just when're you heading out, Alan?" I was being asked by other sailors. A tone of skepticism was creeping into the questions—they knew a bullshitter when they saw one. I had to learn a lot in such a short time, so I borrowed a book entitled *"Survive the Savage Sea"*. I was attracted to the title. That's what I wanted to do—*survive!*

That's when I learned that titles can be misleading—it's all about a family who almost *didn't survive*. Their boat was attacked by killer whales and sunk. For 37 days they drifted alone at sea, drinking turtle blood and all that kind of good stuff. The photos of their pathetic, starved skeletal bodies when they were finally rescued by a passing ship made a lasting impression. I sure got something from that book. *Fear*. I had a fear of storms, being out of sight of land *and now whales*. *That's progress*.

One day I saw a steel boat arrive with a big dent in its side. Whatever had done that to tough steel would have sunk a fiberglass boat like *ESCAPEE* within 60 seconds. *"Whales"* the owner said. I asked him where the whale attack took place. *"That was no whale attack. We just hit a whale sleeping peacefully on the surface*. When we hit it, the whale was irritated and swung its tail to dive--the whale meant no harm. Its fluke hit the side of our boat as it dove. It was all just an accident." Great! I had just learned I could be sunk not only by whales which might attack, *but also by nice, peaceful whales which got pissed off*. *Even if I didn't run into* a *pack of whales who wanted to play "bang the boat," I could still be sunk—by a nice, friendly whale taking a nap*.

I filled up with fuel and *ESCAPEE* was ready to go, even if I wasn't. I would find Hawaii with my GPS unit which I bought at a big discount in Cabo—I was always good at getting deals. *ESCAPEE* could carry only enough diesel fuel for 800 of the 3,000 miles distance to Hilo, so if there was no wind I'd run out of fuel with 2,200 miles to go. I was leaving to "drive" from San Diego to Maine, but would run out of gas in "Colorado"— and there were no gas stations ahead. I was pretty sure I'd end up drifting forever, trapped in the empty, windless doldrums.

That was another of my fears—fear number *four*. Let me list these fears for you—since the list is getting pretty long. *One* was being out of sight of land. *Two* was storms. *Three* was being hit by a whale and now *number four* was running out of fuel in the middle of the ocean.

I was also running out of excuses, so to make it impossible to "chicken-out" at the last minute I set a departure date and told anyone who'd listen. At one of the potluck dinners on the beach, one of the sailors said, *"Alan, you're going to die at sea and I know how."*

"How?" I demanded, shaken to my core.

"Well, forget storms and whales and all that stuff. *You're going to starve to death.* You can't cook—we all know that—so you're going to starve those 20 or 30 or so days it takes to get to Hawaii."

I had forgotten all about that little problem. At that time, I couldn't cook—still can't I can tell by the looks on your faces. I almost always ate in waterfront "palapas" in Mexico and only had breakfast on board. Oh, I could open a can of food, but that was about it. My "cooking" was *so bad* I was the only one who could go to the sailors' potluck dinners without bringing a dish. In fact, I could only go to the potluck dinners *on the strict condition that I not bring anything cooked*—just potato chips or something like that.

So what *was* I going to do for food for 20-30 days at sea? A thousand and one things could go wrong in those 3,000 miles of empty ocean and I sure didn't want the responsibility of taking a cook along. To tell the truth there was another reason I wanted to go alone—*taking a small cruising boat alone across a vast ocean is still one of the few great adventures left in the world and I wanted to see if I could do it.* If I could I'd sail on with Ann. And if I didn't make it—well, it was my life to throw away.

Some cruisers tried to talk me out of going—they damn well knew I didn't have the experience for this long a voyage. But I *had* to get to Hawaii—Ann would most likely come and sail with me if I made it. Then, there was all that talk about going around the world and I knew in my gut the time had come to put-up or shut-up. "Thanks," I said to the guy who had warned me not to try this, "but I'm going."

"OK, but you might wind up being at sea for up to a month, so you better get a cook on board or you'll starve."

But where could I find someone who could cook on a small boat and who could also leave for Hawaii on such short notice? One of the sailors suggested I check the waterfront bars. *"You can find all kinds of people in Mexican bars,"* he said.

That's for sure—and you'd never want to meet most of them.

"That's where I met William who came into my life and graced it with his presence, in a dark Mexican bar on a hot afternoon. He was about 30, had the start of a beer belly and a pockmarked face that had been scarred by acne. He was balding in front, but made up for it with long, greasy black hair hanging off the back onto his shoulders. He had a nervous look about him—the guy could never sit still. I sat on a bar stool next to him, but he squirmed constantly—his eyes shifting to the bar room door every few seconds.

"You Alan?" he asked. "Hear you're going to Hawaii. Looking for a cook. That guy over there told me 'bout you," he said nodding towards one of my sailing friends.

"My name's William—but you can call me William," he said looking straight at me for the first time, sending a clear message to keep my distance and not get too familiar. It took only a few minutes for me to know that this guy was anti-social and didn't want anyone, as he put it, "in my space". *"When're you leaving man? I sort of need to leave pretty soon,"* he said, looking at the bar room door again as though he expected the police—or at least an irate husband or defrauded partner to burst in at any moment.

"William, I've got a few questions for you before we talk departure dates" I said. "First, have you had experience cooking at sea?"

"Oh yeah man, I was in the Navy and sailed everywhere."

"Well, this is a small boat and it rolls a lot."

"No problem man. I once worked on a fishing boat in Alaska. No big deal."

"Look," I said, "I'm sailing the boat. All you have to do is buy the food and cook three meals a day. I'll do all the sailing, but if we have a problem, you're going to have to pitch in and help. Is that OK with you?"

"Sure man. No big deal".

With that settled, I bought him a beer. William was from Southern California, had been in the Navy, done some fishing in Alaska and then got a job doing dry-wall and sheet-rock in construction jobs. He had life all figured out. "I don't need no college, man. I can do drywall and sheet-rock like no one else. *I figure that's the only skill I'll ever need in life, so why waste time going to school and filling my head with all that other crap?* They're always building houses somewhere and as long as they build, they need me. I work only when I need the money. I made a bundle on the last job and decided to come down here to goof off for a couple of months. I've done that and now I'm ready to split. I've heard they's lots of construction jobs in Hawaii. So I'm ready. *When do we leave?*"

I told him, "we have to check out with the Mexican authorities and check in with US customs and immigration in Hawaii on arrival. *Is there any reason you wouldn't want to do that?*" That was a polite way of asking if he was a fugitive or was on the lam. I figured that would scare him off if he had anything to hide. "*No problem man. I do things my way, but I'm not running from no one,*" he said glancing nervously at that door again.

I figured the guy would be quiet, keep to himself and do his job. He's not the kind of guy I'd choose to hang out with, but at the time he seemed OK. So I gave him some money to go buy all the food needed for 25 days, filled the water tanks and got ready to go. William soon returned in a taxi loaded with boxes of food, mostly large cans of beef stew. *But that wasn't all.* He also had a lot of something else, as I was to find out later.

"Why so much of the same thing," I asked.

"Man, great deal on this stuff. Bought all I could. Great price." That's how he talked—*Uzi talk*—short, staccato bursts like an Uzi machine gun. Come to think of it, I never once heard him string a complete sentence together. William was still down below putting away the last of those cans of beef stew when I started the engine, waved goodbye to my sailing friends and pointed the bow of *ESCAPEE* west to Hawaii, about 3,000 miles away.

I was leaving the city limits of San Diego, driving all the way to the top of Maine—*poking along at 5 miles an hour*—and there were no stops, no gas stations, no repair garages, no help of any kind. And there was no place to hide in a storm.

What am I doing? I asked myself as I moved the engine throttle forward and headed out into that huge, empty ocean.

As it turned out, I should have been asking—"*who am I doing this with?*"

"*I was just looking for a cook,*" I later tried to explain to the police in Hawaii.

CHAPTER FOUR

"WHERE'S HAWAII?"

You guys want any more beers before I get to this next part? They did and Susan went down to get some from the fridge and handed them up. They settled down to hear more, especially about this guy, William.

Well, as you can guess, I was one scared guy—leaving the sight of land for the very first time. The next land was a small island—a mere dot—3,000 miles away across the Pacific. I would mark my progress on both the marine chart from Cabo to Hawaii and that US road map from San Diego to Maine.

William quickly settled in and made it very clear he wanted his "own space" and chose the forward cabin. It was his and he told me to keep out. I warned him, "the front part of the boat rolls and bounces a lot more than the center cabin. Why don't you take a berth there?"

"*No way man,*" he said. "I need my space to do my own thing. I've fished Alaska so bouncing seas don't bother me none."

By the second day a pattern had set in. William kept to himself and wasn't interested in anything on the boat, but to give him credit he came out of his cabin right on time to fix breakfast, lunch and dinner. I soon discovered that to him, "fixing" lunch or dinner meant digging out one of those cans of beef stew and heating it up—that's it. After the second day and four meals of the same beef stew, I asked him, "*how about something different for a change?*"

"*Sure man, no problem.*"

At *last* we were going to have something different to eat and I was looking forward to it. William added onions and garlic to the *same* beef stew and presented the next meal as "something different". That's when I realized *he didn't know any more about cooking than I did.* He served those hot bowls of beef stew two times a day and kept out of sight doing his "own thing" as he put it.

It was also on the second day that I found out what William's *own thing* was. He had brought along a huge supply of marijuana for the three-week long trip and I smelled the aroma of pot coming out from under the door of the forward cabin. I had warned William—*no drugs*—and charged into the forward cabin to confront him.

"*Hey, this ain't drugs man. I don't do no hard-stuff shit. That can really screw your head up,*" he said. "*One of my friends fried his brains and can't even wipe his own ass no more. Someone has to do it for him. I sure ain't messin' with that shit.*

This is just pot." I looked unconvinced. *"Hey man, lighten up"* he said. *"You're on your trip. I'm on mine.* Where else could I drop out and do all this shit and not have to do nothin' else— except cook? What better place to let myself go and enjoy this grass? I ain't got nothin' to do for the next three weeks but cook and do grass. But no worries, man. I'll cook like I said and do what I said. Nothin' more. Nothin' less. Outside that what I do is my business. *Now piss off and leave me alone.*"

Now, I got it. I'm slow, but I finally got it— William saw this trip as his perfect chance to do all the pot he wanted with minimum distraction—no hassles, no diversions, no police, no anything, except lose himself in pot. I told him, "boats arriving in Hawaii from Mexico are searched for drugs and if they find anything—*anything at all*—-I could lose this boat and a lot else." He just said, "hey man, I promise you there won't be nothin' left by the time we get there," and at the rate he was puffing away I had no doubt he meant it.

"One other thing," I told him. "I don't want you up on deck when you're on that stuff. It's too dangerous. You could go overboard."

"No problem, man. I don't dig all this sea shit anyway."

I finally woke up to reality. *I was doing a "solo" voyage with a hostile pot-head recluse hiding in the forward cabin*, who couldn't cook and only came out to open another can of beef stew and disappeared again to his mountain of pot.

Good going Alan, I told myself, *you really know how to pick 'em.*

This wasn't starting out well at all. I was stuck with a cook who couldn't cook and on top of that, was trying to set a world's three-week pot-consumption record. Well, look at the bright side, I told myself—I was still sailing "alone" to Hawaii. But that had now become my biggest problem of all—*I wasn't sailing.* I was "driving"—using the motor for three straight days and nights—out into the empty Pacific and there were still no winds. I couldn't keep this up much longer. *ESCAPEE* motored about 5 miles per hour, so in those three days I had motored 360 miles out into the Pacific and there was still no trace of winds. I'd started off with fuel for only 800 miles and had already used up 360 of those miles.

According to the GPS, within a few hours *ESCAPEE* would be 400 miles out and I would've reached what airplane pilots dramatically call *"the point of no return"*. I never liked that phrase. It sounds so final and fatal—like a one-way trip to oblivion. *I always wanted to return.* I was now very close to my own *point of no return* and if I didn't get winds soon, I'd have to either turn around and go back while there was still enough fuel left to get back—or keep on until I ran out of fuel and then drift helplessly, all alone with a hostile pothead .

I was about to panic when I opened my book on weather and winds and read that in an "average" year there's supposed to be trade-winds all the way to Hawaii. *So, where the hell were they*? I only had 5 more hours to go to my own "point of no return". Then what? *Go back --or go deeper into this limitless sea?* In desperation, I called a sailing friend on the long-distance radio—that's the single-sideband radio—SSB for short—and it reaches up to 6,000 miles, depending on the time of day. I asked him to call the weather bureau. "Just ask them where the winds are and when they'll start blowing. I'll call you back in an hour."

An hour later my friend was back with a weather report and said, "the high pressure ridge in the Pacific is out of place. It's called the Pacific High and creates all the winds. It'll come back, sooner or later, but until then you're out of luck. Hang in there." I didn't know what the "Pacific High" was, but it clearly held my survival in its hands.

William wasn't worried—*not one little bit*. He was completely unaware of all this drama taking place around him. *William had already found his own sweet "Pacific High".*

The more I read the book on weather the more certain I was that sooner or later those trade-winds *had* to start blowing. I decided to keep going another 24 hours and if I hadn't found them by then, I'd shut down the engine and drift in the Pacific waiting for wind. Hopefully they'd arrive before we ran out of beef stew or water—I sure didn't want to get into an *"it's-either-me-or-you"* situation out there with William. I had no doubt who the *'lone survivor'*—as the newspapers always called them—would be.

Then on the 5th day—somewhere in northern Arizona on my road map—I was getting ready to shut the engine down and drift when the trade-winds hit. It was as if someone had turned on a giant fan. *"Yes!"* I shouted as I turned off the engine and raised the mainsail. *ESCAPEE* leaned over as the sail filled and started plowing her way through the seas westward towards Hawaii. There'd be no more smelly diesel fumes, no more hot engine, no more throbbing engine noise night and day, and best of all—no more danger of running out of fuel. *The skier had just gone over the edge and was now speeding downhill.*

As the waves became larger I discovered something else about them. Ninety-nine out of a hundred of those large waves coming from behind would rise high up behind *ESCAPEE* and then slip right by beneath her without a problem. But maybe one in a hundred would be a "boomer, hitting the side of a boat at just the right angle to make a very dramatic *"BOOOOOM!"*

When the first "boomer" hit I looked around in panic to see if the boat was still in one piece. I soon discovered those waves aren't really dangerous since they hit with a glancing blow and the boat yields to them, but from inside the boat *it sounded like the end of the world had come.* That first "boomer" scared me out of my wits and I jumped up, fully expecting to see *ESCAPEE* breaking in half and the ocean pouring in. I looked around amazed that she was still in one piece and only seconds later, a wild-haired William burst out of his cabin, his blood-shot eyes filled with total, stark terror. *He had the look of a man who had no more than 30 seconds to live.*

"Sssheeeiiit man--what the hell was that?"

I told him, *"it's OK, we're still in one piece."* He looked around to be sure he was still alive and dry and went back to his cabin—and clouds of smoke poured out from under the door. Not much later, it happened again and this one was even louder than the first. I looked up from the chart table towards William's door and started counting slowly. *"One-one thousand . Two-one thousand. Three-one thousand..."*

The door flew open and William again burst out, his face again frozen in sheer terror and his crazed red eyes clearly expecting to see the Pacific pouring in through the cracked hull of *ESCAPEE.* Maybe he was in a pot-haze, dreaming of some disaster and the "boom" just added the *right* sound effects at the *right* moment. *Who knows?* But as soon as he pulled himself together and went back into his cabin I started quietly laughing. I know it wasn't a nice thing to do, but couldn't help myself.

As if to pay me back for laughing at William's terror, fate prepared the greatest, heart-stopping "boomer" of all—*just for me.* It was about 9 on a beautiful Sunday morning. We were somewhere in "Colorado" on my road map and I'd just finished morning coffee in the cockpit when I turned to go back down below and automatically glanced around in all directions for any sign of a ship. As usual, the sea was empty so I went below to make another pot of coffee.

I had that full pot of coffee in one hand and a bag of used coffee grounds in the other when I suddenly I heard a screaming, ear-splitting *ROOOAAR!!!!* It was like 10,000 motorcycles and 100 ship's air horns—*all rolled into one horrible, deafening roar. And it was no more than* a *hundred yards away. We were about to be run down by a huge ship I hadn't seen!* At least that's what flashed through my terror-stricken mind.

I threw the pot full of coffee and the bag of coffee grounds straight into the air and peed in my pants. In absolute panic I ran up on deck *expecting instant death* from the giant bow of a ship. Instead I saw a small Navy jet plane, which had come out of nowhere and roared over us at mast-top height. *How could that be?* We were at least 1,000 miles from any land—far beyond the range of small jets. I rushed down below to get my hand-held radio and hurried back up, turning it to channel 16— the emergency frequency I *should* have been listening to.

"Good morning little boat," the pilot said, *"did you enjoy your wake-up call?"*

"Wake-up call?" That's what he called the loudest, most unexpected ear-splitting noise I've every heard in my life! I started to ask where the hell he'd come from when he said, " *I tried to call you, but you didn't have channel 16 on as your're supposed to, so I just had to give you that little wake-up call. I see I got your attention."* I could tell from the tone of his voice he had to be laughing his head off. He'd probably *always* wanted an excuse to buzz a small sailboat at mast height and really shake them up and then tell his buddies all about it. Now he'd had his chance.

He said, *"I'm off an aircraft carrier and you're sailing into an area of a naval military exercise. So I strongly suggest you alter course by 15 degrees to the north for about a hundred miles. That'll keep you clear of the live firing. Have a nice day."* Then he zoomed off and I went below—my hands and knees still shaking—and started to clean up the horrible mess.

William! I'd forgotten all about William! I opened his door and found him hiding under his blanket, curled up in a fetal position, *quivering and shaking so much the entire blanket was jumping!* He couldn't have heard me up in the cockpit talking to the pilot on the hand-held radio. He couldn't have known what that noise was—any more than I knew before I rushed up on deck. *He still didn't know.* In his pot-fogged mind, he must've thought that all the demons in hell had come shrieking after him and he was curled up in that fetal position, shaking uncontrollably.

What's worse, *he didn't even know whether the noise was for real or not. It could have been an internal, pot –induced noise* he imagined—the result of his own drug-fried brain. As far as he knew, *the noise wasn't even real*—after all no ships make that kind of noise. Because there were no reasonable *external* sources, William was obviously convinced it had come from *within* him.

At first I planned to deny there was any noise at all and ask, "w*hat noise, William? There was no noise. I didn't hear anything. Man, your brains are cooked and you're imagining some weird stuff. You'd better lay off that pot.*" And maybe for his own sake I should have, but when he finally stuck his head out from under that jumping blanket he was about the most miserable, pathetic sight I've ever seen. He was shaking and trembling and *looked so lost.* But it was the eyes that got me— *I'll never forget those eyes*—those pathetic, horror-stricken eyes! *They were begging for mercy.*

I didn't have to deny there was any noise—*he was already convinced there wasn't and that he'd permanently damaged his brains—just like his friend.* Just a little shove from me now—a denial there was any noise at all—and I think he would've gone over the edge of sanity. The poor guy needed to return to earth in a 'soft landing'. As it turned out, I had to argue with him for at least a half-hour to convince him it *really was* a plane.

"They ain't no planes out here, man," he said. *"Don't be shittin' me. We're too far offshore."*

"William, I told you it was from an aircraft carrier."

"Are you sure it was a plane?"

"*Yes, I told you.* I saw it and talked to the pilot." In the end, I had to show him all those coffee grounds and broken glass everywhere to convince him there *really was* a plane.

"*Oh, holy shit*" he said, with his head buried deeply in his hands. "*I thought I'd really gone and done it this time—just like my friend who's now some kinda' freak.* My friends used to call me '*the king of pot'.* I could do more pot than anyone. Now… I just don't know anymore."

I changed course as the pilot suggested—live missiles coming at me was all I needed now! For days afterwards William had a haunted look and had trouble "cooking" which meant he served the beef stew lukewarm, not hot—a real drop in his normal high standards. He even seemed to cut back on his pot smoking—at least for a day or two.

During William's haunted days *ESCAPEE* continued slowly on her course at about 5 mph—across "Colorado" and into "Kansas" on the road map—and closer to Hawaii on the ocean chart. Until now, I had faithfully stayed up every night in the cockpit, sleeping 20 minutes and waking up to the loud ringing of the egg-timer I kept under my shirt. I looked around for any signs of ships and went back to sleep for another 20 minutes. *Why 20 minutes?* I'd been told that's about how long it takes for a ship to come up over the horizon and kill you. I couldn't really turn loose and sleep during the day, either. Ships can kill you anytime—day or night and I'd just had the biggest scare of my life. My nerves were still on edge.

I could *never* figure out how two vessels on a limitless ocean could wind up being in the *exact same spot at the exact same time*—and collide. There was all that vast, unlimited ocean out there, but they managed to do it all the time and small boats like *ESCAPEE* always came out the loser.

"*Those ships'll never see you at sea*" an old sailor had told me back in Mexico, "*usually, no one's on the bridge watching. They just turn on the autopilot and set a loud radar alarm, which goes off if another ship gets within 20 miles of them.* So most of them never keep a visual watch on the high seas. Your boat's too small to set off their alarm, so they'll never know you're there." I knew that was really true. I had heard that one ship arrived in San Francisco with the mast of a sailboat hanging from its huge anchor. No one on the ship knew anything about it until the harbor police told them on arrival. Somewhere at sea, they had rammed a sailboat and never even felt it—and somewhere at sea, someone had died.

That and the scare from the plane motivated me to keep my 20-minute watch schedule day and night. The problem was that I wasn't getting enough sleep and it was really catching up on me. I started making little mistakes and doing really dumb things due to lack of sleep. One morning I reached for the red and white tube of Colgate toothpaste and instead got the red and white tube of *Ben-Gay deep-heat rub* which I had bought in Mexico—and started brushing *the deep-heat rub* into my teeth and gums!

Have you guys got any idea *how painful* deep-heat rub is when you brush it into your tender gums? I thought it tasted funny at first but just ignored it—and then it "went off". My mouth was a volcano! I sucked ice cubes from the fridge for hours. Some advice—*never, ever rub deep-heat into your gums!*

I needed sleep and thought about asking William to take a watch or two but gave that up when I realized he couldn't be trusted to stay awake. I now had to face a fact. I could keep my 20-minutes on and 20-off watch around the clock and get really worn down by lack of sleep—which would be very dangerous in case of a storm or emergency—or I could just take the chance of a collision and get a few hours solid sleep at night.

I decided to get a few hours solid sleep even if it meant *ESCAPEE* was charging blindly ahead through the night with both of us sound asleep—or one of us asleep and the other stoned. Every morning I woke up I was grateful—*and a little bit surprised*—to still be alive and not run down by a ship or hit by whales during the night. I knew I was really pushing my luck.

If I ever got to Hawaii alive I'd have someone reliable, like Ann, with me the rest of the way. But I had to get to Hawaii first and hadn't even reached the halfway point yet. On the road map we were now in "Missouri," which I'd figured was about the halfway point. We were 1,500 miles at sea with another 1,500 miles to go – creeping along at 5 mph, and I was constantly looking over my shoulder for any signs of a storm. The trade-winds were steadily coming from behind day and night. *The skier was effortlessly gliding down the slope.* There had been no sign of any ships and little sign of William. The bowl of beef stew was sometimes left in the sink at the right time, but he rarely came out these days.

We slowly crossed into "Ohio"—on my road map of the US. In reality, we were moving steadily towards the big island of Hawaii and I checked my progress by GPS several times a day. It faithfully told me where we were—*or at least I thought it did*. One afternoon the position the GPS gave me didn't make much sense—it said we were somewhere in Europe. *Europe?* My heart skipped a beat and I hoped it was just a one-time fluke. I tried to get busy with other things and give the GPS an hour or so to clear things up—it must be some problem with the satellites, I figured. I was out there in the middle of the ocean and that little black box was the *only way* to know where I was. It *had* to work—just give it a little time to get a good position fix.

I couldn't wait the whole hour—the tension was too much—and forty minutes later I checked it again. The fix came in and put us, guess where—*in the heart of Africa*—then it died and the screen went blank. *So much for that big discount!* I fought to control my panic and sat down at the chart table to think it through. I had a sextant and the books and tables necessary for celestial navigation by the sun and stars but I hadn't bothered to take any classes—*who needed to know that in the day of satellite navigation?*

The "Big Island" of Hawaii looks big when you're there but I want to tell you, it's just a tiny dot on a chart of the entire Eastern Pacific. That's the only chart I had and it ended at Hawaii. These winds were so strong and the seas so high, if I missed Hawaii there'd be no going back. It would be like trying to *ski up a mountain*—it can't be done. On top of that with no charts beyond Hawaii I wouldn't know where I was or if there were dangerous reefs dead ahead. As far as I knew the next land would be Indonesia or China. I *had* to find Hawaii on the *first* try and definitely not—*under any condition*—miss it.

William came out to 'cook' dinner and saw the sextant out of its case and the books strewn around. *"What's all that shit, man?"* he asked, reaching for the sextant.

"Don't touch it William, it's delicate."

"What the hell is it?"

I told him it was a sextant. He thought about it for a minute and said, *"man no one uses those things now there's GPS. All the fishing boats use GPS—same's us."*

"William we did use GPS but it stopped working. Now we're going to have to use this sextant." His face went white—absolutely white.

"You mean we're lost? You don't know where the hell we are?"

"Well, I knew where we were yesterday" I said confidently, trying to cheer him up. That didn't impress him one bit.

"Shit man, you're telling me we're lost. How in hell are we going to find Hawaii? What's to keep us from missing it and going on forever?"

I didn't want to admit it, but that's *exactly* what I was worried about, too. I needed to calm him—*and myself*—down so I said, *"people sailed around with sextants for centuries before GPS. If they could do it we can do it."* He wasn't buying that at all. Neither was I—it was all bravado bullshit.

"We're lost at sea," William said softly to himself, *"my God, now we're lost at sea. What else can go wrong on this boat from hell?"*

"No we're not," I insisted, *"I just need a little time to study all this. Now quit bugging me so I can get to work. I need a fix."*

"So do I man," he said, *"so do I,"* and went back to his cabin and the smoke soon poured out. William soon had *his* fix but I still had to figure out how to get mine.

While I studied the books on celestial navigation *ESCAPEE* was charging ahead in the strong trade-winds—faster than ever. *The skier was speeding downhill but was lost and didn't have any idea what was around the next corner—maybe a thousand-foot drop-off!*

I was lost—*just plain lost*—on a very big ocean. I desperately hoped we'd come across a ship to tell us where we were and scanned the horizon with the binoculars, but it was a very empty, big ocean. *ESCAPEE* was plowing ahead and making good time—*I just didn't know where*—so I decided to think it through over-night and tackle it again first thing in the morning when I was fresh. We were still going in the right general direction, of course, but I was going to have to come up with a solution in the next day or two or we'd most likely miss Hawaii and sail off into the endless Pacific. I didn't sleep much that night as I wrestled with my self–doubts. I had *really* over-reached myself this time.

Here I was, a burned-out guy in his mid-forties pretending to be Captain Cook—and had managed to get lost on the biggest ocean on earth. And here's the really scary part— even *if* I figured out celestial navigation and got it 100% right,

I had no way to *know* it was correct until Hawaii was either there—or *wasn't there. If it was there—OK. Great. But if it wasn't there, it would then be too late.* We couldn't turn around and go back to look for it against these winds and waves. *The skier couldn't ski uphill.*

That's when I remembered reading somewhere that finding latitude—the north-south position—is a lot easier than finding the longitude—the east-west position. Finding my latitude would only take a few calculations. The chart showed that the big island of Hawaii was on latitude 20. If I could figure out how to get on latitude 20, I'd just stay on it until I ran right into the island. Mauna Loa, the volcano on the Big Island, was over 13,000 feet high so I should be able to see that 50 to 60 miles away. I'd just sail along latitude 20 until we bumped into the Big Island—at least that was the plan. I shot the sun with the sextant, did the calculations and steered *ESCAPEE* to what *I thought, hoped and prayed* was latitude 20. But how would I *really* know?

We were speeding along at about 150 miles a day under these stronger trade-winds and I figured we were now only about 200 miles from Hawaii—or around "New Hampshire" on my road map. At dawn on the 19th day, I estimated we were close to the Big Island and should be seeing the peak of Mauna Loa dead ahead in front of us. *But it wasn't there.* What did I do wrong? I re-did the calculations all over again.

I didn't *dare* show how scared I was—William was on the verge of panic and I wasn't far behind. He told me he'd smoked every grain of pot on board and I believed him because he was acting like a guy who badly needed something and didn't have it. I definitely should be seeing Mauna Loa by now *but it just wasn't there.* I re-did my figures for the 6th time and they showed us on latitude 20—more or less. So where was Mauna Loa? It should have been visible from 60 miles out and I figured we were only 25 miles away. *Where the hell was it?*

Then I had a horrible, spine-chilling thought.

Maybe the GPS was wrong all the time—all the way from Mexico.

Maybe it had *never* been reading correctly for the last 19 days at sea. *How would I really know?* It's all just water out there.

Maybe we've already sailed past Hawaii.

Maybe I'm on latitude 20—but on the other side of Hawaii heading for China.

Maybe I don't know what the hell I'm doing!

In desperation I decided to try to call someone for help on the short-range VHF radio. It only has a range of some 40 miles so I figured if anyone could hear me, it meant we were within 40 miles of Hawaii. I called twice. There was no answer and I fought the rising panic. I called again and some guy on a fishing boat replied. I was so overjoyed hearing a voice—any voice—I instantly blurted out the only thing on my mind these last few days—*"where's Hawaii?"*

There was a long pause. Then the guy came back and said slowly, *"it's where it's been for millions of years. I think the real question here is—where are you?"*

"I don't know where I am. That's why I'm calling." I told him I thought I was close to latitude 20 and should be within 25 miles of the Big Island. I said, "I should be able to see the mountain, but I can't see a damned thing."

The man must've heard the edge of panic in my voice and said, *"now just relax and wait a few minutes. I'll be right back."* He was soon back and said, *"OK, I've turned my radar on and we've got two radio direction finders on two boats standing by. Count to ten slowly and we'll home-in on your radio signal. Between the radar and direction finders, we'll find you. Ready?"*

"Ready," and I started counting to ten slowly.

"We've got you. Guess what? You're only ten miles out so you better slow down or you're going to crash right into the island. You can't see much because of the bad haze mixed with a bunch of volcanic ash in the atmosphere. Welcome to Hawaii!"

I felt like a ten-ton cement block had been lifted off my shoulders! Two hours later—after 19 days, 8 hours and 31 minutes *and 39 cans of beef stew—ESCAPEE* was safely tied up at the customs and immigration dock in Hilo. The customs officer took one sniff of us and said, "you boys go ahead and shower-up over there first"—pointing to the public shower— "then we'll do the paperwork".

I stood under that shower and let the water flow. It was luxurious beyond belief. We'd had to watch every drop and now I just let it pour over me—-and scrubbed and scrubbed. Long after I had shampooed and washed and was clean—long after I had any excuse or reason to still be there—I let the water keep pouring all over me, onto my head, into my face, down my body. There was no luxury on earth to match that shower. *None.*

After the formalities were over, William said a quick goodbye and rushed off to the Kona Coast muttering something about *"scoring some Kona Gold"*. I offered to buy him a big breakfast at a nearby coffee shop but he said *"no way, man. I don't never wanna be within a hunterd miles of this damned boat no more. I'm outa here."*

On my way to the coffee shop I stopped at a phone and called Ann. I was feeling ten feet tall. I was on a "high" when Ann picked up the phone and by the time I finished gushing out my ecstatic monologue, telling her all about the voyage, she *finally* had a chance to get a few words in. *"Alan, I'm really happy for you. Yes, I want to go with you. I've got some practical things to deal with—some good news and bad news. But I'm coming—just give me a little time and I'll be there."*

I was never a good listener and heard only the "good news"—*Ann was coming.* The *bad news* part just didn't register with me. By the time I got to the coffee shop it was about ten in the morning or so and I grabbed the breakfast menu and ordered a huge stack of pancakes, which I topped off with hot melted butter and maple syrup. For the first time in 19 days, the table wasn't rolling. I held my coffee cup tightly until I realized I could actually set it down and it wouldn't go flying off by itself. *Amazing!*

I ate slowly, savoring every moist bite and sipped my fresh Kona coffee. By the time I finished the pancakes and coffee it was about 11:30 and they brought out the lunch menu— with those *irresistible* photos of hamburgers. I ordered a juicy, half-pound hamburger smothered with fried onions and lots of tomatoes, pickles and Dijon mustard. When that was finished I used the last little piece of the hamburger bun to wipe up the juices left on the plate. When I paid I asked the cashier, *"where's the nearest ice cream store?"*

As I walked towards it I suddenly remembered Ann saying something about *bad news*—dammit why didn't I ever learn to listen! I rushed to the nearest phone and told her, *"Ann, I'm sorry. I was on such a high I heard only what I wanted to hear—that you're coming—but I missed the part about the bad news."*

"That's OK, Alan," she said. *"I didn't have the heart to interrupt you. I figured we could talk later."* She said she could come, but for only 6 months. The job was not the problem—the problem was her mother. She said, *"as it stands, I can't be gone from her longer than six months. Are you sure you still want me?"*

"Ann, I'll take you for a week if that's all you've got. I miss you. Let's start with the six months and go from there."

"OK, that's what I was hoping you'd say, but I had to tell you. Call me in a week or two. I should have the date of my arrival by then. "

Back on *ESCAPEE* I looked myself over in the mirror. I was leaner than I had ever been, despite my feeding frenzy earlier that day. My stomach hurt like hell but I had lost weight during those 19 days of constant motion and flexing my muscles to stay balanced. My moustache was now exactly the way I wanted it. I wore sunglasses and this colored, knotted bandanna over my shaved head and this gold earring I'd bought in Cabo. I thought, what a difference from that paunchy, square guy back home!

Then it hit me—I had said *"back home"*.

ESCAPEE was now my home. Somewhere out there on the Pacific—sometime during those 19 days—she had ceased to be just a boat and had become my *home*. She was no longer just a way to *get* where I wanted to be. *She was where I wanted to be,* and that was the true test of a home—*anyone's home.*

That night I turned loose of all responsibilities and slept like a baby for 11 hours—rocked by the gentle waters of the harbor. It was the best sleep I could ever remember having— tucked safely in the bosom of my home. I didn't have to wonder if I'd wake up swimming—hit by a ship or whales while sailing blindly through the night. It was a life-renewing sleep and I woke up feeling like a new man.

About an hour after waking up a police car pulled into the boat dock and two cops got out. *"Are you the guy who brought a William Reynolds Throckmorton, Jr. here?"* one asked, looking at his notes. *"William who? Oh William yes, he sailed with me here. I was just looking for a cook,"* I stammered.

"Well, it seems he's got himself into a some trouble over on the Kona side. Seems he was picked up trying to buy a really big bunch of pot. *We've got to check out your boat."*

I panicked. Did William get rid of all the pot? Is anything left on board? I could see the headlines in Santa Barbara—*"Local Man Sailing Around World Picked Up on Drug Charge in Hawaii"*—and right next to it my photo looking like a pirate. One look at that photo and everyone—*even my friends*—would say, *"guilty as hell"*. But as it turned out William had been true to his word. He had smoked every bit of pot he had—every last seed, every last grain, every last fragment and *probably even the sawdust* left over from the carpenter's work.

"You're clean," the police said after the search.

"Oh by the way, this guy William said you could vouch for his good character—*sort of like a character witness."*

I didn't know what to do about that—William wasn't really such a bad guy at heart. I wanted to help him if I could and told the police. But the next day he had a message waiting for me at the office. *"Thanks for offering to help, man, but don't need no help no more. Just a little misunderstanding. All solved. Your friend, William."*

My friend? I really *did* miss the guy—*for about an hour or two*. I was sure glad he'd managed to get out of that mess but wondered how William—the *"Uzi talker"* who had never managed to string more than one complete sentence together—managed to talk his way out of that mess?

The next day I sailed towards Honolulu where I took a guest dock at the Ala Wai marina, right next to Wakiki beach. As a new arrival I could stay for 30 days and that was just about the right amount of time—I wanted to head on across the Pacific and on our last telephone call, Ann said she'd be arriving in a couple of weeks.

Michael flew out to spend a few days with me. He's a lawyer and had become my best friend when I met him 13 years before at a conference on real estate law. He was shocked when he got off the plane and saw this pirate standing in front of him. He knew what a fraud this pirate get-up is and said "w*ho're you kidding? What a load of bullshit. This is your friend Michael, remember? I know you."*

"*Shhh,*" I whispered, "Whatever you do, don't tell anyone. I've got an image to live up to."

"*Well, you're sure as hell are doing a good job of it,*" he said, laughing. Michael never understood all this "*man against the sea stuff,*" as he called it. He laughed at my appearance but did admit he saw a very different "me"—leaner, fit, confident and much more self-assured. According to him, whatever had happened to me out there at sea those 19 days had turned out to be good. As he left, he made me promise to write him and keep him up to date on what's happening.

Two days after Michael left I got a message from my daughter, Lisa, who was 22 and worked for a travel agency. She was using her travel agent's discount to go to Asia—and would stop by to see me. I looked in the mirror and wondered *how's she going to handle this?* And I'd sure have to tell her about Ann. I met her plane and as she stepped off she said, "*w*ow, *dad—I like it! I like it! Whoever would've thought my straight-guy dad would turn out to be a rogue and pirate?*"

We hugged and I took her to lunch and told her all about the 19-day passage. She laughed over William and the navy jet that scared him so badly, over my own stupid question "*where's Hawaii*?" and all those cans of beef stew. Then she got to the point.

"*OK, dad of mine—what now? What's next? Where do you go from here?*"

"Hey, hang on," I said. "One question at a time."

"Quit stalling and tell me everything. And I mean *everything,*"

I told her of my plans—first some island hopping across the Pacific, some beach-time, some island paradises—not this Honolulu version of it—and on around the world.

She took that in and said, "OK dad, now another question—one a little hard for a daughter to ask her father—OK?

What about women? You know....women. Come on dad, don't make me spell it out..."

"*Well,*" I said, "*I met someone and.....*"

"*I knew it! I just knew it!*" Lisa said, laughing. "*You old rogue. I hope she's not 18 or younger than me....*"

"No, she's 38 and quite a woman."

"*Yeh, I'll bet she is....*" and let it linger, looking me straight in the eyes. I could feel my face turning red.

"*No, no. It's not like that,*" I protested. *She loves sailing and....*"

She didn't let up for one minute, and said "*dad, you're blushing. Hey, I've made my pirate-dad blush! Come on, you can tell your only daughter. Give me all the sordid details.*" She leaned over to me conspiratorially and asked, "*so where'd you meet this chick? Some dive? Some bar? Some strip-joint? C'mon, dad, you can tell me.*"

That was about enough, so I said "Lisa, cut it out. She's a perfectly respectable lady I met on the beach in Mexico and..."

"*Oh no! A beach pick-up!* You picked up a chick off a Mexican beach...."

Lisa was having the time of her life and had no mercy on me---*none*. She was watching me turn beet-red and had me on the defensive, explaining and trying to justify myself—and she wasn't about to let up.

Carole, you're just as bad—even worse. Why do you women do this to me?

Carole smiled and said nothing, so Alan went on.

Lisa said to me, "*dad, you're a grown-up boy*. You don't have to explain everything to me. But you always told me to be careful who I went with, and now—look at you—*a beach pick-up.*"

"Ann's a very fine woman," I told her. "You'll like her. Hey, give me a break."

"I'm just bugging you, dad. She sounds just like a very nice person."

I begged her, "Now can we talk about something else... *pleeeease!*"

We talked about the family. Carl was doing great at work. Solid and steady—chip off the old block. They were going to have their first child any day now. Finally the talk got around to Sarah. My ex was seeing someone—a banker, Lisa said. He seemed like a nice guy and I hoped he'd make her happier than I had. We hung around together for a couple of days and then it was time for Lisa to fly on to Hong Kong. I took her to the airport and as I hugged her goodbye, she had tears in her eyes.

"Dad, do what you need to do. You know I love you. Carl does too. You'll always have us."

I held her and said, "I know, honey. I love you too. *See you soon.*" From the time she was 3 years old, we had always said "*see you soon*" to each other—even if I was just going to the corner grocery store.

"*See you soon, dad,*" she replied

We both knew that wasn't going to be possible.

This was no trip to the corner grocery store.

CHAPTER FIVE

LIFE AND LOVE ON AN UNINHABITED ISLAND

"Come on Carole, don't you guys want to break for dinner?" Alan asked. He hoped they'd heard enough so he could stop. They weren't buying it.

"Not me, what about you?" she asked Sigrid and Susan. They wanted to keep going too, so Carole said, "OK, you and *'the king of pot'* made it to Hawaii. When did Ann get there? *More, more…* "

Well, I called her every other day and during one of the calls she said she'd be arriving the very next day. When Ann came off the plane, she stopped in her tracks and said, *"Alan! You've changed!* Look at that moustache. It was pretty pathetic when I saw it last. And that earring! Hey, which is the real Alan? That four-square guy I liked in Mexico—or this reprobate I see standing in front of me?"

"You'll find out soon enough," I said and we hugged.

Then Ann said, "what've you done? Seriously, let me look at you." She stood back to get a better view. "All you're missing is a tattoo". Ann saw my hesitation. *"You don't have a tattoo anywhere do you?"* she asked. "I hate them."

"That's for me to know and you to find out. When we get back to the boat, you can do a strip-search and see for yourself."

Carole had tried to stay quiet and not interrupt him but this was just *too* much. *"Ugh, Alan, what a line!"* she said.

"Hey, whose story is this?" he asked and then continued.

Ann settled in on *ESCAPEE* and we started getting ready to cross the Pacific. We worked well together as a team. What I couldn't do, she could—and vice versa. We really got along well—I was sure we would but was still a little nervous about it. It's one thing you know, to have a good few days together as we did in Mexico and another to live together day in and day out—*well, you guys know all about that.* We spent 6 weeks sailing and working to get the boat ready to go.

Towards the end, we rented a truck, drove to a wholesale food company and bought enough food and supplies to last for 6 months. That was one truck-load and I thought poor *ESCAPEE* was going to sink. We'd been allowed to pull into the marina guest dock for an hour to unload and a guy with a group of tourists asked, "what's all that stuff?"

"Heading across the Pacific" I said, as I started passing the boxes down to Ann.

"Hey guys," he shouted to the others who'd gone on ahead, "these folks are sailing across the ocean in this itty-bitty boat. Get your asses back here and let's help'em load up."

"Why so much?" I told him we wanted to wander around the remote islands in the Pacific with no worries about time or supplies. I figured that if Ann and I had only 6 months together—and I certainly doubted that—I wanted them to be the *best* 6 months of her life. I had that small water-maker installed, so we'd have plenty of fresh water for daily showers and bought a new, reliable GPS and *another* as a backup. *No more getting lost!* Well, anyway the day came when we were fully loaded with food, water and fuel and it was time to go. *"We're off to our own deserted tropical paradise,"* I said to Ann.

"You mean there's still an uninhabited island somewhere out there—*in this day and age?* I thought that was only in fairy tales."

Palmyra Atoll is 1,052 miles south of Hawaii. It's a circular coral atoll with a beautiful, sheltered lagoon in the middle. The atoll is the tip of the cone of an undersea volcano and sticks up a bare 4 to 5 feet above the sea-level. It was discovered by the American sailing vessel *PALMYRA* in 1802 when sailing across the uncharted Pacific. It's part of the United States but has been uninhabited for years since the plantation pulled out. During WWII, the US navy installed large water tanks and other facilities so it has an abundant supply of fresh water from the frequent tropical rainstorms which dump an incredible *14 feet* of rain a year. There's no shortage of anything—fresh water or food from the teeming lagoon and abundant vegetation—*just people.* Usually, it's only wandering cruisers like Ann and I who go there.

Palmyra has long attracted people searching for their own uninhabited island paradise. You guys may have heard the story of two sailboats arriving on Palmyra at about the same time—each couple looking for a deserted island of their own. One couple was from San Diego. Mac and his wife Muff arrived on a beautiful, well-stocked sailboat to spend a year alone. Soon after they arrived, a battered and un-seaworthy boat arrived from Hawaii with an ex-convict named Buck and his girl friend Jennifer. By the time they managed to get to Palmyra they were running out of food and their boat was in such bad condition it was doubtful they could make it back to Hawaii.

As the months passed other boats came and went, but in the end Mac and Muff were left alone on the island with Buck and Jennifer. Mac and Muff disappeared and Buck and Jennifer took Mac's boat back to Hawaii where they re-painted it in an effort to disguise its appearance. They were eventually arrested for theft of the boat which Buck claimed to have won in a bet with Mac. *What a lie.* But without more evidence murder charges couldn't be made. Years later, another visiting boat found burned bones which were identified as Muff's and Buck and Jennifer were charged with murder. Buck was convicted but Mac's remains were never discovered. The murder became a best-selling book and film—and Palmyra got the reputation of being a "sinister" and dangerous place.

What a bum rap. *In reality, it's a little slice of paradise*—tropical, deserted, with freshwater and unlimited quantities of fresh seafood, coconuts and hearts of palm.

On the eighth day, Palmyra Atoll popped up out of the empty ocean, dead ahead and we found the pass into the lagoon and started in. We entered the huge, protected lagoon and my heart sank. I saw what I didn't want to see—the mast of a single anchored sailboat. After the murders here, I didn't want to be here alone with just one other boat. Palmyra is beautiful, but it's no place to be alone with a murderer or madman. As we dropped our sails and motored towards the anchored boat I was hoping it would turn out to be a nice, elderly couple or a young family with children on board. But no one seemed to be on the strange–looking, home-built craft.

We stopped *ESCAPEE* near the boat and looked into the palm trees at the edge of the water for any sign of the boat's occupants. There was movement among the bushes—and we saw a fierce-looking man in a tiny string bikini with a huge knife strapped to his leg. The man stared back at us—looking menacingly hostile and threatening. I was spooked and ready to turn around and head back out to the open sea when I saw the "hostile" man, now smiling and waving his welcome. He wasn't hostile—*just surprised*.

He was now getting into his dinghy and rowing out to welcome us. I felt more than a little stupid—and very relieved. Roger was the official caretaker of the island on behalf of its owners, a master French chef trained in Paris and an adventurer. After *ESCAPEE* was anchored he welcomed us on his boat and said he was sorry he re-acted as he did, but was surprised to see us. He'd been there for several months and while there was plenty of food everywhere, he was running low on basic stuff likes flour. "That's no problem," Ann said, "we're loaded to the gills in food and provisions. We're a floating grocery store."

Roger said he would make us a deal—if we chipped in the flour and other essentials he was short of he'd be our personal chef and make a special dinner each night to be served on a small, sandy "dining island" inside the calm reef. What an offer! *We now had our own, private French chef on our own uninhabited island in paradise.* It doesn't get much better than that.

Every morning Roger described that night's mouth-watering dinner and gave us our "shopping list" for the day— fresh crabmeat, fish, hearts of palm, bananas—whatever. Around 10:30 we took off carrying something for lunch and explored, swam, gathered the "shopping list" and had our lunch at some scenic spot. Around four in the afternoon, we returned to present Roger with our "shopping" While he created the evening's masterpiece Ann and I luxuriated in the open-air bathtub which we filled from the huge water tank. We bathed together and as I scrubbed her back, Ann said, "*Alan, every day just keeps getting better*".

I told her, "*lots more to go.*" As it turned out, there were lots more—*but not enough.*

After the bath we sat at the "*Palmyra Yacht Club*"—a run-down concrete naval building which someone there before us had converted into the grand-sounding "Palmyra Yacht Club". We watched steam pour out of the open hatches of Roger's boat and about an hour before dusk each day he emerged—the master chef was ready with his most accomplished creation—just for us. We went to Roger's boat where he passed down the food wrapped in aluminum foil and climbed into his own dinghy, and we took off for our own private "*dining island*". It was a strikingly beautiful little *islet* with white, powdery sand, a "dining table" of sorts, palm trees and baby booby birds—all nestled inside the calm waters of the lagoon. Every evening, Mother Nature put on a magnificent sunset "light show" in the west as we enjoyed the food we had gathered earlier that day, creatively prepared by *our own* French chef—and served on *our own* private "dining" island in *our own* tropical paradise.

"*Am I dreaming all this?*" Ann asked and said, "*this is so beautiful. I don't want it to ever stop. Not ever.*" I guess that's when I lost touch with reality and expected us to be together forever. I probably confused Ann's wishes—and my own—with reality.

I asked Roger about the two dogs which followed him everywhere and he said that when the plantation closed down and pulled out its workers they started to shoot the dogs. They soon killed all of them except for three tough and smart guys who figured out what the hell was going on and hid until everyone had left.

A few months later a sailboat arrived and the crew found the island completely deserted—except for those three tough and smart dogs. The sailors named them *'Army'*, *'Navy'* and 'Palmyra' and as soon as the dogs saw the crew meant no harm they stuck with them night and day. They were tough, smart mongrels but loved the company of people. 'Navy' soon died but 'Army' and 'Palmyra' were alive and well. The cruisers left a note for the next sailors to arrive, giving their names and asking them to look after the dogs. They followed Roger everywhere and at night, when everyone returned to their boats, the dogs stood at the water's edge whining. Sometimes, they swam out to Roger's boat, circling and begging to be allowed to come on board.

They were afraid he would leave them and they'd be alone again. They knew all of us—even Roger—would leave too, someday. The dogs were friendly and affectionate, but they were very tough—they had to be to survive alone on Palmyra. "Army" had a huge hunk missing from the end of his nose and "Palmyra" had large parts of both ears missing and I asked Roger what on earth had done that damage. He laughed and said that he'd show us the next day. We took off as usual to explore the island and harvest the food we needed for that night's dinner and Roger and the dogs came along. On the windward side of the island there was an offshore reef which broke up the big waves thundering in. The reef had created a small, shallow lagoon no more than 6-8 inches deep.

Roger told us to watch carefully while Army and Palmyra stood at the water's edge, shaking with excitement and staring intently into the water. Then they saw what they were looking for—the fins of the black- fin reef sharks. Roger said those sharks were about 2-4 feet long and while no threat to people, they're still sharks and can put up a hell of a fight when cornered.

As if on a silent signal, Army and Palmyra leaped out into the shallow water in great, bounding leaps. Palmyra stopped and waited while Army went on through the shallow water, out to the edge of the reef and stopped. Roger said he was cutting off the sharks' escape route back into the ocean. As soon as Army was in place, Palmyra started on the attack. He bounded out towards a circling fin, took a mighty leap onto a shark and the water exploded in a frenzied fury. Thrashing, swirling bodies were everywhere. *It was total chaos and mayhem*—and we didn't know who was going to come out on top—Palmyra or the shark.

The thrashing bodies and exploding water finally calmed down and Palmyra came back to shore, proudly dragging the dead shark by the tail up onto the beach. His chewed-up ears seemed about the same size—more or less—so apparently the shark hadn't taken a bite out of them *this* time. Palmyra now changed positions with Army, who now stood quivering in excitement waiting for his turn for a fight.

As soon as Palmyra was in place blocking the escape route to the sea, Army started prowling. He soon saw another fin slicing through the water and jumped in great leaps through the shallow water and landed right on top of the shark. Again, a furious melee followed, with sound and fury and thrashing bodies everywhere. It soon calmed down and Army came back towards shore, dragging another dead reef shark.

Roger said that was how they lost parts of their ears and noses and that's why he couldn't tell us—we had to see for ourselves. Neither dog lost any more of their ears or noses this time and victoriously dragged the sharks up into the sand to bury them as a future source of food.

"It's show time," Roger said one day as the three of us sat in the shade at the "yacht club" on a hot afternoon. A large spotted eagle ray—a manta ray with 'wings' at least 4 feet across—swam gracefully in towards the edge of the water in front of the "yacht club." We watched in fascination as the ray's huge wings moved slowly up and down with the gracefulness of a ballet dancer. The ray swam in closer to the edge of the water

where Army and Palmyra were waiting, quivering with excitement. "Watch the old ray torment the dogs," Roger said.

The manta ray circled around several times, each time coming in a little closer to the water's edge, as Army and Palmyra crept to the edge, shaking with excitement. They both crouched and got ready to make a great leap onto the ray when it got close enough. It circled around coming closer each time, taunting and teasing them. On its next circle, the ray came the closest yet. Army and Palmyra couldn't resist any longer and both leaped into the air towards the ray. While they were still in the air the ray flicked its tail and shot off. Army and Palmyra landed with a big splash into empty water—exactly on the spot where the ray *had been* milliseconds before. Everyone laughed and Roger said the dogs were embarrassed and you could see the embarrassment on their faces as the two wet, frustrated dogs came back ashore..

"Who says creatures of the wild don't have a sense of humor?" Ann asked, laughing.

We soon discovered that Roger was a major character of his own. He was not only an incredibly good chef, but an adventurer and risk-taker at heart. Watching him catch the huge coconut crabs was one of the scariest things I've ever seen. The coconut crabs on Palmyra are the largest land-based invertebrates on earth. They're commonly called *"coconut crabs"* because they're very big and their claws are so powerful they crack coconuts open and eat the insides. *Can you imagine the awesome force it takes to crack a coconut open?* I put a hard broom-stick between the claws of one of the coconut crabs as a test and the huge crab cracked it in half *as if it had been a piece of cooked spaghetti!*

One day Roger invited us to go with him to catch another coconut crab. Ann had something to do, so I went along. He said he'd show me how to do it and then I could catch one on my own. Not likely, I told him. He was always very protective of life and vegetation on the island and only took what he needed for food. He really loved that island and took wonderful care of everything on it.

The coconut crabs live inside hollowed out trees or in holes they've dug in the palm trees that have fallen over and I asked him how he got them out. He said he just reached in and grabbed them before they could grab him. He looked into a hollowed out tree trunk and said he saw one...a big one.

"You're going to put your hand in there?" I asked unbelievingly

"*Why not*," he replied. I could think of ten reasons why not—*my fingers!*

He reached his hand far inside the dark crevice where the huge coconut crab was hidden. "Here's the secret," Roger explained, as if I was going to do it next. "You put your hand in and hold it open and pressed hard against the back wall of the tree. The crab can't grab it if your hand is pressed hard against the wall. *Your hand becomes part of the wall and he can't get it*. Then you move it slowly around behind him. If you feel him trying to grab you, don't panic and try to jerk your hand out— he'll get you for sure and could cut an artery. Just keep your hand flat and hard against the wall all the time."

"*Got it*," I said to humor him.

"When you're behind him, then—*and only then*—you grab him from behind and pull him out. That's all there is to it. *Anyone can do it*."

Sure, I thought and watched unbelievingly as Roger put his hand and arm in so far his shoulder was pressed up against the opening in the tree and moved his hand around in that dark hole by feel alone. He moved slowly and I expected him to withdraw a bleeding hand with a missing finger at any moment.

"OK, OK, easy now....g*ot him!*"—and he pulled out an angry coconut crab, furiously clicking its huge and powerful pincers into thin air.

Roger invited us to go swimming near the reef by the pass. We anchored the dinghies and dove in with our fins and snorkel gear on and to our shock we saw a large 8 to 9 - foot shark swimming in lazy circles, watching us. We told Roger there was no way we were going to swim with that big shark around. He agreed it was big, all right, but said it wasn't a Great White or man-eater, so we shouldn't worry.

He said that eight out of ten of those sharks were harmless—though very territorial and didn't like their space invaded. He said I should keep an eye on the shark and if he got agitated, then we should get out. Usually, he assured us, they're not aggressive. As long as the shark was swimming in circles around us, there was no problem. On the other hand if he stopped circling, we should get out—*quickly*.

I *still* don't know why Ann and I did it—Roger just seemed so sure we just went along with him. Here we were— invading the territory of an 8 or 9 foot shark and I was supposed to let everyone know if he gets pissed off. *Then what?* He's *"usually"* not aggressive, Roger said. *Is this a "usual" time— with three swimmers invading his territory?* Eight out of ten are harmless—now what the hell does *that* mean? Do they 'take numbers' or something—and what number was he?

The simple fact is, he was big and had the powerful jaws and size to kill anyone. *All he needed was the intent*—and that could come at any moment. And what would you do with a shark bite on a deserted island a thousand miles from the nearest hospital? *The infection alone would kill you within a day or so.* The big shark kept circling with one eye watching me every second. Roger soon had enough and swam to his dinghy —and we were right behind. As soon as we were out of the water, he said there was no need to "push our luck" any further.

"Luck?" Here we were, a thousand miles from any medical aid, invading the "space" of a big shark which had everything needed to kill us—except the intent—and we were counting on luck? I told Roger he was crazy and so were we to

swim with that shark. He said we were now one of an elite few—how many people could honestly boast that they swam alongside a big shark?

Now, I could say I did. Doesn't that impress you girls? *Or does it just tell you how really stupid I was?*

The bird-life on Palmyra is beyond belief—this is the only nesting place in a 450,000 square mile area of the Pacific. One research group estimated there are more than a million birds on the atoll. All I know is there were so many, at times they seemed to darken the sky and most were unafraid of people. They had never been harmed by anyone so had no fear and we could go right up to them.

Palmyra is home to the rare red-footed booby birds. The cute 'baby boobies' are so fluffy and puffed out with feathers, they look much larger than the adults. But it's all just "fluff". The babies have great black eyes set in a big, white, soft, pillow-like body. Ann fell in love with one on the dining island and every evening after dinner, she walked a few feet to pet and stroke her favorite baby booby bird. The parents were equally unafraid and watched a few feet away with no concern. No one had ever harmed them, *so why be afraid?*

Palmyra is covered with boobies, frigate-birds, terns by the thousands, tropicbirds—and others. The terns laid their eggs on the ground, without any fear of harm except the occasional egg-feast Army and Palmyra indulged in when they got tired of eating reef sharks.

Palmyra really belonged to the birds which had never learned to fear anyone, to the two dogs with pieces missing from their noses and ears, to that old manta ray which tormented and teased the dogs, to the powerful coconut crabs—*and to the three of us* who'd been fortunate enough to find this little piece of paradise in the remote Pacific. We had shared this island paradise with Roger for quite some time now, completely forgetting the calendar. We swam, fished, made love, ate

Roger's wonderful food and enjoyed everything about this isolated paradise. Some other cruising boats had come and gone while we were there—and it was about time for us to move on as well.

Ann said, "this is turning out to be the best time of my life. It's like we're living some kind of a charmed life. *Sometimes, I get afraid—how long can such wonderful times go on?*"

I told her we'd just take it one day at a time.

Ann must have had some kind of premonition.

Neither of us had any way of knowing that we were about to experience a *horrible nightmare* on the high seas.

CHAPTER SIX

HIGH SEAS RESCUE

"*Hey, how about a break now*?" Alan asked. "*We can finish this tomorrow.*"

"*No way,*" Carole said. "*You've got us this far and you're not going to leave us in Palmyra.* We want to hear about the rescue. Let's just take a short break and get some sandwiches, but then we want to hear the rest of it—right?"

Susan and Sigrid agreed.

After a break and some sandwiches, Alan started in again where he'd left off.

We left Palmyra and headed south towards Tonga where I met you guys. This route took us directly across the doldrums and within 2 days we ran out of wind. The sea was like glass. Ann looked at her reflection in the still sea while brushing her hair and said, "this must be what they mean when they say 'a mirror sea'." As you guys may know the doldrums are a belt of windless seas, which more or less straddle the equator around the globe. During the age of sail, sailors feared the doldrums above all other dangers at sea—far more than storms. Many were trapped in them and drifted helplessly, until water and food ran out.

We motored about 300 miles through the airless doldrums until we found the Southeast trade-winds and suddenly everything changed. Now there was plenty of wind—sometimes too much. Every few hours fast-moving squalls came through—like the one that hit us in the channel coming to Fiji. About an hour after the last one passed, a huge black squall was approaching from far off on the horizon. It was the mother of all squalls. *That's when I was lost overboard.*

I'll start at the beginning. I'd just seen that black squall and Ann was asleep below, exhausted from her four- hour watch. As I said, *this was the mother of them all.* I looked around *ESCAPEE* to make sure everything was ready for the beating we were about to get and saw that plastic "jerry jug"—the one that holds the gasoline for the outboard motor coming loose at the back of the boat. It had to be re-tied and lashed down before that squall hit. *OK, I should have put a safety harness on, but figured it would be a quick, easy job.*

I stayed low and held onto *ESCAPEE* as I made my way to the back of the boat. I'd just reached the back and started re-tying that loose jug, *which took both hands*, when a wave came out of no where and hit *ESCAPEE* on the side. It wasn't even a particularly big wave—it just came from an unexpected direction and shoved the boat sideways while I was using both hands to tie the jug down and I was thrown overboard.

I knew I was dead even before I hit the water.

A split second before I landed in the ocean, I got off one call for help. But before I could call out again, the next wave crashed over me. I swallowed a lot of seawater and fought my way back to the surface—choking and gasping for air. By the time I got the salt water out of my throat it was too late to call for help again. *ESCAPEE* was already *much too far away. She was sailing away, steered by the wind-vane with Ann sound asleep below.*

I was left behind, *350 miles* from the nearest land.

I knew I was a dead man. No one has ever gone overboard from a small vessel in mid-ocean—*without anyone on deck to know about it*—-and survived. Even if a *full crew* of three or four *saw* me swept overboard, by the time they could turn the boat around and come back it would be very hard to find me—just a small head sticking about 12 inches out of the water, hidden behind the 6 to 8 foot waves.

I was still in shock—*one minute I was on ESCAPEE and the next I was alone in the ocean, watching her disappear off in the distance.* Each wave lifted me to its top for a few seconds and then dropped me back into the troughs or "valleys" between the waves. Sometimes when I was up on a wave top I could see *ESCAPEE* getting smaller and then I fell into the troughs and saw nothing but "walls" of water all around me. Remember, my head was only 12 *inches* or so above the surface and I was looking *up* at 6-foot waves, which sure looked big from my point of view. All I could do was tread water—just trying to keep from going under and suddenly it hit me—"*so this is how I'll die*". I guess we all sometimes wonder when and how we'll our lives will end. *Well, now I knew.*

Then something very strange happened to me—my mind just "shut down" and I couldn't think. I couldn't process thoughts. I guess I was far too shocked to think rationally. Instead of thinking, I just *felt* and was overwhelmed by a series of powerful "feelings" which swept over me.

The *first* thing I felt was a *feeling of complete acceptance*. This was how I was going to die—and I felt a calm acceptance of it. I didn't feel any anger or bitterness or curse my fate. *I've cursed more when I smashed my finger with a hammer than when I went overboard to my certain death*. I was a dead man and that was all there was to it. I now think I was so calm and accepting because of the sheer *finality* of it all. *I simply had no chance of survival and knew it*.

I think I now know a little of what some people feel when facing certain death—such as on a doomed plane. Of course there's shock, fear and horror, but I'm now sure that some—in the end—feel a sense of acceptance, as I did.

The *second feeling* which quickly overcame the first was a *sense of relief*. That's right—*relief*. Remember I wasn't thinking—I was *feeling*—and that feeling came from being aware Ann would be OK. She's an excellent sailor and I felt such a *sense of relief* knowing she'd be OK and could sail on to the nearest port by herself. *There'd be only one victim*. She'd be safe and that meant *everything* to me. It was such a relief and comfort and *the one bright spot* in this nightmare.

That feeling of relief was soon replaced with a *third* wave of feelings—*feelings of deep sadness*. *It was all so damned sad*. I don't mean for me only but for both of us. In two or three hours Ann would wake up and find me gone and she'd have to deal with the shock of my being lost at sea *and* face all the practical work of sailing to Samoa by herself. She'd call out to me as she always did when awakening—*"how's it going up there?"* This time there'd be no reply. I felt really guilty about that—and the mess I had left her in. I desperately wanted to say, *"I'm sorry, Ann. I love you. I'm sorry I left you in this mess."*

If could've left her one last note that would've been it.

ESCAPEE was gone and I was now swimming alone. The Pacific down here isn't that cold but I knew hypothermia would set in when the sun got lower. I was now fighting for survival—*wave by wave.* To tell the truth I don't even know *why* I kept swimming—I really don't. *ESCAPEE* and Ann were already gone. *So what was the point?*

The *fourth* wave of feelings swept over me and I felt a *really overwhelming need to connect with Lisa and Carl before I died. I needed to say good-bye and send them a farewell message that I loved them.* Maybe it's not logical, but remember I wasn't thinking—just feeling. I closed my eyes, called out each of their names and focused on all the love I felt for them—and said *I love you.* I hoped that wherever they were at that moment, they'd somehow *feel my love.* Later, when they got news of my death, I hoped they would put two and two together *and understand I had been saying goodbye to them.*

Love is a wonderful and powerful thing and no one really knows its limits—so maybe they *could* feel my love halfway around the world and understand. I know it's not rational but stranger things have happened—and it was *something I had to do.* Until now I hadn't been able to think—*just feel.* I remember that special moment when I was able to get my run-away mind back in control and start to think again. For some reason, that was a really big moment for me. I can't explain it—it just was.

All this time *ESCAPEE* was sailing farther away. The afternoon had been warm and I had gone overboard wearing only a light shirt and a bathing suit but now that the sun was getting lower I began to shiver—the first signs of hypothermia. As I said, it'd been about 5PM when I had gone overboard and I knew I could tread water for only a few hours, if that.

I knew I'd die sometime early that night and for some reason, dying in the darkness of the coming night frightened me far more than dying in the daylight. It doesn't make any sense of course—*dying is dying*—but it just seemed much more terrifying to die in the darkness. I'd read enough about drowning to know that it isn't a painless or easy way of death. I'd even heard that some suicide victims—*who wanted to die*—fought to live during the last horrible moments of drowning.

I also knew my body would never make it to the bottom. As I sank the intense sea pressures at about a thousand feet would burst my body open and the sea creatures would feed on the rest—I'd read that in some sea book. Long before my body got to the ocean floor, there'd be *no body left*. I knew that was what was going to happen that night.

I knew I could go down in one of two ways—either struggling and fighting all the way, or just *give up and go peacefully*. It seemed far better to just turn loose of life and go peacefully when *I* was ready rather than go down struggling and fighting at the bitter end. Anyway, why keep on swimming and struggling like this? *What for?*

That's when I felt that *fifth* and most painful wave of feelings. *I felt so lonely. It was* a *soul-crushing and unbearable loneliness*—far beyond anything I'd ever felt before. To die out here alone in the ocean at night, hundreds of miles from land and far from those I loved was the loneliest I've ever felt in my life. The pain of that unbearable loneliness made me *want* to get all this over. If I had any doubts whether to *turn loose of life now*, instead of having it *taken from me later*, that decided it. *It was now time to go* and I heard myself say, "*Goodbye Ann. I love you*". I was ready to swim downwards as far as I could go, take a big lungful of water and let my body keep going down.

About then another wave lifted me up to its top and I scanned the horizon, hoping for a last glimpse of the back of *ESCAPEE* sailing away. During the few times I'd caught a glimpse of *ESCAPEE* I'd always seen the *back* of the boat as she was sailing away from me, but this time I *thought I saw her side*. I fell back into a wave-trough before I could tell, but on the next wave-top I saw it—off in the distance I clearly saw her *side*. It wasn't my imagination. *ESCAPEE was turning around to come back for me.*

Ann later told me she'd been sound asleep when I was thrown overboard but had heard my single call for help That's really amazing because of all the noise a boat makes in heavy seas—the seas break, the boat strains and the wind howls through the rigging. On top of all that, she was sound asleep and exhausted from her own watch and when she heard my shout, thought it was just a dream *and went back to sleep again.* Soon after drifting off to sleep, something hit her—she jumped up wide-awake and realized *that call for help was real* and it was from a *distance—from off ESCAPEE.*

She said she called out my name and when I didn't reply she wasn't surprised. She rushed up on deck to release the sails and let them flap wildly in the wind and then started the motor to turn around and come back to search for me. That's what was going on when I saw *ESCAPEE'S* side far off in the distance.

As I watched *ESCAPEE* turning back, I realized it was almost dark by now and daylight would soon be gone—and with it *all* chances of rescue. Whatever could be done had to be done soon or it would be too late. There was *no* possibility of rescue in the darkness—I had no life jacket, no flares, no lights. *It was now a desperate race against time.* If that squall got here first, I was a goner. If night got here first, I was a goner.

When I was momentarily up on a wave-top I saw both that approaching black, stormy wall of the squall with flashing lightning—*and ESCAPEE* pounding back towards me. Ann was driving her hard, smashing through those waves. I could only think of one thing—*"hang on Ann! Hang on! ESCAPEE* was rolling sickeningly as she smashed through the seas, drove up and over the tops of the waves, plunged down into the troughs and back up again—under full engine power—bullying her way through and sending spray flying everywhere.

That squall was closer and you guys *know* what they're like. Ann would have to face the squall's fury exposed on deck and I'd face it even more unprotected—swimming in the sea. Just imagine swimming in a squall like the one which hit us in that channel coming to Fiji—the driving rain, no visibility—there's no way I could survive that.

ESCAPEE was now much closer. *"Be careful Ann!"* I pleaded. I knew it would be taking all her strength just to hang on—much less steer the boat and search for me. Before long Ann had brought her the full distance back to where I was but was about 100 yards off to the side. Even that close, the hull of *ESCAPEE* often disappeared from my sight into a wave trough, leaving only the sails and mast visible. Then it hit me—if I couldn't see the hull of a 40-foot sailboat in the wave troughs only a hundred yards away *how could Ann see something as small as* a *my head*?

ESCAPEE was now so close I could occasionally see Ann standing behind the wheel, gripping it tightly and trying to keep her balance, but she was focused on something on the *other* side of the boat. She was staring in that direction—the *wrong* direction. I raised one arm out of the water and waved to try to get her attention—but she was still looking the other way. There was no way I could shout to her—the winds, noise and my own throat sore from all the seawater I had swallowed made that impossible. Back on the top of the next wave, I saw diesel smoke pouring out of the exhaust—Ann was leaving. The engine was on full power and *ESCAPEE* was *driving away from me*. I knew she'd never return to search this part of the ocean again.

"No!" I cried out hoarsely. *"Here! I'm here!"*.

I sank back into the next trough and into a deeper despair. It would've been *far better* if she had never turned back—-for her own safety and for me too. I stopped swimming and gave way to the sea, overwhelmed by despair—despair for myself and for Ann who'd tried so hard. *"Go, Ann. Go on to safety! Take care of yourself!"* I pleaded, as I watched the stern of *ESCAPEE* driving away.

The outcome wasn't surprising—there'd *never* really been a chance. For a few minutes it looked like there might be a miracle but it was clearly not to be. Back up on the next wave-top I could see her driving further away, staring intently ahead. The black wall of the squall was almost here now and would soon hit and I could never survive it. *It was all over* and I heard myself saying, *"take care of yourself, Ann. I love you..."*

She said later she realized that whatever she thought she saw ahead of her, it wasn't me. She stopped *ESCAPEE* and turned around looking everywhere—her eyes sweeping the horizon and never stopping in one place. Ann was as desperate as I was. Then—at the *exact moment* when her scanning eyes passed the *exact wave* I was hidden behind—the wave lifted me to its top *and our eyes met.* I quickly fell back into the trough and swam up on the next wave-top, waving my arm again. She saw me waving, waved back—and put the engine under full power to turn *ESCAPEE* around, aiming the bow directly at where she had last seen me.

She *had* found me. The *"needle in the haystack"* had been found, but I still had to get back on board *before* that black storm wall hit or Ann would lose sight of me again. You know what it's like—*someone turns out the lights*—and you can't see a thing. I'd be lost again and even if I survived the squall—which was very unlikely—by the time it passed it would be dark. It was now a *desperate race against time*—between the squall and Ann. It was just a question of which would get to me *first.*

Ann brought *ESCAPEE* right next to me and I tried to climb back on board from the side. It was far too high and I'd never get back aboard that way. My best chance was to try to get up on the back of the boat, but I had to hurry—*that squall was about to hit.* The wind-vane steering gear was attached to the stern and was something for me to grab and hold on to. I not only had to hurry, I had to be very careful. *ESCAPEE* was going up and down like a *rocking horse*—first the bow plunged down and the stern shot up with each wave and then the bow rose on the next wave, plunging the stern into the sea. Back and forth— like a rocking horse. *But ESCAPEE was a deadly 27,000 - pound rocking horse.* If the stern hit me when it plunged down it would crack my head open like a ripe watermelon.

I pulled myself as close to the rising and plunging stern as I dared get. My plan was to get close enough to grab the wind-vane when the stern plunged downwards and hold on, letting it jerk me up and out of the water when it shot up again. I would then pull myself on deck and to safety. I inched in closer; watching as the stern lifted, paused and then crashed again into the sea, trying to get the timing right.

Too far away, and I couldn't reach the wind-vane. *Too close* and I would be crushed. If I lost my grip and fell back in the water, the stern would land on top of me the next time it crashed down.

I came in as close as I dared to get and looked up at the stern, which now seemed to be directly over me. Every instinct within me screamed—*get back!* I *forced* myself to stay in place as the stern paused at its upward arc and came crashing down into the sea. It hit only *inches* in front of my head and threw a wall of stinging water into my eyes, blinding me. I couldn't see a thing but reached out blindly, groping for that wind-vane. I found it and held on as tightly as I could when the stern shot back up into the air, taking me with it. As the boat paused at the top of its arc I pulled myself onto the deck and grabbed something to hold onto. *I was exhausted, drained, shivering and choking with seawater—but I was back!*

We both crawled from that bucking and tossing rear deck to the safety of the cabin below and collapsed into our berth where we held each other tightly—in total silence—*far too traumatized to say a single word.* Up above, that squall hit. I would never have survived it if I had still been in the sea.

As I said, Ann and I held each other in *complete silence.*
It was all just too overwhelming to say even a single word. After
a few minutes Ann started shaking and crying. *She just couldn't*
stop. *That's when I realized it had been far worse for her than*
for me. She had held a life in her hands. Someone would live of
die, depending entirely on what she did. That was terrible
pressure and on top of that, she'd been operating on a massive
flow of adrenalin and super-human strength from the moment
she heard my call for help and woke up. Now that it was all over
and she could turn lose *it hit her really hard.* I want to tell you—
the shock and trauma of it all was almost too much for her.

After holding her tightly for an hour or two, I went up on
deck and got *ESCAPEE* underway again. The seas and winds
had calmed down a lot by then and I set a new course for the
nearest port—Apia, in Samoa. We were wiped out and needed
to get somewhere quiet and pull ourselves back together.
ESCAPEE steered herself by wind-vane until we got to Apia
where we anchored in a quiet part of the harbor. We hardly
moved for the next couple of days and kept to ourselves—
slowing getting over that horrible experience.

After a couple of days, we were ready to head back out
to sea again—we needed to move on and try to get all this
behind us. Ann was also very aware of those six months and that
the clock was ticking—*I had just tuned all that out.* A few days
later we sailed into into Tonga and Ann steered *ESCAPEE*
towards the main harbor of Neiafu, where we all met.

ESCAPEE came around the corner of the channel into
full view of the town of Neiafu and we saw at least twenty to
thirty sailboats anchored in the big bay. They were from the US,
Germany, France and other countries. The large Moorings
charter company was over to the side with its fleet of charter
boats—*the ones you and your group chartered, Susan.*

I dropped the anchor and we settled in off the Paradise
International Hotel, which seemed to be the cruisers' hang out. I
anchored about 100 yards from the boat you were on, Sigrid.

That night, Ann and I stayed on board and after dinner and the subject of her departure hung over us. I asked her again if she could just forget her job and find someone else to look after her mother. *"If it was just the damned job, Alan, I would—in a flash,"* she said. *"But I've got to take care of my mother. There's no one else."*

We threw ourselves into enjoying the time we had left and the weeks passed like a beautiful dream. Life aboard *ESCAPEE* was slow and tranquil, but it was also becoming increasingly sad. Every wonderful day that passed brought Ann's departure *one day closer.* The night before Ann had to leave, I held her all night—I didn't want that moment to ever end. The next morning after an almost silent breakfast, I took Ann to the airport and we said goodbye.

I went back to *ESCAPEE,* which now had such a sad and *empty* feeling about her and fell into an exhausted, emotionally drained sleep. I slept the rest of that day and around eight in the evening I woke up *needing to be around people.* I went up to the Paradise Hotel and when the bar closed I rowed back to *ESCAPEE* and sat in the cockpit, thinking of Ann. She and I had had so many wonderful times together. We had shared everything. She had saved my life—a*nd now it was all gone.*

At first I called her several times a week and then agreed to talk only on weekends. The following weekend Ann said, *"Alan, we've got to face it. It's not going to work out for me to come back to ESCAPEE*—at least as far as I can see. I can't leave mom alone. She's got no one else. Maybe I can meet you in Fiji or somewhere later."

We both knew in our hearts that would most likely never happen. I knew I was losing her. I didn't know it at the time, but I had already lost her.

But even the blackest cloud has a silver lining.

That's when I met you guys

CHAPTER SEVEN

POLYGAMY— OR JUST GOOD FRIENDS?

"Well, you asked for the whole story—so there it is," Alan said.

It was now past eleven. Alan had been talking since around six and they had skipped dinner, just snacking. It had been a roller-coaster evening—at times they had been deeply moved and at other times they were laughing hilariously at William and Alan's attempt to get to Hawaii in one piece.

"That's it—the good, the bad, the ugly," he said. "Now, you know almost as much about me as I know about myself— probably a lot more than you want to know. Like you said Carole, *'what you see is what you get.'"*

"Ann was a wonderful person and we're sorry you lost her," Susan said. That part had touched each of the girls. *"Well, now you're stuck with us."*

"I hope so," Alan said, *"I'm counting on it.* There's nothing wrong with any of us—we've just got to turn loose of the past and look ahead. *Me too."*

It had been an emotional evening and they crashed into their berths—each with his or her own feelings and thoughts. It's not easy making your deepest feelings known to others but not one of them felt they were on their own any longer. *Sometimes, just having someone beside you is all you need to find your way through your dark tunnel and come out safe on the other side.* When they first met they had been four strangers—each alone and struggling with some very big issues—but no one was alone any longer. They had each other.

It was time to head back to Malolo-lai-lai and load up with provisions. As Sigrid and Carole steered *ESCAPEE*, Susan sat up on the spreaders watching for the dangerous, dark clusters of coral patches and shifting sand banks. Alan had something special he wanted to do before they left this magical place. He checked his chart and put a big circle around that first island— the one where the *"arrangement"* to share him had been made. Someday, he told himself, when he was old and gray he'd get this chart out in some elderly care center somewhere and show everyone that circled island *and tell them exactly what happened to him there*—and they'd walk off muttering, *"dirty, senile old man"*.

Sometimes, as the cliché says, truth *is* stranger than fiction—*and life on ESCAPEE was certainly turning out that way!*

When they got close to Malolo-lai-lai they had to get back into the habit of wearing clothes again—even if it was just bikinis and a bathing suit. They'd worn nothing in the "*clothes-free zone*" for so long it took some getting used to and Susan—*who'd been the last to ditch all clothes*—was the *first* to complain about being "over-dressed".

"*That girl is changing,*" Alan said to Carole.

"*Told you so, and she's not finished yet.*"

Now what's that mean? Alan wondered.

A fax was waiting for Alan from his best friend, Michael, the attorney from Santa Barbara. He was in Hawaii on a vacation and was getting bored with the same old Hawaii. His fax said, "I'm only five hours from Fiji and with you going overboard and everything, I figure I better come down and see you before you do something stupid and kill yourself. So call me here at the hotel and I'll hop a plane and be right there." Alan had written Michael about going overboard and it had really shaken him up.

How's he going to react to all this? Alan wondered.

Alan called him, "sure Michael, come on down. Great to have you. The yacht club—if you can call it that—is close to the international airport. Fax me your flight number and I'll be there to pick you up." Michael faxed back saying he'd arrive in 2 days—at 11 in the morning. As they had dinner in the restaurant that evening, Alan told the girls all about Michael and when he'd be arriving.

"He'll be staying a few days. We're crowded and he doesn't like boats, so I'll put him up at one of the guest rooms here on the island. But since I have to go pick up him, let's sail to Lautoka, near the airport. It's a big town and we can load up with all the food and supplies we'll need for the next several months, hit a couple of Indian curry restaurants and pick him up at the same time. *That OK with you guys??*"

"Sure, how far is it?"

"Well Miss Navigator here," Alan said, gesturing to Susan, "will figure it all out when we get back to the boat."

Susan smiled. She really liked the trust Alan had in her. He was the first man—*the very first man*—who ever thought she could do anything on her own. Her father and brothers sure didn't. They just bullied her around and treated her like a helpless baby and a failure. When they got back to the boat Susan opened the charts and books and worked away with the dividers, parallel ruler and all the gadgets needed for precise coastal piloting. As before, she plotted the complex, zigzag course through the dangerous patches of coral reefs and sand bars—right up to the anchorage at Lautoka. *She was good.*

They left the next morning and reached the worst part of the coral reefs at eleven when the sun was high and behind them, giving them the best visibility—exactly as Susan had planned it. They arrived in Lautoka in plenty of time to get settled in and go ashore for some of the Indian curry Lautoka is famous for. There are more Indians than native Fijians living around Lautoka and the curry is out of this world.

While they were having dinner, Alan said, *"Michael doesn't know about our—well, our 'arrangement,' so...."*

"I'll tell him," Carole said, *"if you're too chicken to."*

"No, that's not what I mean—and you know it." Carole smiled innocently.

"Oh come on, he'll admire you even more if he knows you're taking care of three women—well, OK, two. Don't go keeping your old buddy in the dark. Oh, all right then, we won't tell him a thing, but I'm not saying we won't *show* him a few things—you know, like falling all over you. *We can put on a pretty good show, you know."*

"Come on, you guys. This guy really is as square as they come and...." Alan stopped dead in mid-sentence and knew he'd

made a big mistake saying that. He hoped the girls would let it pass and give him a break—*just this once*. But that false hope only proved how bad his "comprehension problem" was if he expected any "slack" or mercy from these three. They attacked.

"Hold on. Are you saying what I think you're saying—that he's squarer than you? No way! No one could be," Carole said, and Sigrid and Susan both vigorously joined in on the attack.

"You square," Sigrid said and glanced at Carole to see if she'd said it right.

"Alan, you're hopelessly square. You've got the market cornered in 'squarness'," Susan chimed in. They were at it again and it was his own damned fault. If he wasn't so *easily* rattled and bugged it wouldn't be *so much fun*.

"OK girls," Carole said, *"let's get serious here and support Alan. Let's put on our long, black dresses and long faces for his friend. Alan's little friend is coming over to our house to play and we're going to behave ourselves like nice little girls—aren't we?"*

Alan knew they sure as hell wouldn't—*but what could he do?*

They all went into Lautoka the next morning—Alan to pick Michael up at the airport and the girls to do a massive shopping to load up on everything they could possibly need for the next few months. They wanted to be free to go anywhere and stay as long as they wanted, without running short of anything. As usual, the girls paid more than their share of the food and supplies—they always insisted on it.

Michael's flight arrived and after getting his luggage, Alan grabbed a taxi back to Lautoka. During the taxi ride, Alan asked about things in Santa Barbara. Sure enough, Shirley had married that banker. Business was about the same. Alan's friends were about the same. *"Hell, everything's about the same,"* Michael said.

"So, everything still about the same with you, too?" Michael asked. "Go swimming in mid-ocean again? Man, that letter about going overboard really shook me up. I read it over and over. *My God, don't go doing that again."*

Alan laughed, "I don't plan to." Alan filled him in on Ann, her departure and that it was more or less certain she wasn't coming back.

"Oh man," Michael said, *"that's bad news. It must be awful to be out here all alone."*

"Well, I'm not *exactly* alone."

"What do you mean? Oh, you've got someone sailing with you. Hey, that's good, given your habit of going swimming in mid-ocean."

"I've got three *'someone's* sailing with me, Michael. I'm not going to tell you any more—you'll just have to wait and meet them. So, here's the story—I've got a room for you tonight at a local hotel. I know how you hate sleeping on a boat. We'll all go to dinner together, tuck you in and come and get you tomorrow. Then we'll sail about 6 hours to the yacht club—and I've got a room for you at a lodge on the same island. When it's time to go, I'll take you back to the airport."

"Sounds great," Michael said.

They stopped at the hotel to leave Michael's suitcase and headed for the boat. Sigrid saw them coming and rowed to shore to get them. She had her bikini on and those large breasts in that tiny bikini top were still defying the laws of physics. Michael wasn't missing a thing.

"Wow," Michael said, *"you're doing OK for yourself."*

Alan introduced Michael to Sigrid and she grabbed his hand and vigorously pumped it up and down, just as she'd done when she first met Carole. Michael whispered into Alan's ear as Sigrid rowed them out, *"that woman's got a grip!"* *If he only knew*, Alan thought.

The girls had already returned earlier and put away most of the supplies and provisions but a few grocery sacks still sat around, waiting to be emptied. *"Guys,"* Alan said, *"I want you to meet my good friend, Michael. Michael, this is Carole and Susan and you've already met Sigrid."*

"Welcome," Carole said, "Alan's told us all about you." Michael was stunned—*three* good- looking women.

"You fellows go on up on deck and we'll pass you some beers," Carole said. "It's a little crowded down here until we can get all this stuff put away. Then, we'll come up and join you. Anyway, you've got a lot to get caught up on."

As soon as they got to the cockpit, Michael said *"Alan— three of them! You never told me about three."*

"Well, I guess I skipped a few details in my last letter"

"You sure as hell, did buddy. *Three of them."* He couldn't get over it.

"OK," he said, moving closer to Alan and lowering his voice. *"Which one is yours? It's the German, isn't it?"* he said, answering his own question. *"The one with the big ...you know. I can tell it's her. I just know those things."*

"I don't have one, Michael," Alan said quietly.

"Oh come on, I don't believe that for a second—*not a second!"*

"It's true, Michael. I don't have one."

"Alan, you're full of bullshit and you know it. All three of these good-looking women *and you don't have one? Buuuuullshiitt!"*

"No Michael, I don't. It's the honest truth. I'll take an oath to that—so help me God. *I don't have one.*"

Michael shook his head in total frustration. He *knew* he was being lied to. Something wasn't right here—*not at all.* Alan had worked that line for about as long as he could, so he said, "I swear I'm telling you the truth, Michael. I don't have *one*"—and let it sink in.

Michael's face went white. "*oh shit. You don't have one—you've got them all? Alan Richards, is that what you're telling me? You've got them all?*"

"*Well, more or less.* The young one, Susan, is a little too young so I only have two. For now. But Susan will come around any time. "

Michael stood up and turned completely around, looking off into the distance to the left and then to the right, shaking his head and then sat back down. "*I can't believe this!*" Michael said. "*I just fucking can't believe this!*"

"Michael," Alan whispered, "come closer so they can't hear me. I've got to tell you something urgent. I was going to slip a note into your pocket—but they're not listening so maybe they won't catch me. *Michael, save me. I'm being held captive as a sex slave on my own boat.* "

"*You dirty, rotten, filthy, old man!*" Michael exploded.

"*How the hell did you do this?* Here you are, captain of your own boat, sitting out here in paradise with three— *count'em*—three good-looking women at your beck and call. Alan, guys who're rich, intelligent and handsome can't get three classy women like these at a time—not if they know about each other. And let's face it --you aren't rich. You sure as hell aren't handsome—not even your own mother ever claimed that. And in the brain department, you're certainly no rocket scientist—*so how the hell did you pull this off?*"

Alan answered with what he hoped was a modest, "*aw shucks*" kind of shrug, and said, "well, this is not my doing. *It's their arrangement.* They decided it and just *informed* me. Look at it this way—I'm just an *innocent victim* who was overpowered by superior numbers and intellect."

"*What bullshit!*" Michael exploded. "These are not some dumb bimbos. These women are something else—smart, intelligent, good-looking—any one of them would be a prize. *What the hell can they possibly see in you? Alan Richards— you've just blown away everything I've ever believed possible. Everything!*"

Alan gave another modest, "*who me?*" shrug.

Michael said, " You know what burns me up about all this. I can't even go back and tell anyone back home. No one would believe me. They know you, Alan. They'd just say, 'no way, not *our* Alan' and accuse me of smoking something. Hell, they'd claim I made it all up—gone crazy or something. Who wants to hire a lawyer like that? So I can't tell a damned soul. That really drives me up the wall."

Michael's face suddenly changed, "*Hi ladies,*" he said brightly as the girls came up to join them in the cockpit.

"*Hi Michael,*" they all three said very sweetly and at the same time.

Alan shot them a look that could kill—he *knew* something was wrong. *The girls were being far too nice*—and he'd learned the hard way that always meant something was about to happen. *Always.*

He glanced down into the cabin and sitting there all by itself right in the middle of the table—in full sight of Michael— was a *large, economy -size box of condoms, with a ribbon on it.*

"*Carole!*" Alan hissed.

"Well, it's just a little gift from us girls to you. You told us to get everything we'd need for the next few months. So we did. *You know how obedient we are to our captain."*

"That's not what I'm talking about and you know it. Get that box out of there, please, before he sees it. Please!"

"Oh OK, spoilsport," Carole said smiling. "But I really think Michael knows all about the birds and bees." She went down and put the giant, 'gift box' of condoms in a drawer and said, *"there, you happy now?"*

Alan rolled his eyes. When would he ever learn he was no match for these women?

They returned to Malolo-lai-lai the next day and the time with Michael passed quickly. After his initial shock—if you can call a *three-day long state of shock* "initial"—things settled down and he quit staring at the girls and quit asking that same damned question over and over—*"how the hell did you pull this off?"* He must have asked it at least a dozen times. The poor guy clearly was having trouble dealing with all this—and that was understandable. After all, this was Alan. *Their* Alan. *The* Alan from Santa Barbara—square, solid, stable—even a little on the slow side. Not handsome, not rich, certainly no rocket scientist—but somehow he'd managed to be out here in paradise, captain of his own boat and had three good-looking, smart woman living with him.

"Why's the world so damned confusing sometimes?" Michael asked Alan, bewildered by it all. *"You think you get it all figured out, then something like this comes along."*

Michael was also burning with curiosity. *"So, how do you do it...I mean, how does it work?"* he asked Alan.

Alan knew he'd get around to that question so he had made up a mock *"schedule"* to put up at the chart table right next to the radio and weather schedules. It was headed simply, *"Alan's Schedule"* and had a grid of boxes with days of the week across the top and the names of the three girls down the left side. It was all a sham of course but Alan was laying it on thickly with Michael. Alan knew the poor guy was now so shaken and gullible, he'd probably buy it all—hook, line and sinker. Alan brought Michael to the boat the next morning and said, "*you might as well see for yourself how we organize things.*"

He took him over to the chart table to show him the schedule he'd just pinned up. "*Ok, here are the schedules we live by on ESCAPEE—the weather schedule, the radio schedule to keep in touch with people we meet, and look, here's what the girls call 'Alan's Schedule'—the one where the girls schedule our play times together. You see—the girls pencil in the day they want to have some fun—and no one gets in each other's way. I can take a look at it as I pass the chart table and see how things are shaping up for the week to come.*

"*Look, here's Sigrid three days in a row—Friday, Saturday and Sunday. Wow, she's got some high hopes. But notice this—she takes a break for a few days and Carole has two days in a row, skips a day and then is back again.*"

Michael looked at it dumb-founded. He smelled a rat of course but with Alan and this incredible situation *you could never be really sure.* Normally, he would have laughed at it as total bullshit. But that was "*normally*"—and if there was one thing clear to him by now *it was that there was nothing "normal" about life on ESCAPEE.* Of course his instincts said not to believe it. But then he wouldn't have believed it if Alan had told him he had three women living with him—*and that turned out to be true. So maybe this was too.*

Who the hell knew anything, any more?

"Look," he said. "You've got Susan's name down, under the other two. You told me she's not part of all this."

"Well, she wasn't, not at first. Still isn't, but I have definite indications it won't be long before she'll start filling in her own boxes on the schedule." Michael fell for it and said, *"this is the most cold-blooded, heartless thing I've ever seen.* What about spontaneity? What about something just hitting you and you go do it on the spur of the moment? What about liking one more than the other? I mean, that's possible. *What about all that?"*

He had fallen for the mock "schedule". He bought the whole story and Alan took enormous satisfaction in seeing one of the rarest sights in the world today—*a naïve, gullible attorney being jerked around.*

"Well, nothing's perfect," Alan said, "we all have to make sacrifices sometimes."

"You know something," Michael said, *"you are one obnoxious, arrogant son of a bitch—and you know something else? I would be too, if I were in your shoes.* OK, this is how you schedule it—but how does it work out, you know, in practical terms?"

Now the truth itself was enough—*no more bullshit.* Alan told him the simple truth with no embellishment—how two of the girls slipped off to the beach, leaving two of them alone on *ESCAPEE*—or if they were all on the beach, how two of them went back to the boat. That part was all true—and it rang true to Michael. He still didn't know what story to buy—*or how much of it.* He was suspicious of that "schedule"—it sounded too damned cold and planned to him. He already knew enough about these women during these few days, to know *they got what they wanted, when they wanted it*—so a schedule just didn't fit the picture.

But then…on the other hand…

Soon afterwards, Alan admitted the "schedule" was a joke on Michael and that *really* pissed him off. He decided to make Alan pay before he left—*no one made a fool of him and got away with it.* The night before Michael was to leave, Carole and the girls insisted that Alan and Michael have dinner together and spend a little time alone. The two of them went to the bar at the yacht club to have a few beers before dinner and that's where they got into a fierce argument—an argument only an attorney like Michael would think of or pick a fight over. *And Michael was in the mood for a good fight.*

No one should have it as easy as Alan—and he had *really made a fool of him* over that phony schedule. Michael was ready to rough him up and make him pay. The first cold beer was hardly poured when Michael fired the first salvo of the fierce battle to come. *"You know what? I've been thinking about all this. You're a damned polygamist, Alan. That's what you are—a damned polygamist."*

"No way," Alan said, rising to the fight. He knew Michael was spoiling for a good verbal brawl and he was ready. They'd had a few good, rollicking verbal battles before—it was part of their friendship. "A polygamist is a man who is married to several women at the same time. Everyone knows that. I just live with these women. *You're nuts. How the hell do you keep any clients with such a weak, flabby mind?"*

"Well, I rest my case," Michael said. *"You live with them. You just admitted it. That proves you're a polygamist."*

Alan shot back, *"you haven't got a case to 'rest'. What're you talking about? Define 'polygamist'*—it's all in how you *define* the word. Polygamy is when a man chooses to be married to several women at one time. We're not married—just living together. *And this is their deal*—they set it up and just *informed* me. I had no say in it."

"That's exactly my point. You're living with three women who are, in all the important, practical ways, your wives—at least two of them. And the third one—Susan—it looks to me like she's about ready to join the party any time now. *That makes you a bona fide, 100% polygamist."*

"The hell it does. Your thinking is all screwed up," Alan insisted, enjoying this verbal fight with his good friend. By this time they had gone through several beers, which helped

illuminate the finer points—and certainly increased the noise level—of the 'legal arguments'.

Alan said, "*look, if you take a couple of women for a ski week-end, does that make you a polygamist? Of course not.*"

"*Alan, this isn't a week-end ski trip.* You've lived with these women for a long time now and you already told me you're going to stay together indefinitely. That's not a ski weekend, buddy. *Face it—you're a full-fledged practicing polygamist— one of the very few in the world today.*"

"You've had too much sun. Look, *first*, we're not married. *Secondly*, we're not together for life. *Third.....*"

Michael broke in, "well, buddy of mine, *you look. First, you're doing all the things married people do—and then some. Secondly, who's together for life anymore? No, my friend, you're a fucking—pardon the pun—polygamist.*"

"Don't try your smooth legal tactics on me," Alan said. "I was going to say, before you interrupted me, third –or is it *thirdly? Now look—see what you just did?* You made me completely forget what I was going to say—*you and your clever lawyer tricks.*"

By this time they both had had a little too much to drink and the friendly argument grew louder, getting the attention of the others at the bar. "*Look,*" Alan said, "*there's lots of guys who are married and have a girl-friend or more than one on* the side. I'm not saying it's right, but we just don't live in a monogamous society as much as we used to. So here's a question for you—*in your feeble, tort-ravaged brain do you call them polygamists, too?*"

"*No way,*" Michael shot back, "*they don't know about each other and even if they do, they live separately. You, on the other hand, live with these three women together in one place. They know about each other and take turns bouncing the mattress with you—the same mattress. So don't try to wiggle out of it. You're a true, practicing polygamist."*

"*I want a jury, dammit,*" Alan demanded. "*You're an attorney—a pro. I need someone impartial.*" He looked at the guys lined up down the bar and said, "*you guys—come help settle an argument for my buddy and me.*" About six guys gathered around. They'd already overheard parts of the argument and wanted to hear more. They were also an enthusiastic—and very well lubricated—"jury".

Michael said, "*I'm going to present my brilliant prosecution for the crime of polygamy. Then my buddy will present his incoherent, brainless defense. You guys are the jury and have to decide who's right—me, the brilliant attorney, or this beach bum who's screwed his brains out.* I say he's a polygamist because he's living full-time and long-term with three good-looking women. They do everything a polygamist would do—well, you get my meaning. They plan to stay together indefinitely. Now, in my book, that makes my buddy here a *certified, A-1, bone-fide polygamist! What do you guys think?*"

By this time a crowd had gathered around—men *and* women. It's not every day you hear a hot debate about *polygamy*—especially one argued by a high-priced attorney.

"*Hey, wait just a minute*" Alan objected. "*I haven't presented my case yet.*" He drank down another beer, and stated his case. "I'm not married to these lovely ladies, nor do I intend to be. Just as well—they've got taste. OK, we're living together. We don't have kids—I am not a father with any of the three women. We haven't exchanged vows or rings. We don't have a marriage certificate—or certificates. We have never told anyone we're married. So, I am not—*repeat am not—a true polygamist* under the strict definition of the word."

One of the guys jumped in, "*just a minute here. I'd like to say something in defense of this man accused of polygamy.*"

The room went silent, waiting. *"But I can't think of anything,"* he said—and everyone laughed.

"What say ye, jury?" Alan called out. *"Bring me to the bar of justice—or jus' to the bar."* By this time, he'd had several beers and was feeling free and loose.

"The jury has to ruminate and ponder this question," one of the guys on the jury said. They huddled a few minutes, talked it over and the "jury foreman" returned with the verdict.

"We, the jury in the case before us, find the accused defendant guilty as hell of polygamy. We declare he is a polygamist, living in an illegal state of polygamy on the vessel ESCAPEE. We condemn him to have his over-worked balls castrated at dawn tomorrow. The execution of this eminently just and fair sentence will be suspended only under one condition—if he tells us how the hell he did it, so we can do it too."

A big cheer went up in the bar.

The beer flowed and there was one—*and only one*—subject at the bar that night—polygamy and all of its merits, demerits, forms and variations. In all of recorded history there had probably never been such an enthusiastic examination of this subject conducted by a more well-lubricated group.

The next morning Alan and Michael nursed hangovers as Michael said goodbye to the three girls. He and Alan walked to the small commuter plane which would take Michael to the Nadi International Airport. On the way to the plane Michael said once again, *"I'm so burned up.* Here's the best story to hit Santa Barbara in ages—and I can't tell anyone. They'd just think I was crazy—not the best reputation for a practicing attorney."

As they hugged goodbye, Michael said once again, "I just don't know how you did it, buddy. As I said, handsome, millionaire geniuses couldn't get three women like these, especially if the women knew about each other. But you have and they're great ladies. So keep well and write to me."

The same day Michael left, *ESCAPEE* left Malolo-lai lai to spend another two weeks hanging out at the small, uninhabited sandy islands, which they had all to themselves. It was a sun-filled, lazy two weeks of just loafing around in a place everyone who has been there agrees is about as close to paradise as you can get. As soon as they got out of sight of Malolo-lai-lai, they stripped off the bikinis and bathing suit. Susan was the first and *ESCAPEE* became a *clothes-free zone* once again, as they went back to the same easy-going, laid back pattern of living they had before Michael's visit. When they felt like fresh fish, Alan and Sigrid took off in the dinghy with the snorkel gear and spear gun and always came back with fish. Sigrid was such an incredible swimmer she could chase a fish deep down among the coral patches and spear it. Pity any poor fish Sigrid decided she wanted.

They barbequed the fish on the beaches, swam, sun-bathed, read and slipped back to *ESCAPEE* to make love whenever someone felt like it. All that fresh sea air, the isolation, the islands, the sand, the nudity—all whetted their healthy appetites, food and otherwise. It just happened—unplanned, spontaneously—time and again during those two weeks. There was never any embarrassment or awkwardness — just four very good friends, three women and one man, living a completely natural life in their own little world—respecting and liking one another and as they say, "doing what comes naturally".

One day Carole and Sigrid took off for the beach in the dinghy, leaving Alan on board with Susan. "*Hey, Susan,*" he said, "*race you to the beach*" and got ready to go into the cockpit, dive over and swim to shore.

"In a minute, Alan, but first I need to ask you a question."

"Fire away, what's the question?"

"You don't like me very much do you? I mean, not as much as the others. You like them better than me."

"Susan! You know better than that. Of course I like you as much as Carole and Sigrid."

"No you don't. I can just tell."

"Yes, I do!" Alan was astonished and searched his mind—what had he ever done to make Susan think he didn't like her as well as Carole and Sigrid? Poor girl's probably been carrying this around for a long time, he thought. *He felt terrible—and guilty as hell* for giving her that impression.

"I can just tell, Alan. You like them better than me."

"Susan, that's just not so. I like you. I like you very much—every bit as much as I do Carole and Sigrid."

"Well then, show me. Prove it to me," she said and put her arms around him and kissed him, pressing her body hard against his.

"Susan!" a very shocked Alan moved back.

"See. That proves you don't like me. I told you so."

"Susan, I do. Come here." and he held her close to him to reassure her. *That's really and truly all he intended to do—* re-assure her—but in just a few seconds he felt something happen that he had no control over. Susan pulled him towards the berth and within moments they were making love. He was astonished at her enthusiasm. He'd heard the shy, quiet ones often turned out to be the most passionate—*and now he believed it!* While they were making love, Alan occasionally felt the pangs of guilt but managed to overcome them. *"Go away! I'll deal with you later,"* he told the guilt. After it was all over—and it was quite a while—Susan lay exhausted in his arms and Alan said, *"Susan..."* and she put her finger to his lips to silence him.

"Don't talk, Alan. Just hold me."

He did and Susan dozed off in his arms and he held her quietly as she slept. He couldn't get over how sweet she was—*soft* and sweet. When she woke up and smiled at him, Alan said, "Susan, I've *got* to say something. I'm really sorry if I made you think I didn't like you as much as the others. I really am. I do like you very much. You're a wonderful girl and ...."

"Alan, hush! I always knew you liked me—I never doubted it. But I knew you'd never make love with me unless I said something crazy like that—so I just made it all up," she said, smiling sweetly. It'll be easier next time, Alan. I won't have to make up all those dumb things."

He pulled her close and said, *"Susan, you're very special to me and have been since the day we met. I mean very special and it's got nothing to do with this—making love and everything. I hope you don't live to regret this. Anytime you have second thoughts—anytime—we stop, OK?"*

"I know what I'm doing, Alan" she said softly. "Remember when you said, *'never say you're sorry when we're being ourselves'?* Well, I'm being myself and I'm sure not sorry."

"Dammit!" Alan roared—suddenly sitting up and trying to put on his most fearsome, outraged look—*"you manipulated me! You made up that whole damned story and made me feel guilty as hell. I went crazy trying to figure out what I'd done to make you think that. You manipulated me, you little brat!"*

She looked at him with that patented, sweet smile of hers and said, *"who, me?"*

"Come on," he said, *"let's hit the beach"* and they dove over the side and swam ashore.

"Well, look at you. Robbing the cradle, huh?" Carole said to Alan when they got to shore.

"Correction, my esteemed captain. You didn't rob the cradle —you crawled into the cradle. Shame on you." Then

raising her voice, she called out to Sigrid, *"put out a sex-criminal alert—dirty old man in our neighborhood likes to play with little girls"*.

"*Ja*," Sigrid said and rattled off a phrase in German. Alan figured it couldn't be very flattering.

Alan knew he was hopelessly outnumbered and *outclassed*. He might try to look like a pirate *but these women were the real pirates.*

Now, he was—how did Carole put it—*"on call"* *to all three of these pirates.*

No place, however seemingly perfect, is ever *really* perfect. There's always some flaw or another—even in paradise. In the South Pacific that "flaw" is the hurricane season stretching more or less from December to April. The hurricane season was fast approaching and Alan and the girls needed to leave soon. They planned to head west to hurricane-free Bali in Indonesia— with stops in New Caledonia and Australia.

Alan and Susan spent hours huddled over the charts and sailing guides to plan their route and timing and checked the weather forecasts daily. He'd once seen a marker in Fiji a *half mile inland* showing how far the horrendous hurricane-driven waters had reached. When the planning was finished, they gathered around the chart table to look at it. They'd sail from Malolo-lai-lai directly for New Caledonia. Noumea, the capital, was like the "Paris" of the Pacific. It was culturally French and about the best way to see Paris if you lived in the South Pacific. It would make a great change of pace from the deserted, tropical islands they'd enjoyed for so long.

"*It's about 800 plus miles*," Susan said, "and if we leave in the next day or two, we should be there—let's see—by the middle of next week." She then pulled out the local chart of the western area of Fiji, where they were and said, "we need to leave here at the crack of dawn to clear the last reefs before dark." She showed them another complex, zigzagging course she'd plotted through the shallow waters, coral patches and sand bars of the gigantic lagoon.

"*We have to be safe in the deep, open ocean before night—that's for sure*," she said. "We can't get caught out in these reefs in darkness." No one questioned Susan any more. Alan double-checked her—as she did him—but he never had to correct her. Susan sent the same carefully timed fax to her father telling him they were headed west, all was well and they were leaving tomorrow. That's what she wanted her family to know. She really didn't want them to worry—*she just didn't want to hear back from her father.* Alan figured the controlling, dominating old fart must be chewing the fax cord in anger about now.

Being a little on the slow side, it had just recently dawned on Alan that *all along* Susan had been intentionally sending the faxes too late to get a reply. He'd fallen for that himself in Tonga. *Manipulative little brat*, Alan thought and smiled.

That evening, they celebrated their last night in Fiji with dinner at the yacht club. They reminisced and laughed about Big Margaret at the hospital in Suva and even about *the Kava thing*. "*Come on Alan*," Susan said, "*show us how Carole was trying to find her lips in the mirror*"—and Alan pantomimed that all over again.

"OK," Carole said, "*my turn. Now show us how you had to help Susan pee.*"

"*Hey, that's not fair*," Susan objected. After dinner they said goodbye to the friends and acquaintances they'd made among the other crews—who were surprised that the crew of *ESCAPEE* was not only still together but such an obviously close-knit group. They crashed in their berths that night and were soon sound asleep. The door to Alan's forward berth was open—no one had any need for privacy anymore. They were far beyond that.

The next morning they left as soon as the sun was high enough to help them see the many underwater dangers. Susan expertly guided them on her course through the maze of coral patches, shallows and sand banks while Sigrid and Carole took turns at the wheel. Alan watched them work as a team—expertly maneuvering *ESCAPEE* past those underwater dangers where a number of boats had come to grief. They did it perfectly all morning and into early afternoon. They would get *ESCAPEE* safely through the lagoon and into the safe, open Pacific where Alan would take over for the long first night.

He didn't want them to think he didn't trust them in these dangerous waters, so about 2 in the afternoon he went down below to take a break to be ready for the first all-night of sailing. If anyone had ever told him that one day he'd grab some sleep below while his boat—*his home*—was in dangerous waters *he'd tell them they were stark, raving mad.*

Alan knew these women were the *real* pirates but they were also serious, highly competent women and he trusted them completely with the safety of his home—*which was now their home.* By late afternoon, the girls had taken them safely beyond all the reefs and out into the deep, safe waters of the rolling Pacific. Now they could relax and as *ESCAPEE* began to roll in the gentle ocean swells, Alan and Susan set a course for New Caledonia. They had done their share. Now he would do his. Alan took over for the first night—always the most difficult to adjust to after weeks in quiet bays and regular sleeping hours. After a quick dinner in the cockpit, the girls crashed for the night—they'd had a very intense day of dodging coral reefs. Tomorrow they'd start sharing normal "at sea" watches of 3 hours on and 3 off, around the clock.

The next day dawned hot and they had to wear something to protect themselves from the intense sun, but as soon as they got into the cabin or found a shade everything came off.   Even with the trade-winds coming in from behind them, it was hot. During the first couple of days, they relaxed, sun-bathed, took it easy and got used to the open sea again after all that time in calm, sheltered water. The wind-vane was steering and the gentle trade winds were always the same—coming from behind them. *The skier was on a gentle downhill run.*

There was nothing much to do, since *ESCAPEE* was taking care of herself. Carole was on watch which was really just watching for ships and keeping a general eye on the sails and Susan was reading in the cockpit, where the sails had created some shade.

They were on their way to beautiful Bali in Indonesia, *some 4,500 miles distant* and in a totally different part of the world—*Asia.*

CHAPTER EIGHT

"THE FIVE S's"---SUN, SAND, SEA, SAILING AND SEX

During the 6-day cruise to New Caledonia Alan wrote Michael a mock—*but accurate*—"research report" on their lives on board *ESCAPEE* en route from Fiji to New Caledonia.

The "research report" was Alan's way of paying Michael back for the rough time he'd given him at the bar. That night had earned poor *ESCAPEE* the nickname of "*the polygamy boat*" and Alan wanted revenge. The "mock report" was a true account of what happened on that cruise, *but Alan wrote it in a way he knew would drive Michael up the wall.*

Research Report:

<u>To</u>: Michael Andrew Gilbertson

<u>Research Subject</u>: The *5 Practical Problems* Of Practicing

'Polygamy' In A Small, Crowded Space

By Captain Alan Richards

RESEARCH VESSEL *"ESCAPEE"*

SOMEWHERE AT SEA BETWEEN FIJI AND NEW CALEDONIA.

ESCAPEE has been converted into an ocean-going "research vessel" for this cruise to New Caledonia. We're not researching whales or ocean temperatures or such "standard" research subjects, but something a little more unusual—*the practical problems of practicing 'polygamy'*—as you wrongly insist on calling it—*on the high seas, when we're all confined in a small and crowded space.*

The 6-day cruise from Fiji to New Caledonia is our *first time at sea* since the girls made the "arrangement". It's one thing to live our life-style while we're anchored at beautiful islands—where two take off for the beach and leave the other two of us alone on board with all the privacy we want. *But it's a very different situation here at sea* when everyone is stuck together in a very small space and where there's little, if any, privacy.

I wondered *how* this would work —*or even if it would work.* These are ladies and none of us are into voyeurism so I knew we'd have to call a halt to the "arrangement" while we were at sea—*unless* I could find some practical solutions to the problem of privacy. Needless to say, I was highly motivated. Unfortunately, my first efforts to solve the problem of privacy on board turned out to be a disaster—*a complete disaster.*

The disaster started quietly enough when I was at the chart table and noticed Sigrid standing besides me. She sat down on my lap and said, *"come with me, Ellen,"* took my hand and guided me towards the forward cabin. I knew what she had on her mind—*and why not?* These were slow, gentle days at sea and there's just something about the open sea, the fresh air—anyway, you get the picture. We slipped into my berth in the forward cabin—*the one that bounces around so much at sea*—and closed the door behind us to get our privacy. That was the *only* place we'd have any privacy on board so we had no choice. Well, things soon started to happen—*and happen.. You know Sigrid— all strength and endurance.*

During all this time the forward cabin was being tossed around by the seas. It's so bad I *never* go into that cabin at sea— it's *much too rough*—but that's the *only* place we could get any privacy. We made love and bounced around in the closed, small cabin—*which itself was bouncing around*—and before long I wasn't feeling all that well. *Not at all.* Sigrid has a stomach of iron so all the movement didn't bother her one bit—*and that girl had plenty of movement of her own.*

The whole damned forward cabin was just one big *"movement,"* Michael—*the boat, Sigrid and me.* All of a sudden I felt seasick. I mean *really seasick!* I was about to throw up and it was a race against time.

I didn't know which was going to come first—me or the seasickness.

I was about to throw up all over Sigrid and needed to get out of there *fast* but we were locked in a certain position and I couldn't get loose—*you know what a grip that girl has.* Suddenly it was all over and Sigrid looked at me as if to ask, *"that's it?"* She didn't like it one bit—it was much too fast for her but I just *had* to get out of there. As it was I'd come very close to throwing up all over her *and I didn't think she'd like that very much either. What a disaster!* I apologized and told her, "it'll be better next time"

"*Vat ve do, Ellen?*" she asked, so concerned. "How ve do it?"

I want to tell you Michael, that Sigrid is as soft and sweet in her own way as Susan. Anyway, I quickly found the solution—I'd just take the mattress from one of the berths in the main cabin and put it on the cabin floor. The floor of the main cabin moves far less than any place on the entire boat—*and there's more room*. Why hadn't I thought of that before? But that solution—good as it was—*created a new problem*. The problem was we could be seen from the cockpit. Clearly, that wouldn't do. These are ladies and to them everything—*and I do mean everything*—has to be done in good taste.

The obvious solution was to close the cockpit door and lock it from inside so it didn't bounce open. Then we'd have all the privacy we wanted, but in a much larger space with little movement. It was a perfect solution *or so I thought at the time*. I told Sigrid, "next time, we put the mattress here."

"*Ja Ellen..here, tomorrow, ja?* "

"Tomorrow," I said.

That's when I ran into *another problem*—a "*traffic jam*" I guess you could call it for lack of a better word. I discovered Susan had more or less 'penciled me in' for tomorrow on her *own* schedule. As soon as I realized a *traffic jam* was developing I quietly talked to Susan. "Day after tomorrow then," she said and the traffic jam was over. *That's the first and last time that ever happened.* The next day Sigrid and I went down below, locked the door behind us and found that the mattress worked just great *and* gave us plenty of room to move around. It was a great solution, but that solution opened up *still another problem*—one we hadn't thought of.

The problem was sound—*noise*. The seas were calm and quiet and as Sigrid and I made love the sounds must have carried—*after all Carole and Susan were only a few feet away.* They said they didn't hear us, but I could tell they heard everything—it was that look on Susan's face. Sigrid was upset when Carole admitted that, yes, we had been heard. I can tell you these ladies do not want *any* audience—visual or audible. We're not talking about dramatic or earth-shattering sounds, Michael—sorry to disappoint you—just the inevitable sounds of two people making love a few feet away.

Well, leave it to Carole to find the answer. She's a born problem solver and came up with an immediate solution that was *so simple.* When I went below with Susan the next day, Carole popped a cassette into the cockpit stereo and turned it up loudly. It was that cassette of Pavarotti and The Three Tenors we played back at Malolo-lai-lai when you were aboard. At least I think it was—I wasn't really focusing on the music at the time.

Carole's solution was great. Even though Susan and I were only a few feet away from the others *no one could hear anything* over that cassette. Great solution, right?

Wrong!

That cassette had its own problems. As I said, our sounds were being completely covered by the cassette but what we didn't realize *soon enough* was that the tape volume often suddenly drops way down. The problem was that when the cassette volume dropped off—*our volume didn't.*

Susan was mortified and so was I. It's kind of hard to explain it, Michael—*everyone knows what's going on a few feet away*, *of course*, but no one wants to have it sort of pushed into our faces like that. These are classy ladies and none of us are into that kind of thing. We love those tenors—Pavarotti, Carreras and Domingo—and don't want to switch to another cassette and leave those boys out of it. Any other cassette would have the same problem, so we all carefully listened to the cassette again and found that there really aren't *that many* quiet spots—*we just needed to know where they were*. After we heard it a few times, we each wound up knowing exactly where those quiet spots were—and from then on when the cassette's volume went down, *so did ours*.

As you can just imagine Michael—*trying to make love "in synch" with the rising and falling volume of a cassette is a challenge*. The key thing was to get the *timing* of those "*quiet spots*" just right. Everything's in the timing, Michael. Just picture a conductor with his baton, and then picture...*no, don't!*

As a side note—I could kick myself for not bringing my cassette of Tchaikovsky's *1812 Overture* with cannons. Can you just imagine you and your lady getting *your "grand finales"* in synch with *that finale!*

With that final, finishing touch, we had at last perfected our "*at-sea system*"—even if we did have to follow the progress of the music a little more than we wanted. One by one, the practical problems of practicing what you call 'polygamy' in a small and crowded space were identified—*and solved*. Now, I can just hear you saying "*what a load of bullshit*," but that's a highly unworthy and unscientific response to such a serious research effort as this. The ladies and I have managed to identify and solve the practical problems of the "*arrangement*"while crowded here together on *ESCAPEE* in mid-ocean. And remember, this is all *their* arrangement. How could I—being only one person—possibly resist the combined power of these three mentally superior people? *And come to think of it, why should I?*"

I really shouldn't say this, Michael—I don't want to disillusion you and your fantasies—but it isn't all the "*five-S's*" out here—*Sun, Sand, Sea, Sailing and Sex*. There are those "*five-S's*" of course, but there's more to it than that.

Yes, these are three healthy young women and yes we're out here together in the beautiful South Pacific living in the natural when we're alone—so that all leads to a high frequency of activity. That's just normal under these circumstances. But don't forget, there's *still* a boat to sail and jobs to do. There are watches to keep, lots of equipment to maintain and food to prepare and serve. *It's hell Michael*—and I hope you're feeling sorry for me about now.

After the "traffic jam" four days passed and nothing happened. I mean *nothing. Nada. Zip.* For some reason or another none of the girls was in the mood. That led to yet *another practical problem*—what if the girls aren't in the mood, but I am? They had agreed it worked both ways—they were "*on call*" too, but that's a problem I sure never had before.

So after four days of inactivity I almost stepped in to get some action started myself. But when I thought about it I decided not to. That could lead to *still another problem*. This is a great arrangement they've come up with, Michael, but I figured it's far better if I wait and *they chose when*—instead of me jumping in and *choosing who*. As you can imagine, my choosing *who* could possibly turn into a problem—I don't think so knowing these ladies, but why take the chance of upsetting this great arrangement? That's just one more practical problem identified and solved through this research.

So I just waited and things soon got back to normal. It's sometimes feast or famine with these girls—or should I say, in this case, *famine and then feast?* Anyway, the combination of the mattress on the cabin floor—together with the locked door and Pavarotti and his buddies singing their hearts out worked just great—*as long as we got the timing of the quiet spots right.* It's not quite the same as sitting at anchor in a beautiful bay with the other two off the boat and away on the beach *but our "at-sea system" has been perfected and works.*

Through dedicated, disciplined and highly-focused research I've been able to identify the *5 major problems* of practicing "polygamy" in a small, crowded space. They are:

Where—functionally.

Privacy—visual.

Privacy—sound.

When—if they're *not* in the mood.

What to do—if they really *are* in the mood and a "traffic jam" develops.

I don't know whether you've noticed it yet, Michael, but things seem to come in "*5*'s" on *ESCAPEE*.

There's this "*gimme 5*" from Sigrid. She keeps on doing the "high five" after we make love—it's become our private joke now.

There are the "*Five S's* "—*Sand, Sun, Sea, Sailing* and *Sex*.

Now, there are the *5 practical problems of* "*polygamy*"*in a small, crowded space.*

And yes, I do admit to some tiredness at times but as your great hero John Wayne used to say, "*a man must do what a man must do.*"

Now, I know you—*so quit shouting "bullshit"* at this scholarly Research Report. You'll upset your secretary and alarm your clients *if you have any left*. Read and weep amigo— *all this really did happen on that passage.* This is just life in the tropics, on the good ship *ESCAPEE*.

End of Report

While Alan was busy with his *"research,"* ESCAPEE sailed steadily westwards towards New Caledonia under the gentle breeze of the constant trade-winds. No one had to change the sails or steer—just keep watch for ships and read. *The skier was effortlessly gliding down the mountain.* Now that the *practical* problems of what Michael insisted on calling 'polygamy' were solved, the voyage settled down to what passes for *"normal"* on *ESCAPEE*. Later Alan wrote Michael a brief cover letter to be sent along with the Research Report. It said:

On the 6th day, we arrived in Noumea. It had been a slow, easy passage and we were ready for the bright lights, cafes, bars and restaurants of the *"Paris of the Pacific"*. You should have seen their eyes when the girls saw the patisseries and French ambiance. This place is French through and through, so we bought a bag of freshly-baked croissants and wolved them down. People dress more formally here too, so the girls wear bikinis only on the boat.

We each dug out the best clothes we had. Susan and Sigrid were OK but Carole had been backpacking—and you know me. But we managed and I didn't want to embarrass the girls, so wore a sun hat instead of my knotted handkerchief and slipped the earring off. We made quite a hit—one guy and three good- looking women. Those Frenchman didn't like that one bit—I think it must have offended their well- known egalitarian tastes.

As usual some guys tried to move in on the girls a few times when I wasn't around, but Carole *"dispatched"* them—as she called it—with a few choice words. *"Nice, but clear words,"* she said. I don't doubt they were clear, but *"nice"*—I just don't know. That girl doesn't like rude, pushy people and sure knows how to handle them. Sometimes we found people standing around looking for the guy and three good-looking women he lived with. I always thought the French were sophisticated, Michael, but some of them were like country-bumpkins coming to town on a hay-wagon and seeing their first shopping mall.

Carole and the girls took off shopping in those French stores while I worked on the water maker. We use a lot of water and need to keep it in good working order. After the work was done we took a 3-day tour around the island. It's beautiful but we had a little trouble explaining the sleeping arrangements we wanted—all sharing two beds in one room, but they soon got the picture and no problem. *They're French, after all.* They said it would be too crowded for four people in one room, but after being on *ESCAPEE,* the room seemed like a tennis court.

I don't know what it was—maybe the romance of the French culture all around us—but frequently and as if by pre-agreement, two of them would just walk off the dock to go window-shopping and leave the other two of us alone. You get the picture. What can I tell you, buddy? *It doesn't get any better than this.*

So we've been here about two weeks or so, eaten French food, shopped, seen the tourists sights and serviced the water-maker. Now we're getting ready to head for Bali, with a quick stop in Townsville and Darwin, Australia.

I'm going to end this letter with a confession. Michael.

I'm falling in love!

Which one? you ask.

Each one! I reply.

I'm truly falling in love with *each one* of these women—individually and separately. There isn't one of the three I couldn't go bananas over. In fact, I already have. They're very different from each other *and very special.* You know me—I'm as mushy as hell and an incurable romantic. They're a lot more realistic than I am and their feet's on the ground. Mine are not.

I'm in love, Michael—*with each one.*

Keep well, Amigo.

After all the shopping, seeing New Caledonia and mailing the letter and the mock "*Research Report*" to Michael, it was time to get moving. *ESCAPEE* still had a very long way to go. Alan and Susan studied the charts and Susan calculated the sea distance from New Caledonia to the fabled island of Bali in Indonesia to be around 3,800 miles. They'd have to break it up into two or three "smaller" trips, but even the first leg—New Caledonia to Townsville on the Northeast Australian coast—was about 1,300 miles. Altogether, this was going to be by far their longest period at sea together—*at least a month or more*. Alan was *very* glad the "research" on the trip from Fiji had been so successful.

While Susan was working out the routes, Alan had another concern—hurricanes. It was now mid-November and the hurricane season started in December. Even though most of the hurricanes—or cyclones, as they are called in this part of the Pacific—struck in January and February, they were getting uncomfortably close to the active hurricane season. One of the most destructive hurricanes in recorded history—Hurricane Tracy, which almost blew Darwin, Australia off the map—struck in December. They were due to stop in Darwin around Christmas—the *same time* Hurricane Tracy hit a few years ago. Alan knew they should have left earlier but with so much happening and Michael's visit, it was hard to focus on schedules.

Everyone gathered around as Susan showed them the route she had come up with and Alan told them about the hurricanes. Their trade-wind route took them right through the center of the hurricane belt most of the way. Most cruisers went south to New Zealand to get out of the hurricane belt quickly, but since they were going to Bali, they needed to go west—and that kept them in the hurricane zone much longer. With El Nino and the crazy, unsettled weather in the Pacific there was always the possibility of an early-season hurricane and they needed to talk it over.

"We're all in this together" Alan said, "so here's the situation and I'd like to know what you think." They were long accustomed to working as a team and sharing the major decisions which would affect them all.

"What's the alternative?" Carole asked, as they got the picture.

"Not very good. There's almost never any hurricanes at the equator, so we could go north and over the top of New Guinea to Bali, that way. But it's *much* farther and there's almost no wind up there. We'd have to motor forever and stop and pick up fuel all along the way."

"Well, generally, the first ones hit in January, right?" Carole asked, "so why don't we just get moving and get beyond the hurricane area into Indonesia by the most direct route possible? We could be safe in Bali long before the first one hit."

Sigrid and Susan nodded in agreement.

"OK, I agree," Alan said. *"Let's do it. Bali, here we come."*

They got *ESCAPEE* ready for sea in record time and Susan dashed off to send her *"I'm OK, but it's too late to reply"* fax to her father. This guy wanted to be in absolute control of everything and everybody, but good luck trying to control this girl—*not any longer.* They topped off the boat's food and supplies, filled up with fuel and water and took off. It was hot as they left and the gawkers were treated to the sight of three women in topless bikinis—French style after all—leaving with that American pirate.

The trade-winds were in full swing and *ESCAPEE* flew along on a direct course for Townsville in Northern Australia. The weather was perfect. After all the rush to leave and the tiring motion of the sea after that time ashore, everyone was worn out the first three days. But the weather was beautiful, the sun was out, the clothes were off, the trade-winds were gentle and soon a familiar, easy-going pattern settled in on *ESCAPEE.* *The skier was having one of the best runs ever.*

Alan re-read those words of Ralph Waldo Emerson— *"the good ship darts through the water all day, all night like a fish… sliding from horizon to horizon.*" That was a perfect description of *ESCAPEE.*

On the third day out, Susan and Alan were huddled together over the chart table checking their progress when they closed the cabin door for some privacy. The *"at-sea system"* which they had worked out en route from Fiji worked—cushion on the floor, door closed and locked from the inside, Pavarotti and those nice Tenors singing their hearts out just for them. It worked very well—*as long as they got those quiet spots right.*

Then it was Carole and Alan in the cockpit on the night watch together. They looked around for any ships, closed the cabin door so not to disturb Sigrid and Susan who were asleep below, and made love as quietly as possible under the stars on one of the two full-length, cushioned cockpit seats. It was *very* romantic with all those stars above—*until they rolled off the seat and hit the cockpit floor with a thud.*

The boat was gently rolling in the following seas and had rolled them right off. To make it even worse, it happened at a very critical time and spoiled the night's *grand finale* for both of them. The rolling was never a problem when you were sitting upright and gently holding on or restfully bracing yourself with your legs—you hardly even noticed it. But they had been *lying down and holding onto each other*—not the boat. The boat wasn't rolling much, but it doesn't take much of a roll to dump you if you're lying down and hanging onto *someone else* instead of the boat.

After that highly untimely dumping, they realized there was just *no way* they could hold each other and make love without rolling off. For Carole a problem was nothing more than a challenge and she quickly found the solution. She named Alan the *"designated holder"*—sort of like a *"designated driver"*. His job was to hold onto the back of the seat and to keep them from rolling off *while Carole held onto him and more or less took care of everything else.* It took a little creative experimentation at first but they soon were making love again—and often—under the stars on those long night watches. Where there's a will, there's a way and Carole was not only an experienced and creative lover but was *loaded with will.*

Now they had an *"under the stars"* system as well as a day- time *"at –sea system"*. *Things were certainly looking up.*

There was nothing planned about any of it—just lazy, carefree, sunny days *and nights* at sea with one man and three women. As usual, ESCAPEE was still a *"clothes-free- zone"* and one day while the girls were in the cockpit getting some sun and reading, Alan slipped below and did something he had been planning to do for a long time—he shaved off his moustache. The damned thing added to the appearance he wanted but was just too much of a nuisance—and it could be hot as well. After he had finished, he called up to the cockpit and said, *"OK, you guys, get ready for a surprise,"* and came up into the cockpit, wearing nothing—*not even that moustache.*

"Alan!" Susan called out, shocked. *"You shaved your moustache off. Why? You look…well, naked!"* The girls took one look and agreed—with that big moustache gone he now *really* looked naked. Sigrid starting laughing and Carole joined in and said, *"Oh no—now we've got to look at all of him—and I do mean all.* At least your face was partly covered up 'til now. Now we've got to look at every last bit of you. *Ugh! Who wants to wake up to that face each morning?* That's not nice, Alan," she said, changing into a serious tone of voice, *"you really should've asked us first. After all, we've got something to say about it since we have to share you."*

"I know," Susan said brightly, *"when we—you know— share Alan, why don't we just put a sack over his head?"*

As soon as Sigrid understood she said, *"Ja—gut idea. Pillow sack is better.* I make one for him, with eyes cut out. Ve no let him touch us without pillow sack over head. *All agree with zis?"*

Alan said, *"hey, what is this, a strike or something? You guys threatening a strike, huh? OK, let's just see who can hold out the longest.* I could use some rest, you know. I might just be the one to go on strike. After all, I've been feeling a little *used* lately. *You three just use me and throw me aside until you're ready to use me again. That sure hurts a boy's feelings. I may just have to go on a strike to get some respect around here."*

"Oh, poor baby's feeling used, is he?" Carole asked. *"You just try to hold out on us, Bubba.* All we've got to do is get Sigrid rubbing those boobs of hers up against you and the strike's over—or have Susan sit on your lap and wiggle around—we all know how you like young girls. So don't try any of that 'strike' stuff on us. *We'll break you down. We'll destroy any will-power you think you have. We'll turn you into a blathering idiot begging us for it."*

"OK, OK," Alan said, laughing and giving up. *"Bad idea. You win.* If you want me to glue the moustache back on, I will. But come on guys, have a little mercy. It was hot and just too much trouble. Anyway, I'm keeping the earring and bandanna."

"Well, there goes our pirate-lover," Carole said, *"melting away before our very eyes. Next thing you know, he'll look as square as he really is. Before you know it he'll be just 'John Doe, blah real estate broker' again. And have you ever seen a pirate without a moustache?* You've blown it Alan—you'll never get that pirate job at Disneyland when you get back."

Alan shrugged his shoulders. *He just couldn't win with these three*—they *always* had the last word. It all just seemed so damned one-sided and unfair—they had wit, intelligence and were fast while he had that damned "comprehension problem" of his.

Oh well, he thought, *there are compensations.*

They were soon approaching the Great Barrier Reef— the world's longest chain of reefs, stretching 1,250 miles from north to south off the coast of Australia. The Great Barrier Reef is also the world's largest living object. The reef was formed over millions of years, by billions of tiny calcium-producing organisms and grew into the world's longest reef—*and it's still growing*. It's called a "barrier" reef because it forms a huge barrier blocking off the thundering Pacific rollers and creating sheltered water for the entire Australian coast behind it. There are several large, well-marked channels through the reef and Susan had picked the one which would take them the most direct way to Townsville.

ESCAPEE passed through the Great Barrier Reef in a wide, well-marked channel. What a difference from that channel on the way to Fiji! Three days later they motored into the modern marina in Townsville and were met by Australian authorities who came on board and confiscated all their fruit and eggs and anything else on the "not allowed" list. They did this to protect Australia's agriculture from foreign diseases.

When the formalities were done they all headed into town to find an ice cream store and a salad bar—the two things they'd missed most at sea. They didn't know it, but a great deal of sadness was waiting for them in Townsville. As usual they stopped at a large hotel and Sigrid called her family in Germany to check in with them. She faithfully did that in every port but this time she got the shocking news that her father had died of a heart attack five days ago while they were still at sea. The family had tried to reach her but it had not been possible and they had to go ahead with the funeral.

Sigrid came out of the telephone booth, her eyes red with tears and they went straight back to *ESCAPEE*. Alan gave her the forward cabin for privacy and to be alone with her grief. *Their hearts broke for her*—they knew how close she was to her parents and especially her father. After an hour or so, she came out and they each hugged her and tried to be any comfort they could. She needed to talk it out. She was *especially upset* that her father had been dead for five days and she hadn't even known. Not knowing he was gone bothered her almost as much as his death, she said.

Over coffee, she talked on and on about her father. He had wanted her to take this trip, she said, and kept a big world map on the wall with pins marking all the places she visited. He read all her cards and letters over and over and told her he was seeing the world and all those exotic places through her eyes. He especially loved those photos of all the multi-colored reef fish Sigrid had taken and sent back to him. In all his life he had never been more than a hundred miles from home, she said, so she wrote him often and at length and through those letters he was living her adventures right alongside her.

She knew he had a heart problem and the entire family had talked about it when she flew there from Mallorca before she left on the German boat. But they all wanted her to go. They knew the *hell* that life with Rolf had become and encouraged her to get away—especially her father who was heart-broken over what his baby daughter was going through. His world was so different from Hamburg and Rolf and all that madness. He just couldn't understand it and it hit him hard, she said.

Sigrid went on talking about her father throughout the afternoon and then explained that during the call some of her brothers and sisters were at the family home with her mother. Her mother was doing fine and her brothers and sisters were close by. She was a strong woman—physically and emotionally—and they told Sigrid she would be all right. Three of the five children lived nearby and told Sigrid they would be with their mother and take care of her. They all agreed they wanted Sigrid to go on with her cruise—*because that's what her father would want.* When she insisted she would fly right back they tried to talk her out of it, telling her that was too late to say goodbye to her father and her mother was doing fine. The family didn't want her to rush back, she said, because they knew she'd have to go ahead and deal with Rolf, the divorce and all that mess waiting for her once she got back. That was one reason, of course, *but mostly they all knew her father would want her to continue* and in the end that's what persuaded Sigrid to stay and not fly straight back.

After talking about her father for a long time—their lives together, her childhood and how she admired him—she went back to the cabin and slept through the rest of the afternoon. That was very unlike Sigrid, but they knew it was a way of dealing with her feelings. That evening they had quiet dinner together in a small, almost empty restaurant near the marina. They took a table in a far corner for privacy and Alan asked if there was anything any of them could do.

Sigrid again said that her mother was surrounded by the family and everyone—*including her mother*—wanted her to go on with her cruise. *"I sink about zis much,"* she said. *"I luf my family. My mutter is OK. Zey say so. I go back someday, but I stay now. My fater—he would want me stay. I know zis. My fater would say zis. So I do what he like. Und, you guys also like my family."*

That was just a little more than Alan could handle—it had already been an emotional day, seeing someone they cared for very much go through all that—so he got up, went around the table and gave Sigrid a big hug and said, *"we love you Sigrid and we are your family—one of your families. You have more than one, you know."* Susan and Carole reached across the table and took her hands.

The next day Sigrid wanted to get off the boat and *go do something—go somewhere.* Susan had been dying to see some kangaroos and koala bears and they all wanted to see an "outback" cattle ranch. They picked up some tourist brochures from the local tourist office and rented a car. Alan found a guest ranch on the tourist map, called to make a reservation and they took off to go sightseeing for a couple of days. They were racing the calendar and the hurricane season but they also wanted to see a little of Australia—and Sigrid needed a break to help get her mind off her loss.

The ranch looked close on the map but was over two hundred hot, dusty miles away. Australia is an unbelievable huge country and seems even bigger because the bumpy roads and monotonous, endless miles of dry bushes go on forever with little change. Much of this area looked like West Texas must have looked 50 years ago—a rugged "out-west" feeling with endless miles of bumpy roads and hot, desolate, brown countryside. After a long hot trip through the burning countryside, they finally arrived at the guest ranch which had the cute little Koala bears, kangaroos and a big swimming pool under shade trees—*exactly what they were looking for.*

It also had a desk clerk from hell.

Alan had reserved a room for the four of them under his name. The desk clerk on duty at the guest ranch assumed that it was a husband and wife and two children. When they arrived to check in Alan ran head on into the desk-clerk—a huge, tall, heavy-set woman in her fifties with a foul temper and who obviously considered it her personal, moral duty to examine and supervise the morals of everyone who came on the ranch.

"These three women with you," she demanded to know, her eyebrow raised suspiciously, *"who are they?"* she barked rudely. *"I was expecting a family—husband and wife with children."*

"We're one group," Alan said, smiling and hoping to charm her. He might as well have tried to charm a rattlesnake.

"I know that. Do you think I'm blind or stupid? You came in one car. *Now, which one's your wife—and who are these other women?"* she demanded loudly. The woman was plain nasty and Alan realized they were about to be thrown out by this morally out-raged busybody. They had just driven two hundred hot, dusty miles to get here and the nearest flea-bag hotel was at least sixty miles back where they had come from.

The girls were outside, petting one of the kangaroos and couldn't wait to get out of their hot, dirty clothes into the pool. This place was *exactly* what they were looking for and no one was in a mood to pile back into the hot car and drive another sixty miles back to some dump.

Alan knew he had to talk his way past this woman. He could tell she was just looking for an excuse to throw them out, so she could boast about "upholding moral standards" and impress her friends with her integrity. Self-righteous people are like that, he knew—it's no fun being "righteous" if you don't let everyone know you are. To Alan she was the female version of squint-eyed Clint Eastwood's *"Dirty Harry,"* saying *"come on— make my day."* She was big, mean, nasty—and self-righteous—a *deadly* combination.

Alan quickly chose his wife and said, *"the tall, blonde lady is my wife.* I met her in Germany and we were married when I was there on business. The other two are my sisters—you can tell from their American accents that my sisters and I come from the same place."

She gave him a highly suspicious sideways look and said, *"she looks a little young to be your wife."*

"That's exactly what her parents said at the wedding in Munich last September." He stood his ground, looking her steadily in the eyes—he'd heard that a truly honest person looks people straight in the eyes. This was a good time to see if it worked with this suspicious, self-righteous woman. It apparently did and she said, *"well, I guess it's alright.* If I had two rooms, I'd split you folks up, but seeing we got only one room left, it'll have to do. It has two double beds—one for you and your wife and one for your sisters. I guess it'll have to do. *OK, sign here."*

While he filled out the form, this stern upholder of other people's moral standards came from behind the desk to the window to look the three women over. She obviously smelled sin in the air, but couldn't *quite* put her finger on it. She turned back to the desk, took his credit card imprint and handed him the key.

Alan went back out to the car to get their bags and Susan ran up squealing, *"Alan, this's so great! Did you see that baby kangaroo? Thanks for bringing us,"* and threw her arms around him, giving him a quick kiss.

"Susan," he said, holding her back a little while quickly glancing towards the office, *"we've got a little problem here,"* and he motioned for the Sigrid and Carole to join them. He quickly gave them the story and could see fire beginning to burn in Carole's eyes. He hoped she'd keep her cool but knew that Carole would do something outrageous before they left—*that was just Carole.* They got their bags and carried them through the front office, right past the glaring, still-suspicious desk clerk towards their room.

As they went past the clerk, Alan said, *"Sigrid, honey will you go ahead and open the door? I'll bring the bags,"* and he handed her the key. *"Thanks, sweetheart."*

"Hey, brother of mine," Carole said, *"remember when dad used to take us to western movies when we were little kids? Well, this ranch reminds me of those western movies. Now, go on and catch up to your wife. Sis and I will be right behind. Boy, I wish mom and dad could've seen all this."*

That was good, Alan thought. He'd have to compliment Carole.

Carole then marched straight up to the woman at the front desk and asked if she had another room. *"You understand, my sister and I feel—well, sort of strange—you know, sleeping in the same room with my brother and his wife,"* she said shyly. Carole knew, of course, there were no more rooms available.

"Oh, I perfectly understand," the big woman said, visibly relieved. "But, I'm really sorry. We only got that one room. I guess I could have one of the workers move the bed to

the other side of the room and put up a clothesline between the beds and hang a sheet over it. That would give you and your little sister some privacy."

"Would you do that, please? That would be so nice and would make my sister and I feel better. I'm not a prude, you know.   I just...well, I just don't feel comfortable—you understand."

"I sure do, honey. It's so refreshing to see young people with a sense of modesty like yours these days—not too many young people like you around any more. Now don't you and your little sister worry about a thing. I'll get someone to do it while you folks are having dinner."

"Oh, thank you. You're so nice," Carole said.

The two "sisters" went to the room while the vigilant desk clerk visibly relaxed—the morals of the guest ranch were not going to be corrupted that night. When they got to the room, Susan told Sigrid and Alan what Carole had just done. They had a big laugh about it all, put on their bathing suits and hit the pool. Before they left for the pool, Alan said *"now come on, Carole. I know you.* Whatever you've got planned, hold it till we leave tomorrow after lunch. The old witch could still throw us out."

They swam and hung out at the pool a couple of hours, cooling down from the long, hot drive. They showered and around seven went to the dining room where Alan pulled out the chair for his *wife* but let his *sisters* pull out their own chairs. Sigrid really got into the spirit of the "act"—playing the role of wife with aloof superiority over the lower-class "sisters"—really hamming it up and having fun. Throughout the dinner she spoke only to her "husband," and studiously ignored her "sisters-in-law" who were—after all—*just tagging along like excess baggage* on her trip with her husband.

Kangaroo meat was on the menu but Susan made it very clear if anyone had any meat from those "cute kangaroos," she'd walk straight out of the restaurant—*right then and there*. After dinner, all the guests adjourned to the big lounge where they were treated to music and tribal story-telling by an Aboriginal tribesman. Evening tea was served and then it was time for bed.

They returned to their room to find someone had moved the "sisters" bed to the side of the room and had hung up a sheet between them—all for modesty's sake. Alan took out a flask and they went out to sit on the big porch and passed the flask between them. The desk clerk was already in bed so they could relax and be themselves. Later Alan and his "wife" found the bed a little cramped, so they switched. Susan slept with Alan in the one bed and Carole and Sigrid made do in the other. The long drive, hot weather, swimming, food and the flask all combined to put them to sleep within minutes.

The next morning they woke up and Carole said, *"OK, guys. We're all going to play our roles while we see the kangaroos and Koala bears and have lunch. But just before checking out, I take over and we shift to my plan, OK?"* Alan didn't know what Carole's plan was—*he didn't want to know.* He'd just go with the flow. He could never figure that woman out—any of the three for that matter—*so why try?*

They had a huge breakfast and spent a few hours petting the Koala bears and playing with the kangaroos. They watched a boxing match between a big, male kangaroo and a ranch worker—the kangaroo won by a mile. They had a quick swim before lunch and after lunch went back to the room to get their bags and check out. Carole said, *"OK, just follow my lead. First we make up this bed,"* she said, pointing to the one by the wall. *"We make it look like no one's slept in it."* In no time, it looked completely unused—just the way they found it. *"OK, let's go,"* Carole said.

Carole walked towards the desk clerk to give her the key and stopped suddenly, turned to Alan and said, *"hey brother of mine, you know that fun we had in bed last night?* Well, I want to do it again," and she gave her "brother" a deep, long kiss. The big woman behind the desk was stunned—totally stunned.

"*See,*" Carole said, "*like I told you in bed last night, kissing your sister can be just as much fun as kissing your wife.* You saw that I've got the same equipment she has and know how to use it. Now give your little sister a kiss, too—*can't leave her out.*" Alan got Carole's drift and put his arms around Susan and gave her a long, sensual kiss.

"I told you kissing and playing house with your sisters isn't boring. *We should play like that more often.*" The clerk was now *beyond stunned.*

Carole handed the key to her and said, "*by the way, that sheet you had put up made us feel sort of cut-off from one another. As you can see, we're a very close family so we all slept together in the same bed. It was a really tight fit, but we managed. We did have one problem though—Sis and I just couldn't keep my brother's hands off us. At least I think it was my brother's hands all over us—with his wife there in bed with us you never know. She likes girls. Anyway, the other bed's still made up—never been used. Go see for yourself. Bye now.*"

The woman was shocked speechless and her slack jaw and mouth hung open in utter astonishment. Her eyes were wide—clearly and graphically picturing the horror of the scene Carole had just vividly described. Minutes later she was still in a state of speechless, stammering shock as they got into their car and took off.

"*Carole!,*" Alan exclaimed after the laughter in the car finally died down, "*you're bad. That wasn't very nice.* That poor lady could have had a heart attack. I think she almost did. *She still may.*"

"*No way,*" Carole said. "Those kind die old and grouchy, making life miserable for everyone around them right up to the last minute. And she was real nasty to you. Anyway, we did her a great favor—just think of the stories she's got to tell now. She'll be very popular now and I'll bet that telephone's burning up all day. Hey, look at it this way—we brought excitement into her boring life. Anyway, people shouldn't try to impose their own way of thinking on others. *Right?*"

"*Right*" Sigrid and Susan said forcefully.

These three are something else, Alan said to himself.

They returned to Townsville and used the car to shop and load *ESCAPEE* with provisions and supplies.

It was time to go.

Actually, it was past time.

CHAPTER NINE

THE SURVIVAL STORM

They left Townsville and headed north to the top of Australia where they would turn left—or west—and go *"over the top"* towards Darwin and Bali. Carole was steering *ESCAPEE* northwesterly up the coast of Australia through the narrow channel and Susan was checking progress on her chart.

Since they were inside The Great Barrier Reef the seas were flat. The massive reef really was a *barrier* and blocked off the thundering Pacific waves. The winds were gentle and still behind them and it was nice, gentle sailing. *The skier was just coasting along.* But it was also near the end of November and they needed to get a move on—time was not on their side. Distances in Australia are vast and it was still more than 500 miles from Townsville to Cape York—the northern point of Australia where they'd make their left turn for Darwin and Bali.

The route up to Cape York at the top of Australia was a well–marked but often very narrow channel through dangerous reefs. Stay inside the channel markers and you were completely safe. Go outside them and you'd hit a reef—*for sure*. It was a designated international waterway so they figured they could go 24 hours a day but that very first afternoon they ran into a very bad surprise.

All the ships and most of the smaller boats passing through here had radar which made it easy to follow the channel markers *day and night*. But for *ESCAPEE*, which had no radar, *it was "eyeball" navigation* all the way. To their surprise the channel markers were so far apart Alan and the girls had to often use the binoculars to find the next set of marker buoys so they could stay safely inside the channel. During the day it took a lot of concentration and work. At night the lights on those channel-markers just couldn't be reliably seen—not well enough to safely follow. If they tried, sooner or later they'd wander out of the channel and hit the reef.

This was a major setback. They had expected to keep moving 24 hours a day and Susan had counted on that in her planning. This unpleasant surprise *doubled* the time it would take—time they couldn't afford to lose. Now they had to stop before sunset every day, anchor and wait for daylight. It was like driving a car without headlights—you could drive fast during the day but had to stop every evening before sunset. Normally that wouldn't be a problem—and they'd enjoy the little sandy islands and a quiet dinner at anchor each evening— but they were in a race against the beginning of the hurricane season and had counted on moving 24 hours a day.

It would now take them a lot longer to get out of the hurricane belt and they knew this delay could have serious consequences further on. Around four that afternoon they had to stop and anchor. It was too early to stop but Susan said they couldn't get to the next safe anchorage before dark so they had no choice. After dinner and a swim, they called a "war conference".

"It's still over 500 miles to Cape York at the top of Australia," Susan said. "We may be able to go only 8 hours some days—depending on where the anchorages are. We sure can't be caught out in the dark, so some days we may have to stop early, like today. I think we'd better be realistic and count on an average of only 50 miles a day. That will take us ten days to get to Cape York. That'll make it around Dec. 10—more or less. After that we've still got to make it past Darwin which is another 800 or so miles. With these light winds that's maybe another ten days, moving 24 hours a day. Altogether that's 20 days to get to Darwin and we're still in the hurricane belt all the way. Look what happened to Darwin when *Cyclone Tracy* hit in December. The city was blown away."

She summed it up by saying, *"we're cutting it pretty close."* The mood on *ESCAPEE* was somber as everyone took all this in.

The Australian weather radio was already talking about the hurricane season. Even when they reported, "no tropical cyclone activity" it made their sense of vulnerability more real. *"Let's push on,"* Alan said, " *do the best we can and remember, the first hurricanes usually don't hit until January or even February."* Everyone agreed that was the best plan but it didn't help much when a big Australian cruising boat shot past them the next day and the guy shouted, *"better get a move on".* He had radar and could go day and night. They couldn't.

The days developed a rigid pattern—totally unlike the normal, casual and unstructured days they were used to on *ESCAPEE.* They were up and had breakfast before dawn and left at first light. If the winds were too light they motored—determined to keep their speed up. Around two each afternoon

Susan fixed their position and identified possible anchorages for the night. Everyone hoped they could anchor around dusk but sometimes the choice was between stopping at four—too early— or around eight—too late.

What Alan appreciated about these women was they were smart enough to know they needed to hurry but mature enough to keep cool and relaxed about it. As Susan said, *"ninety-five percent of the things people worry about never happens, so why worry?"* While everyone understood they needed to keep moving no one was overly concerned. *ESCAPEE was still a relaxed, happy boat and a "clothes-free zone."*

After stopping each day they unwound by going swimming and explored the little islands they had sought shelter behind. Some of the islands were large and were well worth exploring. Everyone fell in love with those little anchorages and if it hadn't been for the time of year, they would have taken two or three months to wander through this magical water-land behind the Great Barrier Reef.

Each night they lost themselves in the magic of the place. After a swim and dinner, the stars put on a show like nothing they'd ever seen—*not even in Fiji*. Some nights the skies were full of "shooting stars" streaking across the heavens in an incredible celestial 4th of July show.

They sat for hours in the cool cockpit or on the sandy beach each night after dinner looking at the heavenly light-show. From time to time as they sat watching the show above them, someone would nudge Alan and they'd slip down below and close the cabin door. One of the two left in the cockpit reached over and absent-mindedly put Mr. Pavarotti and his friends back to work. It had now become so familiar and routine that no one thought anything about it. It was just something natural happening—like those marvelous shooting stars and star-filled sky.

After one all-day run, the sun began to set and the little island where they planned to anchor was still not in sight. Sigrid revved up the engine to the maximum and they sped through the channel. They'd made less speed than they thought that day and it didn't look like they were going to make it before dark.

"*What if we don't get there in time, Alan?*" Carole asked, "and get caught out here in the dark?" Sigrid looked over. She wanted to hear the answer to that one, too.

"We don't really have a choice. We can't keep moving in the dark so we'll have to anchor right here in the middle of the shipping channel and watch out for ships," Alan said. "I don't want to do it if we can help it—*it's like parking all night in the middle of a freeway with your lights off.*"

Carole finally spotted that little island which was their safe refuge for the night—but it seemed to be getting no closer. Finally they were in the channel off to the side of the island when the sun disappeared. Susan was sitting up high on the spreader trying to get a better view.

"*Do we go for it or not, Susan?*" Alan called out.

"*I can't see it. Too dark. It's your choice, Alan,*" she called out.

"*OK, we're going for it,*" Alan said, "*hang on in case we hit something.*"

Susan hugged the mast with both arms as Sigrid steered *ESCAPEE* very slowly towards the dark mound which was the little island. Carole stood with Alan on the bow, watching as best they could in pitch darkness. They both expected to hear a crunching noise at any moment, but they made it and soon dropped the anchor in the sheltered water behind the island. Susan climbed down and they all had a cold beer.

"*I don't want to try that again,*" Carole said and Sigrid shook her head in vigorous agreement. It was sheer luck which got them to the safe anchorage—*and at sea you don't count on luck.* A lot of boats—and a lot of lives—have been lost counting on luck.

The next day an Australian coastal "spotter plane" flew low over *ESCAPEE* and everyone waved to them. When they saw the girls, the pilots circled for another low altitude run. The girls stayed put and waved back. This part of Australia is *so remote, so empty and so far from anywhere* the authorities send a spotter plane over every day to keep an eye on the huge, remote region. *In many ways this area is far more remote and isolated than even the famed "outback" of Australia.* The aircraft were there to keep an eye on boats making this passage, watch for any illegal activity and to be available in case of an emergency in this distant frontier.

Alan went down to the short-range VHF radio and switched it to channel 16. *"Hello ESCAPEE"* a voice came on and identified themselves. *"Nice view"* the pilot said, seeing the girls in the cockpit . *"Everything OK?"*

"Yes, we're just heading north and it's too hot to wear anything. Hope you don't mind."

"Are you kidding?" the pilot came back.

"OK," the pilot said, all business now, "this is the middle of nowhere, so we'll be by daily to keep an eye on you."

"Thanks." Alan said. "And thanks for the visit"

"Thank you. As I said, great view," and he zoomed off.

Late the next afternoon, they were back again, flying by low and slowly while everyone was stretching their legs on the sandy beach.

"Everything still OK?" the pilot asked.

" *Just great,*" Alan replied.

The plane came by faithfully every day—circling slowly and at low altitude. It was their duty, of course and the girls waved to them. Usually *ESCAPEE* was still underway and she was still a *clothes-free-zone.*

A few days later they had already anchored and were swimming when the plane flew over. Alan grabbed the hand-held radio and heard the pilot say, *"you'd better get all your swimming in now. As you move further north, you might want to stay out of the water.* There's lots of saltwater crocodiles and poisonous sea snakes where you're heading—lots of nasty sharks, too. If I were you, I'd swim now, but stay out of the water after a few days. *You can't believe the weird sea life in the waters where you're headed."*

"Thanks again." Alan said and they flew on.

Alan told the girls what the pilot had said about snakes and crocodiles—and from that moment, no one would go in the water. And for good reason. The extreme northern part of Australia is the hot, tropical home to sea creatures no one would ever believe if you didn't see them. A few days later they could see hundreds of the poisonous sea snakes in the translucent water of the small breaking waves. *They were everywhere.* Alan started putting a split plastic plate over the anchor chain as a barrier, just to make sure nothing crawled up the chain. It probably wasn't necessary but it made everyone feel better.

As the channel moved close to the land and rivers the huge 20–25 foot-long salt-water crocodiles were a real danger. One high-tech racing sailboat with an open stern anchored for the night. The next morning the crew stepped out into the cockpit and on top of a sleeping salt-water crocodile which had crawled up through the open stern during the night. After they finally got it off, they got on the radio and warned everyone.

One large, aggressive fish in this area has huge jaws and only two teeth—one on the top and one on the bottom. They look perfectly designed for snapping off the toes of anyone they caught swimming or wading in the ocean. *And that's exactly what they do.* A picture of this big, aggressive toe-removing fish appeared on the cover of a guidebook for the area. A photographer was able to take the picture when the aggressive fish chased a swimmer all the way up onto the beach and became stranded.

The deadly box jellyfish up here were very poisonous and almost impossible to see and avoid. There were even poisonous sea shells which, if stepped on, would ruin your whole day—*or your whole life*. Workers at a seafood plant in Cairns— in the far north—were filleting a huge codfish for the fish market and found a man's head inside. Apparently a fisherman was lost overboard and his head somehow ended up in the huge fish's stomach.

That's the kind of place this far-northern part of Australia is.

One day, as they watched the poisonous sea snakes in the breaking waves, Alan said, "I read somewhere that one of those snakes crawled up through the toilet discharge hole in the bottom of a boat. The guy opened the toilet seat cover and there was the head of one of these snakes, staring right at him—at least that's what the article said. *Can you imagine his shock over that?*"

Susan sure could! Carole and Sigrid soon forgot all about it, but not Susan. She imagined the head of a snake looking at her when she lifted the lid, or *worse*, coming up to bite her when she was sitting on the stool. No way was she going to sit on that seat and she was soon in such anguish Alan was really alarmed.

"Susan, what is it? You look like you're in pain."

"*I am*," she almost shouted. "I've got to go to the bathroom bad."

Alan was confused. "*Just go to the head, Susan. Use* the head." "*I can't! Not with those snakes.*"

Alan then got it. *Damn, he wished he hadn't told that story.*

"Susan, I don't even know if that story is true. But for us, there's no way anything—much less a snake—could come up through the closed valve in the head. I'll go right now and make sure nothing's hiding in there and we'll keep the valve closed from now on, until the moment we're actually flushing it."

"*Hurry Alan, do it now!* I got to go real bad," the poor girl said, leaning over and clutching her tummy.

As they neared the very top of Australia, Alan said, "I've never felt *so far away* from anywhere in my whole life—not even in the middle of the Pacific." Sigrid had the same, eerie feeling. This far-north tip of Australia has an unreal *end-of-the-world* atmosphere. Maybe it's the special planes they sent out to check on you, since you are so far from anywhere. Maybe it's the extremely weird and dangerous sea-life all around them—but it's a real feeling.

These were not the happy blue, tropical waters they had swam and played in during the last few months. These were waters that bred the most unimaginable and deadly sea-life on earth. That and the extreme remoteness made everyone on *ESCAPEE* felt they were now at "*the end of the earth.*"

ESCAPEE rounded Cape York on the 11th day out of Townsville and stopped briefly at Thursday Island to get supplies and load up with diesel. The crew went into a dark bar to have a cold drink and get out of the heat and humidity. As they sat on their bar stools they heard a voice coming from out of the darkness, "*G'day mate. You made it. Good on you.*" It was the voice of none other than *Crocodile Dundee*—right next to them. They all looked over expecting to see Paul Hogan, the Australian movie actor. Instead, they saw a man who was, as Carole said later, "*the ugliest human being on earth.*"

The man had a huge, grotesque head—almost a perfect oval—but everything within that circle was seemingly deformed, contorted and misshapen. In the middle of that twisted, seemingly deformed face, were eyes which were all kindness and gentleness. He was a native of Thursday Island, he said, and was half Aboriginal—the prehistoric natives of Australia—and half New Guinea tribesman. Aboriginals are thought to be the oldest, continuously existing civilization on earth. Two of the most primitive peoples on earth met on these islands between Australia and New Guinea before recorded history—*and he was the result.*

Everyone was fascinated and insisted on buying the man a soft drink. They moved over to a table and talked with him for almost an hour. He told them about his life, his family and their traditions and they told him of their voyage and where they were going. He was simply the kindest, most gentle man any of them had ever met. Afterwards, Carole said, *"I've just met the ugliest person on earth who also happens to be the sweetest person on earth."*

As they got up to leave, the man said, *"my people will remember your voyage in our prayers. Go in God's hands."*

As they left, Carole said, *"beauty sure isn't skin deep, is it?"* In the days and events ahead they would all remember the man's parting words.

They bought some treats—ice cream and vegetables flown in from "down below" in Australia—and Alan and Sigrid filled the fuel tank with diesel from the extra plastic fuel jugs they carried on deck for this long trip. They left Thursday Island with full fuel tanks and extra jugs of diesel lashed down on deck. This late in the year they might not have enough winds—and they needed to keep moving.

The good thing about the route over the top of Australia to Darwin was they could go day and night—24 hours a day. *The bad thing* was the trade-winds seemed to be dying out so they'd have to motor and keep going. That meant it would be hot and noisy down below. They all pitched in and rigged up the big sun-awning to cover the entire cockpit and even some of the deck to give them shade throughout the day. It would be blown away in real trade-winds but these winds were light. As they moved westwards across the top of Australia it rained a lot and they soaped up and had rain-shower baths every day, luxuriating in the unlimited fresh water.

Life on deck settled down. They went down into the hot, noisy cabin only long enough to go to the head or get the food and drinks for the breakfasts, lunches and dinners they had in the cockpit under the big sun awning. As usual no one bothered with clothes—the sun awning kept the sun away from them so there was no need to cover up for protection. They ate, slept, showered and lived on deck under the awning as *ESCAPEE* motored towards Darwin in calm seas.

Back at Thursday Island, Sigrid had stayed behind to help Alan fill the diesel tanks while Susan and Carole were shopping. After they'd finished, they scrubbed the diesel off each other's hands and one thing led to another. Sigrid put the mattress on the floor and with the fans going full blast they made love. *Alan almost died of a heat stroke.* "*Gimme five*," he said to Sigrid afterwards. She laughed and gave him a "high-five".

Alan checked the weather twice daily. He also listened to a weather forecast put out by Paul, a sailor who was spending a few months in an Australian marina while passing through on a round-the-world voyage. He was a self-taught weather expert and with lots of time on his hands he prepared special weather reports for sailing vessels underway at sea. Weather was his hobby and passion. He understood the special needs of slow-moving sailing vessels at sea and broadcast his weather reports to them daily on the long-distance SSB radio.

Paul spent many hours a day gathering all the weather information possible and prepared a separate, *individual* weather report for each sailing vessel which requested his service. These individual reports took hours to produce but were far more valuable to those at sea than the generalized weather reports put out by the government.

On the fourth day out they were about 500 miles on the way to Darwin with another 300 to go. Alan had listened to Paul's broadcasts from time to time and thought it was now time to ask him to prepare one of his daily weather forecasts for them. He listened to Paul's broadcast at 8 AM the next day and introduced himself and *ESCAPEE*. "*We left Thursday Island 5 days ago for Darwin and have about 300 miles to go*," Alan said. "*Four on board. What's the weather look like for us?*"

Paul took a minute to look it up and said there would be thunderstorms and lots of rain but nothing to be concerned about. Alan thanked him and said he would check with him daily at the same time.

The next day, as soon as Alan checked in with Paul by radio, Paul said, "*I've been trying to contact you Alan. A nasty tropical depression is forming behind you in the Arafura Sea between Australia and New Guinea—about where you've come from. It's tracking west, just like you and is going to catch up and slam you. It's already strong but it's getting stronger by the hour, feeding on all that warm water up there. It could turn out to miss you altogether, but I don't like the looks of it. It could become a full tropical storm in no time at all. We've sure got to watch it. Check with me at 8 in the morning and again at 4 in the afternoon—twice a day—while this thing is around.*"

"*Thanks Paul*," Alan said, "thanks a million. We'll keep on trucking as fast as we can."

"*You do that*," Paul said.

Alan told the girls about his talk with Paul since they couldn't hear the radio, which was down in the hot, noisy cabin. "*What do we do?*" Carole asked.

"*We just sit tight, keep moving and see what develops.*" *ESCAPEE'S* maximum speed was about 5 miles per hour and the storm was heading towards them at a much faster speed. The next morning at eight, Paul got right to the point, "*it's become dangerous, Alan. The barometric pressure's falling fast and it's started a rotation.* It could be the beginnings of a tropical storm. It's feeding on all that warm water up there, as I said, and getting stronger. It's going to get a lot worse and could even be a full hurricane—or cyclone as it's called here—by tomorrow."

"*Which way's it headed?*" Alan asked.

"*It's coming right at you, Alan. It's following your westerly track and is going to catch up to you.* We sure gotta watch this. Can't afford to make any mistakes on this one."

"*But it's early,*" Susan said as they talked it over in the cockpit.

"*Unfortunately, hurricanes don't go strictly by the calendar, Susan.* Any time the seawater's very warm—I think it's 79 degrees Fahrenheit or something like that—hurricanes can get started. They feed on all that warm water." Each took the news very well, Alan thought and it was Carole who spoke for them and asked, "*OK, what do we do to get ready for this?*"

"*Well, first we keep moving as fast as we can. We can't out run it, of course, but we can keep moving.* Next we make a plan in case the damned thing hits us. We get ready. *Inside*, we make up sandwiches, prepare food and hot coffee in advance. We put away anything that can move or fly around if we're rolled upside down. A lot of people have been hurt by stuff flying around *inside* the cabin. So we put everything away and seal up all the cupboards and floor hatches.

"*Outside*—that's where most of the work is. We keep this sun awning up as long as we can. In the meantime, we get the storm sail ready. Sigrid, you and I will go ahead and get it out of the bag and hooked onto the mast. Carole, when the time comes, take all the scoop-ventilators off the deck and screw the deck plates into the holes. If this thing hits us we can't afford to get any water inside the cabin. You know the small hole where the anchor chain goes through the deck into its locker below? Stuff that hole tightly with rags. A lot of water can get in there.

"We'll go ahead and remove the folding door into the cabin and slip in the storm door." The storm door was a one-piece, solid quarter-inch teak board which slipped into a groove, replacing the lighter folding door used from day to day. *"Susan, plot our position and mark all shallows that might be on our course. We've got to stay away from them. Waves really go crazy over shallow water*—we're in shallow enough water here in the Arafura sea, as it is. We need to stay in the deepest water possible. We'll deflate the dinghy and put it away or it'll take off flying with the first blast of wind. That's enough planning for now. We're not going to jump the gun. *This thing may curve away from us yet."*

At four Alan spoke to Paul again. There had been no change from the morning—*it was still heading right at them.* The next morning at eight Paul didn't waste any time. *"Alan it looks like the first stages of an early-season hurricane.* As I said before, it's getting stronger by the hour. They haven't officially called it a cyclone or given it a name yet but it's packing a dangerous punch. *It's a big one and you're going to get slammed whichever way it goes.*

"This is the same track Cyclone Tracy took and the exact same time of year. A lot of people died in that one. It may still swing southwest and move over land before it gets to you and blow itself out—most of these early-season ones do. But on the other hand, *it may keep heading right at you, getting stronger over all that warm water. If it does it's going to catch you and hit you hard. Real hard. If I were you, I'd forget Darwin and turn north towards Indonesia to try to get out of its track. And I'd do it now."*

"OK Paul. Got it. Let's keep on with our radio schedule. I really need to know."

"I'm right here with you until this thing is over."

"Thanks Paul—a million thanks."

Alan explained what was happening and they changed course and headed north—away from Australia towards Indonesia. Alan said, *"there's no way we can outrun it or escape it, but we've got to get as far away from its track as we can."*

Sigrid deflated the dinghy and tied it down. Carole took off the big scoop ventilators and screwed the steel plates into the holes in the deck. Sigrid and Alan hooked the storm sail on, ready to hoist up the mast. It was very small, made of the heaviest sailcloth and was *triple-stitched*—designed to survive the winds of a hurricane. They wrapped multiple lines around the furled sails so they couldn't blow loose. They took down the sun awning and put it away. They replaced the light folding door, with the one-piece, quarter-inch thick storm door and Carole started making sandwiches and coffee. Susan was bent over her charts. Everybody worked hard and almost wordlessly for an hour or two.

None of them—including Sigrid and Alan—had ever gone through a hurricane in a small vessel at sea. Not too many people have—and many of those who did never came back.

"Sigrid," Alan called out, *"you've had more experience in storms than I have. Have we missed anything?"*

" No, Ellen. Ve go nort fast."

The skies in the east started to darken with heavy clouds and *ESCAPEE* began to be thrown around by big waves coming in. There were no winds yet but those waves were being driven by very fierce winds further away. The waves were already here and the winds wouldn't be far behind. The crew of *ESCAPEE* had done everything they could do.

"OK," Alan said, *"ESCAPEE is ready. Now, about us—* two of us on will be deck at all times—no more. The other two stay below. Put the mattress on the floor and stay on it as much as you can and don't move around unless you have to. You could

really be injured. Keep the storm door sealed tightly. We can't afford to have any water getting down below. You won't be able to see or hear us but we'll be up on deck. We're going to be OK—this is a strong boat. Look at it this way—we're going to be like an empty bottle with a cork in it. You throw an empty bottle with a cork in it into a stormy sea and it'll bounce around and be thrown every which way, *but after the storm it'll still be afloat. We'll be thrown around a lot but that storm door is our 'cork'. We keep it closed and keep water from getting inside and we're going to be OK,*" Alan said and Sigrid shook her head in agreement. Carole and Susan felt better about that.

"As I said, *ESCAPEE'S* a strong boat. We don't have any windows to break, just those small ports. The ventilators are off and their holes are plugged and so is the hole for the anchor chain. *That door is the only way water can get in.*"

The sky now had an evil, sinister look to it as the clouds darkened and the sun was just a weak, round shape—and then it was gone. At 4 PM Alan talked to Paul who said "*it's going to hit you anytime now.* They still haven't made it an official, named cyclone yet but it's very dangerous Alan, especially in that shallow water you're in. There's still a chance it may curve south or southwesterly and just brush you but it's going to be quite a brush. It's awfully shallow up there where you are in the Arafura Sea and those waves are going to be big and square— like boxcars—*huge boxcars.*

"*This is a bad one, Alan. Get as far north as you can— as fast as you can.*"

Sigrid continued north at full engine power and everyone got their harnesses on. "*Ellen*" Sigrid called out, "*those diesel jugs. Zey must go!*" Sigrid was right—*how the hell did he miss that?* Those heavy plastic jugs full of diesel lashed down on deck had to be cut loose now or could get loose during the storm and do a lot of damage or break open and spill foul-smelling, slippery diesel fuel all over them. Sigrid and Alan made sure the lids were tight so no diesel could escape and threw the jugs overboard. They didn't feel good about doing it but those jugs would be far too dangerous when those heavy seas starting sweeping across the top of *ESCAPEE*.

"OK, everyone eat something, *hungry or not*," Alan said. "We don't know how long it'll be before we can eat again." Sigrid had hoisted the small, extremely tough storm-sail on the mast even though there was no wind yet. When the winds came, it would be too late. Compared to *ESCAPEE'S* normal sail, it was so small it was like a tiny handkerchief—*but even that might be too much sail for those winds heading towards them.*

Alan and Susan poured anxiously over the chart. "Draw our course from our position" he said. "See if they're any sand banks or shallows ahead of us. *We've got to avoid those—we'd never survive the waves breaking over them.* We need the deepest water possible." Susan gave them the course towards Aru Island in Indonesian waters. It was northwest, away from the storm track and was free of any extreme shallows. "OK, that's what we steer," Alan said, "*if we can. The storm will dictate that.*" They were now as prepared as anyone can be.

There was nothing to do now but wait.

Both Alan and Sigrid knew it was very likely that *ESCAPEE* would be rolled-over and capsized in those "square waves" Paul had said was heading towards them. In the open ocean—such as the Pacific or Atlantic—the waves can be very high *but their crests are far apart*. They're called "long" waves with a *long* distance—or "period"—between the crests. If a boat like *ESCAPEE* is capsized it has time to recover and stabilize *before* that next wave hits.

Here in the shallow Arafura Sea those "square" box-car-like waves would be *vertical walls of water*—and they would be very close to each other. These are called "short" waves, because there's only a *short distance* or "period" from one wave top to another. If *ESCAPEE* was rolled-over here, there most likely wouldn't be enough time to recover before the next "wall" hit them. A *"short" 25- foot high wave here in this shallow sea would be far more dangerous than a "long" 75- foot high wave on the deep, open ocean.*

Waves themselves are most dangerous when they "break"—when they lose their stability and tons of water crash down with destructive power. Short, steep waves like those heading at *ESCAPEE* break *much more often* than long ocean waves with their very broad bases. The short, narrow base *of* these "short" waves can't support their height. *They quickly become unstable and tons of water collapse—often with devastating results*. Those were the waves *ESCAPEE* was going to have to survive that night.

"Boxcars" was a good word for them—*25-foot high, square-sided boxcars*. Worst of all they would be *breaking waves*—each with tons of plunging, destructive water.

ESCAPEE had a few things going for it that might help them survive. She had what marine architects call "safe numbers". She weighed *27,000* pounds, with *10,000* pounds of that being lead deep in the keel—*6 feet under the water*. The deep keel with that 10,000 pounds of lead down below was designed to act like a *pendulum* to bring them back upright if they were rolled upside-down. She was designed to be *self-righting*—that is, come back upright by herself if capsized.

That and the very small windows called "ports" made *ESCAPEE* actually *safer* in a storm than a large fishing boat *twice* its size. Unlike a fishing boat, she had no big windows to break, no big "deck-house" to be smashed *and* she was self-righting. If they capsized they would come back upright—*if* those walls of water close to each other would let them. Both Alan and Sigrid knew that was a very big *"if"*.

However, all this—the numbers, those small ports, the self-righting ability—meant nothing if water got inside the boat. If water got in everything would change instantly *for the worse*.

The first water getting in would weigh *ESCAPEE* down and make her sit lower in the water, become sluggish and respond to the seas more slowly—*allowing even more water to get inside.* This deadly cycle would be repeated until she went down. Those 10,000 pounds of lead—which were designed to save their lives by bringing them back upright in a capsize—*would take them straight to the bottom.* Alan and Sigrid knew they had to keep water out of *ESCAPEE. They had to keep the cork in the bottle.*

About mid-night the wall of wind hit and was instantly screaming through the rigging. Sigrid and Alan were at the wheel, safety harnesses clipped on and dressed in heavy rain gear. The noise was terrifying. The huge boxcar waves Paul had predicted began to break and crash into the stern and over the top of *ESCAPEE*, throwing her around violently. It was all Alan and Sigrid could do to steer *ESCAPEE* down-wind, trying to take the huge, steep waves on the stern. They "ran before" the waves— going in the same direction—trying to lessen their impact.

Time and again those steep, vertical walls of water broke over them from behind. The weight of the resulting "waterfalls" repeatedly knocked Alan and Sigrid off their feet and the torrent of raging water sweeping across the boat swept them to the end of their safety harnesses. Each time, they picked themselves up and fought the winds and driving horizontal rain to get back to the wheel. They were now fighting to survive what's called a "*survival storm*".

There are generally *three stages* in a storm.

During the first stage, vessels batten the hatches and try to keep moving more or less on the same course while minimizing damage.

When *that* becomes too dangerous, they adjust their courses and speed to the seas—or even stop all forward momentum—just trying to "hold their position" with minimum damage.

During the final and *"survival stage,"* the course and destination are completely abandoned—and the vessel fights for its life. Survival is their only objective. They're not trying to make a course or *"hold"* their position—*their only goal now is to survive.*

This storm had skipped stages one and two and *gone straight to a survival storm* for *ESCAPEE. She was fighting for her life that night.* Sigrid and Alan were standing side by side but the screaming winds and crashing seas were so deafening they couldn't hear one another shouting at the top of their voices. Down below Carole and Susan lay next to each other on the mattress, listening to the waves crashing over *ESCAPEE* and worrying about Alan and Sigrid up there in all that fury. There was no way they could "rest"—just stay low and not be injured by being thrown around inside.

Alan had already decided he was going to have to take the next watch with Carole—it was just too much for Susan. Sigrid would take a short break and then relieve him. *"Rest"* seemed to be a word which belonged to another world—a world no longer theirs. As Carole and Susan lay there looking at one another in fear, one "boxcar" wave after another crashed onto *ESCAPEE* and swept *completely across* her deck.

At first, they wondered if Alan and Sigrid were OK. *Soon, they wondered if they were even still on board.*

Another boxcar wave broke and the tons of water swept across the full length of the boat, completely burying *ESCAPEE* and making her look like a submarine. For a few moments the only part of the boat not covered by the wild, crashing seas was the mast—*which now seemingly came straight up out of the sea.* The deck was submerged and under water until that wave passed—then another hit and broke directly on top of Sigrid and Alan. They were once again instantly knocked off their feet and swept in the raging torrent of waters to the end of their safety harnesses and brought to a halt with a jerk. How long would those safety harnesses take that kind of strain before they broke?

When they picked themselves up, Alan shouted and motioned to Sigrid. She was standing next to him but the shrieking winds and crashing waves made it impossible for Sigrid to hear him. Only by hand gestures and reading his lips, could Sigrid make out what he was saying—*"GO, NOW!"* He knew that one of those huge waves sweeping across the entire length of *ESCAPEE* would soon sweep them both overboard—*safety harness and all.*

"NO," she said, mouthing the word and shaking her head sideways. She didn't want to leave him up there alone.

"GO!" Alan shouted fiercely over the screaming wind at the top of his voice. *"I---COME---NEXT,"* he shouted slowly and with hand gestures to help her understand.

The incredibly tough, triple-stitched storm sail—*made for storms*—started to tear at a seam. The tear was slow at first but then, under the incredible pressure of the violent winds the sail burst at the seams and flailed itself madly until there was nothing left of it but ribbons. Those ribbons then began flapping madly in the wind, cracking and snapping like ten thousand rifle shots, adding to the horrendous noise of the shrieking wind and crashing seas.

Sigrid climbed down into the safety of the cabin and a huge torrent of water—spray and rain—followed her down, soaking the charts, radio and everything below. Alan was now alone on deck. *He had never imagined anything this bad.* Sometimes in the darkness he could see the white breaking water on the wave-tops and they were as high as the spreaders— halfway up the mast. *Time and again, the deck of ESCAPEE was buried completely underwater* from those breaking waves, looking just like a submarine beginning its dive.

A few moments later another boxcar wave coming from out of the darkness broke over the top of *ESCAPEE* and threw Alan violently sideways and off his feet. The resulting stream of raging water swept him to the end of the safety harness, which once again jerked him to a halt just before he was swept overboard. His head smashed into the side of the cockpit and blood streamed from his scalp, down his forehead and into his eyes.

That wave had scored a *direct hit* on the storm door—which was all that kept the sea from filling *ESCAPEE* with water—and cracked it. Alan looked in horror at the huge crack in the door—all the way from top to bottom. One more direct hit would break it in two vertical pieces and there would be *nothing* to stop the tons of water sweeping across *ESCAPEE'S deck* from pouring down below. *ESCAPEE* would quickly fill with water and plunge straight to the bottom.

Alan struggled back to his feet and wiped the mixture of blasting rain and blood from his eyes, trying to see.

They were losing it he knew they were losing it.

He had to do something *before* the next wave smashed that fragile door and those tons of water crashing across the deck poured down below. *He had to protect that cracked door from those waves coming over the back of the boat*. The only way was to *turn the boat around* and take the huge, battering waves over the front, instead of the back. The door wouldn't get a direct hit if the waves came over the front or side. Spray would hit it, but it wouldn't have another *direct* hit. He wiped the rain and blood out of his eyes and tried to look back to see a "gap" between the huge waves so he could turn *ESCAPEE* around.

Turning a boat around in the middle of horrendous waves like these is a very dangerous maneuver—*one of the most dangerous maneuvers at sea*. You only try it in the most extreme situation and then you *wait until you see a gap between the on-rushing waves*. You have to get completely turned around *before* the next wave hits. *You have to*.

If the vessel doesn't make it all the way around *before* the next wave hits it's often rolled over—or a smaller vessel like *ESCAPEE* can be simply *"flipped" upside down—like a pancake*. Alan needed to find a gap between the waves to get safely around but couldn't even look back to see what was coming—the blasting rain and spray, mixed with the blood blinded him and it was pitch black.

He couldn't see—and he couldn't wait.

He'd have to do it by "feel" alone—just after the next wave hit. Alan had no choice. He *had* to get *ESCAPEE* turned around and facing into those huge, square seas or the next wave to hit that shattered door would fill the boat and they'd sink like a rock. He wiped the rain and blood from his eyes, started the engine—and waited until the next wave swept over *ESCAPEE*. *It was now or never.*

He shoved the engine throttle into full power, turned the wheel as far as it would go, held it hard against its stop and started the *all or nothing* turn. To Alan, it was agonizingly, eternally slow.

ESCAPEE was now at its most vulnerable and he knew if one of those waves flipped or rolled them during the turn it would be all over. While they were upside-down, the water pressure would shatter that damaged door, the boat would quickly fill with seawater *and they'd go straight down—still in the upside-down position.* He knew he'd be washed overboard during the rollover but *ESCAPEE* would become the watery tomb for the girls, *plunging straight to the bottom with them trapped inside.*

Alan finished the turn just as the next wave hit with an enormous crash, *burying the entire deck under the breaking wave once again—but this time from the front*—not the back. Now she would take the waves from the bow or most likely from the side. She would roll heavily but since they were now stopped dead in the water, the boat would "give" and yield unresistingly to the battering blows of the seas. They could still capsize but it was less likely now—*and nothing could be done about that.*

After Alan completed the turn into those giant waves, he locked the wheel, moved the sliding hatch back, climbed over the shattered storm door and plunged down below into the cabin. Large amounts of salt water, rain and spray came down with him. He couldn't do any more up there.   The girls saw blood streaming from his forehead, across his face and onto his chest. It looked like his entire face had been smashed in. *"Lie down!"* Carole barked. *"Get his wet clothes off,"* and he felt hands wiping the blood from his eye and pulling the wet clothes off. Carole wiped the blood out of his eye and off his face and found the cut, just above the forehead. It was a nasty cut and he'd need lots of stitches but they were relieved to see it wasn't as bad as it looked at first. Carole held Alan and pressed the cloth against the cut.

"ESCAPEE has to take care of us now," he said. *"We can't do any more."*

The four of them huddled together on the floor while the seas threw *ESCAPEE* around like a little toy—a little toy that might be smashed or rolled over at any minute. What would have been a very uncomfortable *but survivable* 360-degree rollover would now be fatal. One thing was for sure—while they were upside-down, the cracked door would burst open from the water pressure, tons of water would rush in and they'd plunge straight to the bottom—upside down and trapped inside.

Several times, *ESCAPEE started* to capsize—and everyone was thrown onto the wall of the cabin which became the "floor". They lay jumbled together on the wall bookcase— waiting to go the rest of the way over but each time *ESCAPEE* was knocked over on her side they slowly came back upright.

About 15 minutes later what must have been a gigantic wave lifted *ESCAPEE* up and *flipped the 27,000 pound boat onto its side—as easily as a pancake is flipped.* When she landed on her side, Alan and Sigrid could both feel the fatal 360-degree "roll-over" beginning. Their four bodies rolled *from the floor, onto the wall and kept going* to *where the wall met the ceiling—and she was still going over.* As their bodies tumbled and rolled, they grabbed at anything in reach to hang onto. *The ceiling was about to become the "floor" and the top of the mast was now buried deep under the water.*

Just a few degrees more—or if another wave hit them while they were lying this far over—and they would capsize, the fractured door would crack, the sea would fill *ESCAPEE—and it would be all over.* As *ESCAPEE* reached the point of going the rest of the way over, those "numbers" took over and she slowly—ever so slowly—started her *self-righting* movement. It had been a *very severe knock-down*—but not a capsize. They had rolled over as far as a boat can go without going the rest of the way

For hours, waves repeatedly crashed over and across *ESCAPEE,* burying her under the plunging, breaking seas and she was often covered with waves from bow to stern. But she took the breaking waves mostly over the side, not from the back. The door was hammered but didn't take another direct hit that night. They repeatedly suffered knock-downs—some very severe—but they never rolled *all* the way over. *That was what saved their lives.* That shattered door held and kept the seas out and the boat floating.

The "cork" stayed in the bottle.

Around six in the morning, Carole awakened Alan who had fallen asleep in her arms. *"I think it's easing off,"* she said. The wind was still shrieking but Carole was right—it was shrieking slightly less than before. *ESCAPEE* was soon rolling wildly—the wind had stopped, but the big leftover waves were still throwing them around. Amazingly the radio was still working in spite of all the salt water which got down below.

At 8 Alan talked to Paul who said, *"it's turned more southerly over land and is weakening. You were far enough north so it only brushed you. That's why you only had a few hours of it.* You're one lucky guy, Alan. Others may not be so lucky. I've got two boats which were caught right in the path of it and they're not responding to my calls. It could be just antenna problems *but I'm afraid they may be gone.*"

"*I'm sorry to hear that,*" Alan said and was glad his own antenna for the vital SSB radio link with Paul was the heavy wire cable—the "backstay"—that held the mast up. He'd only lose that if they lost the mast. Paul came back, "*I'd get out of there and get into Indonesia and out of the cyclone area if I were you, Alan. This is just the start of the season and that was just a brush. You may not be so lucky next time.*"

"*I understand. Thanks more than I can say for your help, Paul. We're on our way.*"

They had been very lucky. Each of them had been badly bruised and banged up from being thrown around down below and Alan had that nasty cut. But amazingly, that was all. They looked at the damage to *ESCAPEE*—the destroyed storm sail, the shattered storm door and the damage at the top of the mast. *Everything on the mast-top was completely gone*—the VHF short-range radio antenna, the navigation lights and all the wind instruments. *Everything up there had been swept away during one of the many times the mast-top was buried deep in the sea. And they had only been 'brushed' by the storm!*

It had been a *very* close call.

By ten the sun was out and the "leftover" waves were beginning to calm down at last. By noon, the trade-winds were back. They weren't strong but *ESCAPEE* could sail without the noise of the engine. Alan and Sigrid cut off the torn remnants of the shattered storm sail, raised the normal mainsail and got them underway. Alan said, "*Susan, give us a course to Bali—distance and more or less when we should arrive*"

Carole started mopping up the salt water and cleaning the horrible mess in the cabin. Everything was soaked with salt-water. She wiped the radio and electronics with a cloth soaked in fresh water to get rid of all the corrosive salt on them and dried them off. By three that afternoon they were sailing along peacefully under a bright sun in total quietness as the trade-winds pushed *ESCAPEE* gently towards Bali.

Only twelve hours ago they had been fighting for their lives. Things change fast at sea—sometimes for the good and sometimes for the bad.

At four Alan talked to Paul again to thank him once more and tell him their route. *"Like I told you, you're a lucky, lucky guy,"* Paul said. *If you hadn't headed north when you did, you would have caught it full-force—you can just imagine what that would have been like*. After it turned over land, it began to weaken, so it never became a named cyclone. We still can't find those two boats we haven't heard from. As I said, they were behind you and were caught right in its path. I hope they've just lost their radio antennas, but I expect the worst. *They had the same storm you had—but for a much longer time. They may be gone."*

"I hope it works out OK for them," Alan said. *"And again, Paul, I don't know how to ever thank you enough."*

"What's it look like, Susan?" Alan asked as she worked over the charts. *"Hey,"* she chirped brightly, *"who wants to spend Christmas in Bali?"*

"I do!" they all shouted at once.

"Well, looks like we can if we keep up this speed. We'll arrive the day before Christmas."

"Christmas in Bali," Carole said quietly.

"After what we've just been through, that would be heaven!"

CHAPTER TEN

RECOVERING IN BALI

Early in the morning of the day before Christmas, *ESCAPEE* entered the twisting channel into the harbor of Bali and anchored. The four of them were physically battered and bruised from the storm and emotionally drained—an after-effect often experienced by those who survive a deadly storm at sea. They badly needed a break.

While the girls straightened the boat up and tried to dry everything out, Alan headed to shore with passports and boat documents—and a good explanation why they had arrived without the necessary visas and permits Indonesia requires. He had planned to get them in Darwin the way most people did, but a little matter of *survival* got in the way. The best explanation he could give the officials was that nasty gash just above his forehead.

Alan's arrival without those papers created a stir and they *could* have been ordered straight back to sea. But this was laid-back Bali, an easygoing international tourist center which wanted visitors. He was directed to a medical office for stitches and told to come back afterwards to make the necessary arrangements. These "arrangements" would be unofficial and off-the-record—as often happens in this part of the world –and were good only for the island of Bali. When they left Bali, they couldn't stop off anywhere else in Indonesia. That was OK with Alan, since all they wanted was just to recuperate on this beautiful island.

"Welcome to Bali" a young guy said when he rowed up to *ESCAPEE* and offered to sell fresh fruit and fish or show them around. *"Welcome to the island everyone loves."*

"Let's get off the boat and stretch our legs," Alan said and everyone was more than ready. He wore a hat and took off the earring—"out of courtesy". They grabbed a taxi to a nearby five-star beach hotel, planning to treat themselves to a long leisurely lunch. On arrival at the opulent hotel they piled out of the taxi and walked straight into one of the most embarrassing, humiliating moments of their lives. They stood in the elegant lobby gaping at the staff in starched white uniforms and guests dressed in super-smart casual—and there they stood, looking like backpackers or scruffy sailors off a storm-tossed boat who *should* have gone to a grubby water-front dive instead of an opulent hotel.

"Alan," Carole whispered, *"we're completely out of place here. Everyone's dressed so well and I'm dressed like this. They're all staring at us."* Susan and Sigrid felt the same— *terrible*. They hadn't been prepared for this and were caught off

guard. Guests and staff were staring at them in disdain—like a bunch of scruffy street people had just crashed an elegant party. They felt humiliated, embarrassed, completely out of place—and they wanted out *fast*. This sudden and surprising humiliation on top of the after-effects of the storm was just too much.

Alan didn't want these women *who had just gone through hell with him* to feel so badly. Something had to be done—*and done quickly*—to bring the crew of *ESCAPEE* up to Bali standards so they'd feel comfortable. While the girls made a hasty retreat back outside to the taxi stand, Alan had an idea. He went to the concierge and after a few minutes, the concierge gave him a name and address and ordered a hotel car. As Alan walked out of the hotel, the Mercedes rolled up and Alan steered the girls to the car.

"*We're going back to the boat, aren't we?*" Carole asked.

" *Maybe—maybe not. Sit tight and you'll see.*"

All three were dying of curiosity but were still worried. "*Alan, we can't go anywhere like this,*" Carole said. "*Let's get back to ESCAPEE, please.*" One humiliation was enough for one day.

"*No vay,* Ellen," Sigrid said "*ve go back ESCAPEE. Ve look like sheiss.*" Alan could just imagine what "sheiss" was.

The hotel car soon pulled up in front of a large tailor shop and Alan said, "*this is it. We're going to get everyone fixed up with the right clothes for Bali. We're going to enjoy our stay here—and it's my treat*"

"Alan, you can't do that. It'll cost a fortune," Carole said.

"*Who's the captain of this wretched-looking bunch?*" he asked jokingly as they followed him out of the car.

They looked at the beautiful, wildly colored Bali silks, the incredible fabrics and the simple but elegant Balinese styles. Susan picked up some beautiful silk material and one of the attendants expertly draped it over her. In a second she was transformed and looked every bit as elegant as any of those women in the hotel who had raised their snooty noses at them.

"*Like it?*" Alan asked.

"*I love it,*" she gushed.

"*How much?*" he asked the lady. The concierge had already told him the price range but he wanted them to all hear it first-hand. She punched a calculator and said," *twenty one US dollars*". They gasped. It was so cheap and so—*elegant.* "*OK, treat's on me. Get yourselves two nice outfits each. That should do us. And I'm going to get a couple of smart, casuals that'll knock your eyes out.*"

Alan and the three girls took over the tailor shop and for the next two hours picked materials, changed minds, chose again and changed their minds again—there was such an abundance of beautiful silks and fabrics to choose from. Eventually all the fabrics had been chosen, the styles selected and they were fully measured. The manager said, "come back tomorrow at five."

"But it's Christmas tomorrow," Susan said.

"*This is Bali*" he replied and smiled, "we'll do a last fitting and make any changes needed."

Alan paid the deposit over the protests of the girls and said again, "*this is my treat.* Now don't go thinking you're anything special of something—*I do this for everyone who survives a hurricane at sea with me. Have for years.*" They laughed.

"*Shoes...we need shoes!*" he exclaimed. The hotel car took them to a shoe store where Balinese leather workers made beautiful shoes for men and women—at those ridiculously low

Balinese prices. Alan treated them to two pairs each to go to with the two outfits.

The next morning they had a "Christmas brunch" under the sun awning in the cockpit and by four they were back at the tailor shop, carrying their new shoes. It was an hour early *but who could wait until five?* Everyone tried on their outfits and one or two were re-adjusted, but by six they were all done. Alan said, *"this is your captain speaking. Go back to the fitting room and change into the one you like best. And put on those new shoes. We're going out for a night on the town."*

The manager called for the hotel car and it arrived and stood by. The girls each stepped out of the changing room and Alan was stunned—*completely stunned.* Was this the motley crew of *ESCAPEE?* Each was radiantly beautiful in the simple, elegant dress of Balinese women and high heels. What an incredible transformation. None of them had felt "dressed up" for many months and Alan, of course, had *never* seen them in clothes like these. He was shocked.

"Ladies, your chariot awaits."

The hotel car drove them up to the entrance of the elegant five-star hotel and for the *second time* in two days they arrived at this same hotel. The first time had been a humiliating disaster. This time, as the doorman opened the car door, three striking women in high heels got out and made an entrance which 'stopped the traffic' in the lobby—the concierge looked up and stared, the staff stopped to look before rushing about their business and tourists stopped and just stood there. Just yesterday these same four scruffy people had walked in, been humiliated and rushed out. Today, *three princesses* and their escort swept in and looked like they owned the place, dazzling everyone. *They felt* so *good—just to be looking good.*

That night they saw a show featuring a Balinese dance group, which left them in awe of its gracefulness and beauty. They dined on the finest seafood and Indonesian "rice table"—

an assortment of 15 small bowls of delicacies. After dinner they went into the bar to listen to a musical group from the Philippines playing a variety of western music and Alan danced with each of the girls. Everyone in the bar tried to figure it all out—one guy with three striking women. You don't see that every day.

Alan spoke to the waiter and a few minutes later the waiter brought a bottle of fine French champagne, opened it and poured four glasses. Alan lifted his glass and said, "I propose a toast—a Christmas toast to the crew of *ESCAPEE*. *You brought us through a storm to this beautiful place. Here's to much more time together. You're beautiful and I love you all. No,*" he corrected himself and told the truth, "*I love you each one--and Merry Christmas.*"

Alan had asked the concierge to suggest something as a special Christmas treat for the girls and he arranged for a hotel car to take them on a night tour of some of the Balinese temples. Some are lit at night and others are even more beautiful when naturally lit by the moonlight. The temples are strikingly beautiful during the day but are transformed into an ethereal, out–of-this-world beauty when they stand silently alone in the night, softly lit by moonlight. Time and again that night, they gasped at the beauty of it all—and standing quietly beside a temple in the moonlight, they could feel a little bit of the soul and special magic of Bali.

Around three in the morning the hotel car took them back to the marina. They climbed into the dinghy and took their shoes off so the high heels wouldn't puncture it and Sigrid, still dressed in her elegant Balinese dress, rowed them back to *ESCAPEE*. As soon as they got on board, Carole said, "*now, we've got a Christmas gift for you.*" Carole and Sigrid each wished him a merry Christmas and gave him a big kiss—a really big one. Then it was Susan's turn. "*Merry Christmas, Alan, You're a nice man,*" Susan said as she started to kiss him.

"*Yeh*" Carol said, waiting until Alan and Susan were kissing, "*and a pretty good lay, too.*" Alan burst out laughing and sputtering. "*Hey that spoiled my kiss with Susan. I demand another.*" And he kissed Susan again. "*OK guys, my head's spinning and it's four in the morning. Tomorrow we start seeing the real Bali.*"

They went to a great New Year's party at the hotel and later went into town to join the revelers—mostly crowds of tourists and some Balinese—celebrating in the streets to welcome in the New Year. They staggered back at dawn and then crashed on *ESCAPEE* and slept most of the next day. With every day that passed, the terrible storm and their narrow escape became more distant in their minds. The next three weeks were divided between seeing the incredible sights of this magical island and just hanging out at the beach hotel.

Alan had arranged with the manager for them to have full use all the hotel facilities—the pool and private beach area— everything. They attracted a lot of stares at poolside because their bikinis and Alan's bathing suit showed up their many bruises from being thrown around during the storm. The hotel guests looked at them—and at Alan—trying to figure it out. Three women, one man—each one very visibly bruised and battered. Alan could see their questions—*what's the story here? Who abused whom? Who did what to whom*? He was just as bruised as they were and he had that big cut across his forehead. It looked as if they had all been in a big fight and Alan had lost. He was very self-conscious about it and wanted to explain to the gawkers about the storm, but gave it up—*how could they possibly understand the life and death battle the four of them had just been through.*

Carole—being Carole—couldn't let it pass and one day when waiters at the pool hovered over them taking their drink orders, she said loudly so everyone could hear, "*now lay off the booze, Alan. You know it makes you violent and I don't want to have to hit you on the head with a bottle again.*"

Alan just shrugged and let it pass—by now he was so used to this kind of thing from Carole he never even said *"give me a break"* any more unless it was something *really* outrageous. *Anyway, why ask for mercy from the truly merciless?*

After the waiters at the pool heard all that, they started giving Alan dirty looks and a wide berth. From then on they were very slow in bringing the drinks he ordered, especially if they were alcoholic drinks.

As the days passed they swam in the pool and on the beach, read and snoozed in the beach chairs and enjoyed the expansive grounds of the hotel. On alternate days, they went out on a full day's sightseeing tour. One day recovering at the hotel—the next, a full day's sightseeing. There was just no end to the beauties of Bali. Almost every evening they dressed up and had dinner at one of the Indonesian restaurants in town and afterwards strolled down the streets crowded with Balinese and tourists. One day Alan had the navigation lights, VHF radio antenna and wind instruments replaced on the top of the mast. *Hopefully, that was the last time the top of that mast would be underwater!*

Bali is one of the most romantic islands in the world and the hotel was full of honeymoon couples from Japan and Australia. Some of that romantic spirit must have rubbed off on the girls. After a day at the beach or by the hotel pool, they usually returned to *ESCAPEE* around five and settled down in the cockpit under the sun awning for a pre-dinner drink. Every so often, someone would nudge Alan and they disappeared down below and closed the cockpit door. The other two in the cockpit put the cassette in, turned the volume up and read or talked under the sun awning. They had bought some new cassettes but everyone had the timing of the *The Three Tenors* down so well by now why start with a new cassette?

These "after-the-pool" romps down below with one of the girls went so smoothly they seemed to Alan to be *suspiciously coordinated.* Alan swore they planned it all in advance and "complained" to Carole that it took the *spontaneity* out of it.

She replied, *"who, us? Do you honestly think that's something we'd do?"*

He sure did. Thank goodness, he thought, for all the sightseeing that took up a lot of their time and energies every other day—he needed the break. On the days they went sightseeing everyone was often too tired to do anything but have a simple dinner, relax in the cockpit and get some rest. Even with all this sightseeing, they were only scratching the surface of Bali's fascinating beauty.

"Alan, I've got to talk to you," Susan said as Alan held her after making love late one afternoon.

"Something's been worrying you Susan. I couldn't help but notice it."

"I've got to call my dad. If I don't talk to him soon, there's going to be some problems. I want to stay with you and the girls—very much. I can always refuse to go back home now. *In fact, I will refuse—it's my life, not his—*but I'd rather not have a big conflict with him if I can avoid it. I've got to talk to him soon or he'll hop a plane and just show up—I know him—and then we'll have a big blow-up for sure."

"Ok," Alan said, *"let's call him. You and I both."*

"You'd do that?" Susan asked. "That'd mean so much. If he talked to you, I might be able to solve this without a showdown. I'll tell him off if I have to but I'd sure rather solve this peacefully."

"That's the best, Susan. No need for a blow-up if we can avoid it. Let's do it tomorrow."

They figured out the time zones and while Carole and Sigrid relaxed around the hotel pool the next day, Alan and Susan placed the call.

"Dad!" Susan said, *"we're in Bali. In Indonesia. Having a great time."* Susan went quiet and looked worried. Alan knew her bossy, domineering father was telling her to get the hell home—*now!*

"I know, daddy. I know. I've stayed months longer, but this is an experience I'll never get to have again the rest of my life...so I want to...."

"Yes, dad, I do. I know all that. But this is my once in a lifetime chance. I need to do it now while I can."

"The vessel? It's a very good vessel. And the captain's one of the best around," she said, glancing at Alan, who rolled his eyes at that one.

"There's four of us on the staff, daddy. Four. Everyone is very nice and I love it. Just a few more months."

Staff? Did she say *staff?*

"The captain? Yes, he's here. Hang on and I'll get him."

"Captain Richards," she called out loudly so her father would be sure to hear, paused and handed Alan the telephone.

"Hello Mr. Alexander, this is Captain Richards," Alan said in the most official, business-like tone he could manage. *"What can I do for you sir? "*

"Of course we enjoy having her with us and on our... staff."

"No, she's been no problem at all." In reality, the brat was a headache sometimes, but he smiled at her.

"My opinion? Well sir, you'd be very proud of your daughter. She's become a first-class navigator and handles all navigation on board—even piloting us through dangerous reefs."

"That's surprises you? Well sir, I've been at sea for longer than I can remember"—was it 11 or 12 months now? He really couldn't remember—*"and I can tell you she's one of the*

finest navigators I've ever seen. I'd trust my vessel with her anytime—and have."

"*Yes sir, your little daughter.* She's on the official crew list as ship's navigator."

"*Yes sir, that's right. Your daughter, Susan.*" Who the hell does he think I'm talking about? Alan wondered.

"*Yes, I understand you find that hard to believe, but I can assure you it's true. You can be very proud of your daughter.*" That was very true and he said it emphatically and with a ringing conviction.

"*No sir, we stay away from rough areas.* We stay in yacht clubs—high class, safe places. We're calling you from a five-star hotel."

"*No sir, she never goes ashore alone—the staff all go together.*"

"*How much longer?*"

"*Well, I think another five months or so.* That would get us to Italy or at least to Greece where she could fly home. And she'll be bringing a certificate from me attesting to her being a fully qualified ocean navigator. You may not know it sir, but your daughter is probably the youngest, practicing navigator in the world. *Wouldn't that impress your friends?* " Alan knew that would appeal to the image-conscious old fart.

"*Yes sir, the certificate will be framed*—ready for you to show everyone. Susan will bring it with her."

"*Yes sir. I'll make her do that*—call you at least once a month. *Yes sir. I will.*"

"*Very nice talking to you too, sir.* I'll put Susan back on the line"—and he handed the phone to Susan.

"*Yes, I will daddy.* Yes...I promise. Thank you daddy. Yes, I could use some more money. I'll fax you where you can send it. Thanks, daddy. Let me talk to mom. She talked to her mother a few minutes and hung up.

She grabbed Alan around the neck and shouted, *"we did it! Oh Alan, thank you!"* And then she started laughing. *"Captain"* Richards—you at sea *'longer than you can remember'*. *Oh, and that certificate—now that was a stroke of genius.* My dad will love to show that around. How'd you come up with all that stuff on the spur of the moment?"

"Hey, I want my Susan happy and here with us—so I did what I had to do. And I'll keep my promise. I'll have some fancy certificate made up when the time comes—gold seals, beautiful calligraphy, the works. I read somewhere it's easy to get that kind of thing made up in Singapore."

"Alan Richards, I love you!" she said, hugging him again.

They went out to give the good news to Sigrid and Carole and Susan ran towards them, saying, *"I'm staying—and no big fight with my dad."* They were really glad to hear that Susan hadn't had to battle it out with her father.

"You should have heard Alan on that phone," Susan said as they settled down on beach chairs.

She lowered her voice as deeply as she could and said, *"Captain Richards here. What can I do for you, sir"*.

They roared and Carole said, *"you old fraud."*

"Yes sir" she continued in that deep voice, *"she's our vessel's navigator. Yes sir, official staff navigator,"* and she cracked up along with the others. *"Yes sir"* she went on, struggling to keep her voice low, *"she'll have a certificate you can show everyone."*

"You know what Alan said?" Susan asked, now in her normal voice. *"He said he'd been at sea longer than he could remember."*

"You really said that?" Carole asked.

"Yes, and it's true, too. I can't remember off the top of my head if it's been 11 or 12 months—it's one or the other. And he called me Captain Richards."

"Don't get so full of yourself," Carole shot back. *"You called yourself captain. He just repeated it.* He pictured a uniform and gold stripes—the whole nine yards." She looked at the girls and said, "if he could've seen this pirate here, he'd send in the marines to rescue his little girl. But seriously Alan, thanks for helping Susan. We'd be lost without her—in more ways than one."

"Ja, sank you Ellen," Sigrid added enthusiastically.

"Ok *Captain* Richards, what's next? I'm not ready to rush back yet, so count me in."

Sigrid nodded her head in agreement. "Ja, me too."

"So, what other little goodies like Bali have you got to show your *staff*, Captain Richards?"

Alan had been thinking about the route for the new year. He'd talked to some tourists at the hotel and to the tourist desk in the hotel and got a lot of information. Everyone's favorites seemed to be Thailand, the Greek Isles and Italy.

After almost a month in Bali, it was time to sail on to Thailand. They would have to go by the main route—Bali to Singapore and then on to Thailand. There were no more hurricanes to worry about—they were now out of the hurricane belt. They'd see Singapore, load up with fuel, get that certificate made up for Susan's father and head on up to Thailand.

The seas should be calm and the breezes light.

It *should* have been a perfect cruise.

CHAPTER ELEVEN

NIGHT ATTACK

ESCAPEE left Bali a little over a month after they arrived. It had been a time of rest and recuperation after the battering by that storm and a time of immersing themselves in the culture of one of the most beautiful and romantic islands on earth. Each was now thinking ahead to Thailand, Greece and Italy—and countless beautiful islands in between

Sigrid steered them out the winding channel entrance and up the east side of Bali. By sunset they had reached the "top" of Bali and turned left to head northwest towards Singapore. They were motoring with the mainsail up because the wind was light. As night fell, Bali put on one last spectacular farewell show for them. Fiery lava was pouring down the seaward side of the dark, brooding volcano and provided their last spectacular view of this fabled island.

Susan had picked the course for Thailand by way of Singapore. As usual, Alan checked her work and as usual approved it without any changes. It was the only practical course for a small boat like theirs with limited fuel and dependent on fair winds. It was about 1,000 miles from Bali to Singapore—a cruise of 8 days or so—and the course passed between the two main Indonesian islands of Java and Sumatra on the left and Borneo on the right. But there were many smaller islands lying directly on their course, especially as they got closer to Singapore and they'd have to pick their way around and through them. The route would be through the Java Sea and then through the South China Sea to Singapore.

There was one problem with this route, though no one on *ESCAPEE* knew it at the time. *It passed through the most dangerous, pirate-infested waters on earth.*

According to the *International Maritime Bureau*, more acts of modern-day piracy take place in the general area where the Java Sea meets the South China Sea *than in any other single area on earth*—and those are the ones with survivors left alive to tell the tale. The *Piracy Reporting Center* in Kuala Lumpur, Malaysia—the main center for coordinating information on attacks by pirates—says piracy in these waters has increased by *forty percent* in the last few years. There are several reasons for this infamous reality.

First, there's the heavy sea traffic which is forced to pass relatively close to the many islands. The pirates can easily reach the ships even in their small boats.

Second—and perhaps most important of all—there's a centuries-old *"culture of piracy"* in this area. Many of the sea-going people of this area have been practicing piracy for generations—even centuries. It's become a traditional and accepted way of life.

Third, there are hundreds of small fishing boats out every night, which make it easy for the pirates to hide among them until they are ready to attack and retreat to afterwards, disguising themselves as honest fishermen.

Fourth, these waters are truly lawless. There is no effective naval or police presence in these waters. These are the "wild west" waters of the world's oceans. One press report on modern-day piracy calls these waters a *"no-mans land"* and says, *"these waters are the last place on earth you are truly alone."*

All this makes these waters a perfect and deadly *hunting ground* for modern-day pirates.

For six days, *ESCAPEE* moved northwesterly up the Java Sea towards the South China Sea, passing through groups of small Indonesian sailing craft, the first commercial, working sailing craft they had met. These sailing craft carry goods and people between Indonesia's 12,000 islands, making it—along with Zanzibar in East Africa—one of the few places left in the world where sailing craft still conduct commercial business.

Many of the smaller vessels have sails sewn together from plastic sacks. *ESCAPEE* passed one sailing vessel whose sails read, *"Gift From The People Of The United States of America"*. The sails were made from the heavy plastic sacks of flour or wheat given as aid from the USA. One day *ESCAPEE* sailed alongside a small, 18-foot boat loaded with a man, his wife and two small children—and huge stacks of bananas and produce. The family and the crew of *ESCAPEE* were waving to each other when a dark squall with high winds hit. The little overloaded boat disappeared in the rain and violence of the squall and everyone on *ESCAPEE* worried about them. When the squall passed there they were, safe and sound. They re-hoisted their sail and sailed off as if nothing had happened.

These people have made their own boats and sailed between Indonesia's islands for centuries.

The crew of *ESCAPEE* need not have worried about the man and his wife and children. *They should have been worrying about their own lives.* No one in Bali warned them of the dangers of this route through Indonesian waters. This shameful subject is largely covered up or denied by Indonesian authorities—they don't want to admit some of their citizens are involved *and they certainly don't want to admit they have no control over their own waters*. In any case, many of the acts of piracy take place in what are legally international waters and shipping channels—*a real "no man's land"*.

The crew of *ESCAPEE* were unaware they were in such highly dangerous waters as they cruised through the moonless night with their green, red and white navigation lights burning brightly—exactly as international rules of navigation require.

Around one-thirty in the morning on the sixth night out, they were somewhere off the southern coast of Sumatra when they heard a powerful motor approaching them at high speed from out of the darkness. Carole and Sigrid were on watch together and heard the speeding boat coming at them but could see nothing—its lights were out. Suddenly, a high-powered *"panga"*—a solid wooden boat about 20 feet in length—shot out of the darkness and pulled alongside *ESCAPEE*.

Three of the four men in the boat were armed with machetes—long, curved knives—and grabbed the rail of *ESCAPEE* to pull themselves on board. It was a lightning, surprise attack intended to let the pirates overpower or kill the crew before they could re-act. Sigrid and Carole screamed, *"Alan, some men!"* Alan had already been awakened by the approach of the powerful engine and the scream sent him rushing for the distress flare-gun which was kept next to the navigation table. He grabbed it and rushed up on deck. On his way up the steps into the cockpit, he saw the look of horror on the faces of

Carole and Sigrid. Their faces told him everything he needed to know—*there was horror in their eyes*.

He saw the three fierce looking, young Indonesians with head-bands and blood-shot eyes from too much drinking, pulling themselves aboard *ESCAPEE* with their machetes at the ready. He pulled the firing pin back, took aim and fired a rocket flare into the panga just as the three men were ready to attack. The fiery rocket flare burst into flames in the panga and caught all four of the men by surprise. The three men who were boarding *ESCAPEE* with their machetes hesitated and jumped back into the panga to help the other man put out the fire the burning flare had started.

"Go Sigrid, go!" Alan shouted as Sigrid shoved the throttle all the way down. He re-loaded the flare-gun with another rocket flare and kept it ready. Both Carole and Alan then realized their bright red, green and white running lights were on—that's what the pirates had seen in the blackness of the night and what led them straight to *ESCAPEE* in the first place.

"Carole! Turn off the lights. Fast. All of them."

She rushed below and threw the switches but the red compass light was still glowing in the darkness. She couldn't find the switch to turn it off so Alan grabbed the towel they kept in the cockpit and covered it. Now they were "dark"—as dark as a 40-foot, cream-colored boat can ever be.

"Is everything out?" Alan asked *"Look around—quickly. Be sure there's no light on anywhere."*

Susan had been awakened by all the noise and had been lying in her berth, cowering in fear. Now she was standing in the cabin doorway trembling, her face frozen in terror. *"It's OK, Susan—we're getting out of here,"* Alan said. He looked back and saw the glow of the fire on the panga in the blackness of the night. It was still burning, but they were putting it out and would soon be coming after them. Alan looked up—*the mainsail was still up.* It was big and white and would catch the light from any searchlight the pirates might have.

"Carole, help me get the mainsail down!" Alan rushed up on deck with Carole and released the halyard which kept it hoisted and pulled it down. They rolled the white sailcloth into the smallest bundle they could make, tied it securely and got back down into the cockpit so they wouldn't be seen. They all now stood together in the cockpit. Everything had been done to make *ESCAPEE* as invisible as possible.

By now the last flickers of fire were being extinguished on the panga and they heard the powerful motor revving up to start the search for them. Soon, the pirates were speeding around through the black night, racing back and forth and sweeping the seas with a big spotlight.

Alan said, *"Susan, get the chart on the floor and pull a blanket over you. Use the penlight and give us a course to the nearest land. But get the light off as soon as you can."* Susan soon fixed their position and described their location. They were in a channel about 30 miles wide between two smaller islands which lay off the coast of Sumatra. As Susan worked feverishly off in the blackness of the night everyone heard the powerful motor of that panga, speeding around in the darkness, searching for *ESCAPEE.* Their spotlight shot beams of light crisscrossing the seas, hungrily searching for its target.

"They know we're in the shipping channel—either going up or down it—to or from Singapore," Alan said. *"They're going to search the whole damned channel in both directions. We've got to get outside this channel—and now."*

At times the high-powered motor of the panga seemed to be coming straight at them, only to fade away and then get louder again. They were racing around in every direction trying to find them. *Damn that spotlight,* Alan said to himself. It was powerful and its beams shot across the sea. *ESCAPEE* had a cream-colored hull and if the spotlight hit it, it would show up like a Christmas tree.

"If we stay in the channel, sooner or later they're going to find us," Alan said. *"We've got to go where they don't expect us to go—right out of the channel and straight across to the nearest land—that island you saw, Susan. They won't expect that. We've got to get out of the channel and find some bay or river to hide in. We'll anchor behind any trees or shelter we can find. That's the last thing they'll expect."*

"What ze time?" Sigrid asked."

"Two – fifteen." Carole said.

Alan knew what Sigrid was thinking and said *"only three more hours of darkness, more or less."* Susan flipped off the penlight and told Sigrid the course to steer to the nearest land. It would take them about three or more hours to get there but if they were lucky they could be there at dawn and find someplace to hide *ESCAPEE* before full light made them a sitting duck. The pirates would have binoculars *and as soon as it was daylight they'd find them for sure.*

Sigrid and Carole took turns steering them under full power along Susan's course for the next three hours or so. It was still dark but the tropical sun rises early and fast—it's dark and suddenly it's broad daylight. They stopped in shallow water close to the island Susan had picked and it loomed black and large in front of them in the darkness. *"We can't go in any closer,"* Alan said. *"We don't know what's there. Could be rocks, reefs—anything. We've got to wait until we can* see." They sat still and silently in the water. The motor idled and they drifted, watching anxiously for the first glow of early morning in the eastern sky.

As soon as that very first glow began to replace the darkness they started moving. They crept along the coast, avoiding rocky headlands until they saw a little bay which went in several hundred yards. They had no detailed chart of this area and the water in the bay could be a hundred feet deep *or one foot deep*—it was too murky and muddy from all the rains to tell. They'd have to inch in blind and hope for the best. Sigrid gently moved them in while Alan anxiously watched the depth sounder. The water was either very deep or the depth sounder wasn't working—he didn't know which.   If they ran aground now they'd have no chance of hiding or escaping.

"*Over there,*" Alan said, pointing to where the bay bent to the right a little. It would be out of sight of the sea. "*Get as close to shore as you can,*" he told Sigrid. She inched in. The water remained deep all the way and she moved *ESCAPEE* right up next to a steep cliff, which rose vertically out of the water and continued straight up for at least a hundred feet. Alan and Susan tied two lines to bushes growing out of the cliff.

At last they were there, hidden up against the wall of that cliff that soared high above them. Temporarily at least, they were away from the deadly menace searching for them out there in the channel. Now they'd just have to sit it out and wait.

According to the *International Maritime Bureau* and the *Piracy Reporting Center* there are two kinds of pirates in these waters. There are the organized gangs whose favorite tactic is to overtake a large ship from behind at night, throw grabbling hooks onto the ship's stern and climb on board, leaving a man behind in each boat. They're well armed with AK-47 machine guns and other weapons. They often hit a ship with up to 5-10 men at a time and take it over by surprise.

All pirates count on surprise—just as they had with *ESCAPEE.* They first kill or capture the crew and then take their time. They steal the ship's petty cash which for a large ship can easily be thirty to forty thousand dollars. Sometimes, they let the crew go unharmed. Sometimes they kill a few. Sometimes, they kill everyone and hi-jack the ship. In one case, 21 crewmen were murdered and the ship was re-painted and re-named at sea. The entire ship and its million-dollar cargo of fuel was hi-jacked.

The *International Maritime Bureau* and the *Piracy Reporting Center* keeps records of all such attacks on large vessels.

Those thirty to forty thousand dollars for a night's bloody work is very good pay in an area where fishermen normally make only a few dollars a day. And that's what the pirates usually are—fishermen who have become pirates out of need—or greed. All except the largest gangs are "amateurs"—mostly fishermen who know the waters and have turned to crime and violence.

The pirates are as creative as they are deadly. *Some fishermen in small rowboats without motors have successfully attacked large, fast-moving ships*. Several men in two rowboats stretch a long rope across the path of the ship—from rowboat to row boat—which is easy to do in narrow shipping channel. The ship catches the rope and immediately begins towing the pirate-boats—once to each side. While they are being towed alongside the "fishermen-pirates" board the ship with grabbling hooks and weapons and do their "work".

When they're finished they get back in their rowboats, one of them releases the rope and they disappear into the night in the wake of the ship and row home. *Pirates in two simple wooden rowboats with only oars have managed to attack and rob a huge, fast-moving ship.*

Apart from the highly-organized gangs, the *second kind* of pirates—like the men in the two rowboats—are much less organized, more free-lance and impulsive *but just as deadly*. They really are fishermen most of the time but when a slow-moving and defenseless "target of opportunity"—like *ESCAPEE*—comes along they might just attack. It depends on a lot of things—*sometimes it even depends on how good the fishing has been*. These men were going to do what they had to do to feed their families. A boat like *ESCAPEE* has as least $10,000 worth of cameras, electronics, radios and valuables—all which can be easily taken off and sold. The proceeds of one just night's bloody "work" will support one or two families for up to a year. *The problem is the crew—they don't like to leave witnesses*. It complicates things.

Pirate attacks against small boats such as *ESCAPEE*—like pirate attacks in general—have been increasing in recent years. Such attacks are still relatively small in number but they do happen. Sometimes boats just go missing and don't show up to report an attack—their crew has been killed, the boat stripped of all valuables and sunk. *Boat and crew simply cease to exist—and the whole thing takes no more than an hour*. The pirates *always* prefer a surprise attack under the cover of night, as with the attack on *ESCAPEE*. They *always* assume the boat they're attacking carries guns for self-defense, so they hit fast and hard, quickly disabling or killing the crew before they can re-act or defend themselves. They then take their time stripping the boat and if it's a small boat, they usually open a valve and sink it.

That's what they were clearly intending to do to the crew of *ESCAPEE*.

Only a few of the many thousands of fishermen in these waters turn into pirates at night of course, but enough do that this stretch of water has become the worst area in the world for pirate attacks. Somalia, on the horn of Africa, is another very dangerous area and all ships and vessels are warned to keep at least 50 miles offshore. *They can't do that in this area*. These narrow channels and restricted shipping waters often "feed" the shipping right into their hands, just as *ESCAPEE* with its bright navigation lights *had been fed right into the trap*.

Alan had never met one of the cruising world's most friendly and helpful couples—Bill and Kathy Clever, who were victims of one of the most widely-reported and deadly attacks. From all accounts, Bill and Kathy were a cruising couple with a joy for life which touched everyone they ever met. One night three men boarded the boat they were on and brutally murdered Bill, Kathy and two other cruisers taking cash and other valuables.

There's one kind of boat whose crew is almost guaranteed to survive a pirate attack—a boat with small children. The pirates have never been known to intentionally harm a family with small children. Some attacks have started but were stopped as soon as small children were seen. They can slaughter everyone else, but not families with little children. It seems to be their own code of conduct.

ESCAPEE now lay up against the high cliff out of sight from the sea. Alan didn't know what to do next. The attack had been a shocking surprise and he just wasn't prepared for it. *He only knew they had to keep from being discovered.* He had no doubt as to their fate if they were caught—*they could expect no mercy after he had fired that rocket flare into their boat.* By that act of self-defense he had "declared war" and there would be no mercy shown to any of them if they were caught.

"We're *OK here for a while,*" he said. "I didn't see any villages and with these hills and cliffs, I don't think anyone's going to stumble on us from land."

"*What about from the sea?*" Carole asked.

"We'll have to stay here for awhile and figure out what to do next. We're safe for the moment but we're in a real trap. *We're boxed in and they're out there waiting for us,*" Alan said.

"*What about the long distance radio? Can we call for help?*"

"*We're in Indonesian waters, Carole.* Singapore's the closest place around here with rescue boats but it's far away and they'd never enter Indonesian waters."

"*Then what about calling for help from ships passing through the channel on the short-range radio?*" Good question. She had clearly been thinking this through.

"Look at those cliffs Carole. They'd block our VHF signal which is *line of sight.* No one would hear us and those guys out there probably have VHF radios they've stolen from other boats and are listening to the emergency frequency. "

"*So, we 're really on our own?*" Carole said.

"*We're on our own.*"

Everyone was re-acting differently. Susan was still wide-eyed in fear and was trembling. Alan had his arms around her. Sigrid had gone quiet and retreated within herself—it was her way of handling fear. Carole was thinking, evaluating, analyzing—trying to figure a way out of this. She was a problem-solver by nature—*and they now had a life and death problem to solve.* Four very different people faced their fears in different ways, but they shared one thing in common—*they were very frightened.*

Alan knew that several boats were probably combing the seas for them by now. These people—pirates or fishermen—all stuck together. They were probably from the same fishing village and most likely their families were related to one another. By now other boats would have joined the pirates in the search and Alan knew what they had to be thinking—*ESCAPEE* couldn't just disappear up or down that channel. They were too slow. Sooner or later they'd figure it out and come searching the shore. It's hard to hide a 40-foot boat *and once they started searching the shoreline of the islands they would find them.*

"We can't do anything more now," Alan said. "Let's all get some sleep. *We've got to stay rested and ready ....*"

Ready for what, they each wondered. They each got in their own berths but seemed to be *too alone—and this was no time to be alone.* Without saying anything they moved two mattresses to the floor and the four of them huddled together. They felt more secure that way. They were each wondering how all this would end. What would happen? Would they be alive this time tomorrow? They'd been up most of the previous terrible night and one by one, drifted off into a troubled sleep huddled against one another for a sense of security and assurance. *They needed a lot of both.*

Alan went to sleep thinking about what could happen to the three women he really cared about if they were caught. His death might be merciful compared to what they would face. He drifted off into a very troubled, exhausted sleep with Susan very much on his mind.

They slept for a couple of hours and woke up around 11 AM. *"OK,"* Alan said, *"let's make some coffee and talk this over. Let's put our heads together and decide what we do next."* The shock was now over, they'd had a little rest and the four of them were now ready to think it through and try to come up with an escape plan. Over coffee Alan said, *"first, a simple fact. If we stay here they're going to find us—sooner or later.* Am I thinking straight? Do you all agree?" Alan asked.

They did.

"Then that leaves only two questions to talk about— *when do we leave and which way do we go?"*

Carole said *"I've been thinking about it. We've got to leave soon, Alan—tonight or tomorrow night at the latest. The moon's going to come up earlier and get larger each night, so the sooner the better."*

Everyone nodded their heads in agreement

"Let's look at that chart again," Carole said, as Susan passed it to her. *"Look at this—we're sitting on this small island, off by itself. When we leave, we're in the open—exposed and in plain sight with no place to hide. But look back across that channel—the way we came last night. Over there there's this group of small islands and beyond those the coast of Sumatra. If we can get back over there, we can lose ourselves among all those islands or head for the coast of Sumatra, which probably has bays or rivers. We can then hide during the day in coves or rivers and work our way at night up towards Singapore."*

Susan studied it for a moment and said, "*Carole's right, Alan. We didn't know it, but we went the wrong way last night. Now we're stuck out here on this island off by itself. Over there there's this whole group of islands and the coast of Sumatra— lots of places to hide and outside the main shipping channel where they'll be looking for us.*"

They all looked at it and Sigrid immediately saw the problem. "*But zat means ve haf to cross ze channel again. They look for us. Is very dangerous.*"

"*We don't have any choice,*" Alan said. "Over here we're trapped." Sigrid looked carefully and said, "*ja, is so.*"

They looked it over again, and everyone agreed—they had to get off this isolated island and among that protective maze of islands—even if it meant going *back across* that dangerous channel. Susan did some calculations and said, "*we'll be exposed in mid-channel only—let's see—about two hours at the most. And since it's only about thirty miles across we can do it all at night. We can be behind this island—here—before dawn. Once we're across we can weave our way behind that maze of islands and can hide during the day and move at night. And look at these,*" she said, pointing to the large group of Indonesian islands off the Sumatran coast, just south of Singapore.

"*Sigrid, take another look at it,*" Alan said. "*How's it look to you?*" He respected her experience and they *had* to get this right. If there was a flaw in the escape plan they could all wind up dead. She looked it over carefully and thoroughly, taking her time. "*I sink so, Ellen,*" she said, nodding her head. "*I sink so.*"

"*OK,*" Alan said, "*we've got our escape plan. Now, we've got to decide when we make a break for it.*"

Carole had also been working on that, too and quickly said, "*it's got to be tonight. I know there'll be more boats out there looking for us tonight than tomorrow night. They'll be looking for an escape attempt tonight—that's for sure—but tomorrow morning, they're going to start searching the islands *and we're sitting ducks here.* Also that moon's going to be up earlier and brighter tomorrow night. *We've got to do it tonight, Alan.*"

Alan knew she was right. The pirates and those helping them would be expecting them to make their escape attempt tonight and would be out in full force but they just couldn't take the chance of waiting—they'd be all over them tomorrow morning.

"*OK,*" Alan said with a deep sigh, "*we leave as soon as it's dark*"

They covered the furled white mainsail fabric with Carole's dark sleeping bag and covered the white sail bag on the front deck with a dark blanket. They tried to think of anything else they could do to darken *ESCAPEE* or make her less visible. There wasn't anything more they could do—and there was that cream-colored hull—*all 40 feet of it.* No one could eat anything at dinner—their stomachs were tied into too many knots. They knew their lives depended on what happened during the coming night and Alan was feeling terrible *and responsible.* He'd brought these women into this situation. It was his boat and he was the one responsible for getting them into such danger.

Snap out of it, he told himself, *you're not going to function if you keep thinking the worst.*

As soon as the tropical darkness fell Alan and Carole released the lines, Sigrid started the motor and steered *ESCAPEE* out of the bay and into the channel to whatever awaited them.

Their escape attempt had begun.

Susan stood beside Sigrid with the chart in her hand. She would guide Sigrid and mark their progress. No one talked. They were each lost in their own thoughts. Sigrid and Alan had agreed to go at half speed—instead of full speed. The engine was much quieter at half speed. It would take them longer of course, but they had a far better chance of slipping through undetected. The pirates and those helping them would most likely have their own engines shut off, listening for any escape attempt.

No one talked—they knew what they had to do and they knew what was at stake. Their voices would be covered by the engine of course but they still somehow felt if they talked it might cause them to be heard. It wasn't logical but logic was taking a back seat to their fears—anyway it had all been said and everyone knew what was at stake. Sigrid kept *ESCAPEE* right on course and Susan marked off the distance they had gone as best she could in the dark—she didn't dare use even the penlight now.

By around mid-night they were in the middle of the channel, right where the pirates would be expecting them if they made a break for it. They were naturally expecting *ESCAPEE* to go either *up* the channel, towards Singapore or *down* the channel the way they had come. They were almost certainly spread out in *both* directions and if they had made a break for it in either direction they'd be caught in the net. But *ESCAPEE'S* plan was not to go *up*—or *down*—the channel, *but straight back across it* to the protection of the maze of islands on the other side, closer to the coast of Sumatra.

ESCAPEE was now moving in total darkness and with the motor quietly turning over at half speed, trying to cut straight across and get to the other side and behind those islands *before first light*. Alan and Carole gathered around Susan who whispered, *"we're still in the channel—another hour to go."* That next hour was an eternity as *ESCAPEE*—blacked out and moving quietly through the water—cut straight across the deadly channel towards safety on the other side. They fully expected a spotlight to hit them at any time during that next eternal hour and they all huddled together next to Susan as the minutes of extreme danger in the middle of the channel ticked away. Susan checked her watch—she was even sheltering the luminescent dial inside her jacket so it couldn't be seen.

"We're across the channel," she later whispered but it was still much too soon to let their guard down. Sigrid kept them dead on course as *ESCAPEE* moved directly towards the shelter of that island which they *had* to get behind before the sunrise caught them out in the open. *"The moon—where's the moon?"* Carole asked nervously. It was in view up over the horizon now, but was that early moon—only a sliver.

"How much more time to daylight?" Alan asked. That worried him far more than the moon.

"Another, roughly, three hours," Susan said.

"How far to go?

"Another 14 miles and then we've got to swing wide *to get around the shallow water and rocks at the end of the island. Make it 16 or so miles,"* Susan said.

"In three hours?" Alan asked. *"We'll never make* it. *Not at half-speed."*

"Let's hold the sound down for another hour and then get up to full speed. That ought to do it," Carole suggested. She was thinking—a*lways thinking.* After another half-hour they had to choose between the risk of the engine being heard or the risks of being caught out, exposed in the first light of day before they made it around that island. *They went for the speed.* The engine noise increased but so did their speed. They were now far enough out of the center of the channel they hoped no one would hear them.

They sped towards the island and made it around and behind it just as first light started appearing on the eastern horizon. They wouldn't be seen here and weren't going to sit around waiting to be discovered. They hugged each other quietly. There was no celebration—they weren't out of danger yet. They had only made it across the channel and still had to get a long way up the coast of Sumatra to the safety of Singapore. Sigrid bought *ESCAPEE* to a halt behind the island as Susan used the daylight to study the winding, weaving course she had worked out between and behind the islands off the coast of Sumatra and south of Singapore.

For the next four days, they tried to find coves or bays to hide in during the day and when they could, they stayed put and out of sight during the daylight hours. As soon as darkness fell they took off—blacked out and at half-speed for quietness. They inched their way slowly through the winding, narrow channels between the Indonesian islands just south of Singapore. It was intense work to navigate those channels and through the hundreds of small, unlit fishing boats which were out at night. They knew they had to slip by those fishing boats unseen or they could be attacked again.

On the fourth day after the attack they left Indonesian waters and crossed the busy shipping lanes into the safety of heavily-policed Singapore. They headed straight to the Changi Yacht Club near the airport.

There was a very subdued air on *ESCAPEE*. There was no elation at their making it and no celebration. *It had been much too close.* They had been in a deadly trap and broke out to escape only by the best planning they could jointly come up with— *and by plain luck*. They were exhausted from the tension and stress of the last few days.

They felt a sense of confidence—in themselves and each other—*and they felt great being alive.*

But there was no sense of victory.

It had been much too close for that.

THE SURPRISING

AFTERMATH

They anchored in front of the Changi Yacht Club in Singapore and were safe at last. Sigrid rowed them to the dinghy dock and they went straight to the bar. Normally, Alan was supposed to do the paperwork first but that would just have to wait—there was nothing *normal* about what they had just gone through.

They still hadn't talked about what happened. They had still been in danger right up until they crossed those traffic lanes into Singapore's safe waters. They were about to have their first chance to really talk over what had happened.

Some things are so overwhelming and overpowering, a little time needs to pass before you can openly and comfortably talk about them. This was one of those times—it doesn't get more overwhelming than facing the possibility of your own death. As they settled in at the yacht club bar with their beers, Alan was the first to raise the subject.

"That was a terrible experience. *Let's not kid ourselves, we all know what was at stake.* After that ordeal I wouldn't blame you if you guys have had enough of this stuff and want to call it quits. *Who needs this?* So I guess what I'm saying is that it's probably time for you guys to re-think all this—you know, going on with *ESCAPEE.*"

"Susan, you'd be welcomed home in a flash. Carole, you've got your career and Sigrid, there's a German boat that has a card up on the bulletin board looking for crew—I saw it as we walked into the bar. And another thing, too—the international airport's only a few miles away *and you guys could be anywhere in the world in just 24 hours.* So, I guess my point is, I want you to think about whether you want to go on with *ESCAPEE* or not and to feel free to call it quits if you want to. *I have to stay with ESCAPEE—she's my home.* But you guys don't have to.

"Let's not kid ourselves—*that was close—very close.* So I guess what I'm saying in my own rambling way is, *you should really think about whether you want to go on with ESCAPEE or not.* This is a good place to call it all off. "

The girls looked at each other.

"Can I respond to that?" Carole asked slowly and quietly.

Alan completely missed that *certain tone* in her voice which *should* have tipped him off to big trouble ahead but he still had that "comprehension problem" of his. On top of that he didn't listen well—and he was about to pay for it.

"Well, yes, sure Carole. Go ahead."

Carole picked up her glass of beer as if to take a sip and said, *"ladies, Alan's trying to get rid of us"*—and poured the half-full glass of beer over his head, right in front of everyone in the bar.

"That's our response," she said. *"That's what you get for trying to get rid of us before we're ready."*

The girls laughed at the sight of Alan—stunned, shocked and dripping with beer. The others in the bar joined in the laughter as soon as they saw it was all in good fun. The bartender brought Alan a towel and he started wiping off his beer-soaked head and shirt.

As he tried to dry his dripping head, Alan asked, *"do I take it then that this—this gesture,"* he said, pointing to his soaked shirt, *"means you guys want to continue on with ESCAPEE?"*

"You got it." Carole said. *"Hey girls, he's slow and he's old but he's finally got it."*

None of the three were ready to go back and start the next stage of their lives just yet. No one was going to scare them off and send them running.

"You're still stuck with us, Alan." Susan said.

"I can handle that," Alan said. He was thrilled by the "response"—*soaking wet as it was*. He felt he had to openly talk about the risks and ask them to reconsider, *but the truth was the four of them had found something very special together and he hoped it wouldn't end just yet.*

Not now—not like this.

"OK, here's to no more hurricanes and no more pirates," he said lifting his glass. *"Here's to a lot more good times for as long as we're together. Here's to us—and to Thailand, Greece, Italy—and whatever's ahead."*

"To whatever's ahead," the three of them said, lifting the fresh glasses of beer the bartender had poured.

"That is," Carole added, *"if this worn-out old man here can handle it."*

"Carole," Alan shot back, *"give me a break!"*

They'd give him their trust—they knew they could count on him.

They'd give him their friendship—the friendship which by now had grown into a deep bond between each of them.

They'd give him their affection—and all the good times that went along with it. *Pavarotti and his buddies would continue to sing their hearts out.*

But they'd *never* give him a break.

EPILOGUE

By Alan Richards

By the time we reached Singapore I had a chance to reflect on the unique relationship we had.

When we first met back in Tonga I had hoped a friendship would develop, of course, but I think we were all a little amazed at how fast and how far it went.

Before we met we were each alone and struggling—trying to deal with a major problem in our lives. We had that in common, and that may have been what helped make our relationship most uncommon.

Together, we found the strength and insight to face whatever we had to face and come out on top.

As it turned out, *we needed each other.*

We soon realized we were in the right place, at the right time, and with the right people.

I guess it sometimes happens that way.

Given our unusual circumstances on *ESCAPEE* there was intimacy—it's part of life, and it was part of ours.

But before all that and above all that there was a very special friendship. That friendship was the foundation of everything we had together. *First and foremost we were friends*—in the deepest meaning of that word.

My favorite writer, Ralph Waldo Emerson, wrote:

"*A friend may well be the masterpiece of Nature.*"

I knew I was living with *three* masterpieces.

We knew our friendship was going to last *long after* our times together on ESCAPEE.

But I'm getting ahead of myself.

We still had another six months and thousands of miles to go.

This book is available through your local bookstore or on-line bookseller.

For information on special quantity prices for groups or clubs, please contact the publisher at: penhurstbooks@usa.com or by fax at (305) 675 0940